SOCIAL POLICY

AN INTRODUCTION

Ken Blakemore

OPEN UNIVERSITY PRESS
Buckingham • Philadelphia

Open University Press
Celtic Court
22 Ballmoor
Buckingham
MK18 1XW

email: enquiries@openup.co.uk
world wide web: http://www.openup.co.uk

and
325 Chestnut Street
Philadelphia, PA19106, USA

First Published 1998

A catalogue record of this book is available from the British Library

ISBN   0 335 19494 X (hb)   0 335 19493 1 (pb)

Library of Congress Cataloging-in-Publication Data
Blakemore, Ken, 1948–
    Social policy : an introduction / Ken Blakemore.
        p.   cm.
    Includes bibliographical references and index.
    ISBN 0–335–19494–X. — ISBN 0–335–19493–1 (pbk.)
    1. Social policy. 2. Great Britain—Social policy.   I. Title.
HV40.B544 1998
361.6'1' 0941—dc21   97–45910
                                                                CIP

Typeset by Graphicraft Typesetters Limited, Hong Kong
Printed in Great Britain by Redwood Books, Trowbridge

SOCIAL POLICY

This book is dedicated to the memory of Dilys and to the future of Elin

CONTENTS

PREFACE

How did this book come to be written? Every lecturer should have three points to make, but I'm afraid that I have only two.

The first is that I am a child of the welfare state – in a rather literal way. I was born on the very day that the sun rose upon a new National Health Service and other innovations in welfare. The day before, my mother cut a cartoon out of a newspaper. It depicted a worried looking father-to-be pointing a shotgun at a hovering stork (with baby), trying to keep it at bay until the fateful day (5 July 1948). The cartoon was lost and that is a matter of regret (if you happen to come across it, please let me know), but to make up for it, so to speak, here is a book.

The second reason is that I was once (for six weeks) a young student of social policy. However, I found the subject incredibly tedious at that time. I can still remember sitting on the steps of what we knew as the 'Social Admin building' at the university, trying to sell back the five or six dry-as-dust textbooks that we had had to buy to follow the course. The more faithful students bought them and I switched to a course in sociology. Eventually, though, this also became a matter of regret. Social policy gradually became a more interesting and thought-provoking subject than it seemed to have been in the days of 'welfare consensus' before 1979. This book is therefore an attempt to atone for my earlier decision to stray from the path, but also to try to provide a livelier textbook than the ones I had to contend with. Let's hope that you agree.

Ken Blakemore
University of Wales Swansea

ACKNOWLEDGEMENTS

This book was completed during a period of great sadness for me. Therefore I must first acknowledge the kindness and support of Jacinta Evans and Joan Malherbe at the Open University Press; without their understanding and gentle encouragement, this book would never have been published.

Many other friends, colleagues and students also helped me to pick up the threads of life and, in more ways than one, assisted the book's completion. Space does not permit me to mention all, but I would particularly like to acknowledge with great affection the support of Rob Behrens, Yolande van den Brink, Bill Bytheway, Julia Johnson and Steve Taylor; of colleagues Bob Drake, Samantha Clutton, Mike Sullivan and Anthea Symonds; and of all the students in Swansea's Department of Social Policy who showed such sensitivity and kindness in the year 1996–7. In addition, three students – Lynn Jeffrey, Amy Matthews and Sue Merriman – agreed to read a draft of the Glossary and kindly offered useful comments an it.

Any author who claims to have surveyed the field owes enormous debts to others' work and influences, and I am no exception. However, responsibility for this book, warts and all, lies solely with me. It is difficult and rather invidious to select the names of people who have been particularly helpful on my journey into social policy, but I would like to record deep gratitude to John Harris, Frank Laczko and Edwin Griggs (with whom I had fun teaching social policy, at Coventry Polytechnic), to Alf Barrett, Faith Elliot, Brian Ranson and Helmuth Heisler (for other formative influences) and to Nicholas Deakin at the University of Birmingham (who checked my foundations in the discipline, so to speak).

Finally, I would like to acknowledge the following for their kind permission to reproduce copyright material in this book: the *Independent* for permission to publish the cartoons by Riddell (Figure 1.1) and Shrank (Figure 4.1); Robert Thompson for his permission to reproduce a cartoon (Figure 2.1); the Office for National Statistics for permission to publish Figure 4.2; and the Open University for permission to reproduce a diagram to illustrate the financing of community care (Figure 9.1). Last but not least, I would like to thank Maggie Ainley for her special efforts in taking the photograph used in Chapter 8 (Figure 8.2).

1 THE SUBJECT OF SOCIAL POLICY

SOCIAL POLICY: AN IDENTITY PROBLEM?

Social policy can be defined in two ways. First, it is a subject to research and to study. The aim of this first chapter is to introduce you to it. But in the 'real' world, policies are carried out by government, private organizations and voluntary groups, and they are experienced by families and individuals.

What are 'policies'? In one way they can be seen as aims or goals, or statements of what ought to happen. *Social* policies aim to improve human welfare (though they often fail to do so) and to meet human needs for education, health, housing and social security.

As goals and intentions, policies can be found in the form of official government policy (legislation, or the guidelines which govern how laws should be put into operation), party manifestos or a company's or organization's statement of policy on something (for instance, an equal opportunity policy).

Policies are living things, not just static lists of goals, rules or laws. Policy blueprints have to be implemented, often with unexpected and

Figure 1.1   Tony Blair
(Reproduced by kind permission of the *Independent* ©.)

sometimes with disastrous results. Therefore, social policies are what happens 'on the ground', when they are **implemented**, as well as what happens at the preliminary decision-making or legislative stage. There is often a gulf between the concepts and goals that inspire policy and 'real' policy, the ugly result of compromise (see Figure 1.1).

Studying social policy will involve you in thinking about:

- *What* social policies are: that is, what the content of specific government policies is, such as an Education Act or a policy on abortion in a National Health Service (NHS) hospital.
- *How* policies are developed, administered and implemented: for instance, how a new policy on tackling youth unemployment was conceived, what its stated and hidden aims are, how it is funded, how far it meets its objectives.
- *Why* policies exist (or do not exist). Why, for example, was a market approach to providing health and social services adopted in the 1980s and early 1990s? Or why, in Britain, has there never been, until recently, a concerted policy on nursery provision and pre-school care for children?

Social policy and other subjects

Although preliminary definitions of social policy may be helpful, no definition tells the whole story. The challenge facing us, therefore, is more than that of moving from simple opening definitions of social policy to slightly more complicated ones, followed by descriptions of various policies in areas such as education and health.

Definitions and description are not enough. Anyone new to a subject needs something else: an image of the subject to identify with, or a glimpse of the whole thing which gives a 'feel' for the subject, and some way of anticipating what is coming next.

To demonstrate the importance of these things, you might briefly think about a range of subjects that you are already familiar with: English literature, perhaps, or geography, history or economics. Now think of the images that each one calls up in your mind.

English literature brings images of dramas, stories and writers (some of whom, incidentally, are very useful for a broader understanding of social policy); geography might lead to visualizations of the globe, space or particular environments, such as the tropical rainforest or mountain ranges; history might prompt images of particular periods that you have been interested in, a vision of a medieval market, perhaps, or an eighteenth-century wedding; and economics, depending on your personal circumstances, might call forth either an image of a bank overdraft or fountains of golden coins.

Now try the same exercise with the words 'social policy' in mind. Do any images appear? If they do, you may be suffiently well informed to consider shelving this book. If you have no clear image or impression of the subject, on the other hand, this is perfectly understandable – and you need to read on.

Social policy's identity problem – or, more precisely, its problem of *lack* of identity – has a number of causes. Perhaps, as with sociology, social policy's lack of a clear image is because it is a relatively new subject. However, unlike sociology, social policy is considered to be too specialist a subject to be taught in schools as a separate, examinable course. Consequently, not many people considering a course in social policy have a clear idea of what is entailed, because they are unfamiliar with it as a taught subject.

There is another reason for social policy's identity problem: it is a 'magpie' subject, a **discipline** which has taken bright and sparkling treasures from other disciplines such as economics, philosophy, politics and sociology. This does not mean that social policy has no identity as a subject but that, like the magpie's, its nest or its base contains others' pearls of wisdom as well as its own.

The main aim of this book is to show that social policy as a subject truly has developed its own identity as well as being a borrower. In other words, social policy is like any other discipline, in that it has developed its own distinctive body of **theory** which individual scholars and researchers have used to test **hypotheses** about the impact of social policies on people's lives (see Box 1.1). Through the study of social policy as a discipline, therefore, you will gradually gain insights and a view on the world which is distinctly different from, but related to, the viewpoints from sociology, politics and the other social sciences.

Before we leave initial impressions and images, it is important to realize that experienced scholars in social policy have their personal images of the subject, just as much as do people who have only recently begun to study it. For example, Nicholas Deakin gives us this personal impression:

> Towards the end of the War (which is how people of my generation still habitually refer to the Second World War) my mother took to

Box 1.1   Social policy research – an example

Example of a theory	*Some possible hypotheses to test the theory*
Public provision (e.g. of social housing) maintains some fairness in allocation of goods and services; market provision is bound to exclude disadvantaged groups.	(1) Where social housing is sold off, poorer families tend to get left behind in substandard housing; they are excluded from better quality flats or houses. **OR** (2) Where social housing is sold off, the purchasers are more likely to stay; there is a better social mix than if people have to leave their estates to purchase a home.

An example of research which examines these hypotheses – in relation to council house sales and the Afro-Caribbean community – can be found in a study by Peach and Byron (1994). See Chapter 8 for further discussion of Peach and Byron's study.

bringing home from our visits to the children's clinic . . . small brown bottles labelled 'welfare orange juice'. My brother and I gulped down the contents willingly enough: the flavour, bland, but with a slightly bitter chemical back taste, was in every way preferable to the only other alternative on offer: cod liver oil. Now, forty years later, the ghost of the tang that the juice once left still appears unbidden on my palate whenever I first see the word 'welfare'; and it illustrates in a trivial but (to me) highly immediate way how the terms employed in the debate about the future of welfare have developed associations and personal references which are lodged deep in the collective unconscious of the nation.

(Deakin 1994: 1)

It is likely that for the millions of people of Nicholas Deakin's generation and of preceding generations, this particular impression will have a lot of resonance. It expresses a deep attachment to the welfare state and might be termed a **welfarist** image of social policy.

More recent impressions among younger generations may be less pro-welfare or welfarist. For instance, the term **welfare** may be more readily associated with the frustrations of waiting in a queue at a benefits office, or with the way in which poverty seems to be perpetuated by the **welfare system** rather than relieved by it (see Chapter 5).

Images of welfare and social policy (assuming these two terms are used synonymously) can therefore be negative as well as positive. The study of social policy must involve a critical element. Social policies are 'nasty' as well as 'nice'. The aims and impact of social policies and the welfare system (either deliberately or unintentionally) can as often be to control people and to keep them in their place (see Chapter 4) as to liberate them or give them a better life than they would otherwise have.

Thus, a major aim of the subject of social policy is to *evaluate critically* the impact of social policies on people's lives. As mentioned above, this involves developing theories about the role of welfare and using hypotheses to test out what is happening. As another example, we might consider whether the introduction of a Child Support Agency (CSA) really benefited single parents and their children and – if so – how successful it has been, and on whose terms 'success' is measured.

To engage in an honest and objective appraisal, the social policy researcher must, like any other social scientist, try to lay aside personal values and political opinions. For instance, a man who deeply resents paying maintenance to his former partner would probably not be the best choice of person to research child support, but then neither would a militant feminist who believed that all divorced or separated women are exploited.

Despite the importance of **objectivity**, though, the identity of social policy as a subject *is* simultaneously bound up with **values**: that is, expressing what you believe in, and what you think social policies *should be* trying to achieve to make society better for everyone.

How can there be a commitment to objectivity on the one hand, and to personal and political values on the other? Below, this tension and apparent contradiction in the subject of social policy will be further explored, mainly by looking briefly at the development of the subject and the contribution of perhaps its most important founding parent, Richard Titmuss.

Before this, however, it may help to review these opening remarks about the identity of social policy by comparing the different ways in which other academic disciplines could relate to social policy (see Box 1.2).

THE STORY OF SOCIAL POLICY

In order to understand the distinctive character of social policy as a subject, we need briefly to examine its roots and the way it developed in Britain.

Early roots: social work, sociology and social administration

Concern about questions of social policy grew throughout the nineteenth century: for instance, concern about poverty and the squalid conditions that many people had to live in at that time, concern about child labour in mills, factories and mines, and concern about lack of literacy and the threatening power of the uneducated masses (see Chapter 3).

As the end of the nineteenth century neared, it became increasingly clear to a growing number of reformers that the state would have to play a much larger role than before in dealing with the mounting social problems of the day. Although some of this concern was motivated by genuine and progressive aims to improve social conditions for ordinary people, it was mixed with other more controlling and reactionary motivations.

Box 1.2   Examples of links between other disciplines and social policy

Discipline	Examples of social policy relevance
Economics	Looking at the economic costs and 'payoffs' of particular policies and social benefits, e.g. child benefit.
Geography	Insights into the spatial patterns of the distribution and take-up of services, e.g. 'meals on wheels' for older people.
History	Study of the development of social policies through time; comparing present-day services and attitudes to them with examples from the past, e.g. hostels for the homeless today could be compared with 'Poor Law' institutions in the past.
Philosophy	Examining the reasons or justifications for preferring one kind of policy over another; discussing ethical questions, such as the right of a health authority to draw up a policy of withholding treatment to certain categories of patient.
Politics	Investigating the social policy aims of the Labour, Conservative, Liberal Democrat, Green and nationalist parties; or, conversely, looking at the political impact of social policies, e.g. what have been the effects of council house sales on voting patterns?
Psychology	Studying personal perceptions of, and attitudes towards, welfare services. Psychological perspectives are important in investigating individual need and design of services, e.g. the way breast cancer screening is provided, and women's perceptions of this service.
Sociology	Researching the norms, values and other social pressures that affect the relationship between the welfare system and different social groups, e.g. reasons for 'racial' inequalities in access to social services.

The work of those who led the Charity Organisation Society (COS) is a good example of this mix of motivations and aims. The COS, set up to coordinate charitable efforts and to eliminate problems of charities duplicating one another's work, became a highly influential advisory body in late Victorian and early twentieth-century Britain. For instance, several of its members, including Octavia Hill (see Chapter 8), served on a government commission on the reform of the Poor Law between 1905 and 1909.

In general, the COS and those who shared similar opinions were looking for a more efficient way of managing the existing system of poverty relief, rather than a radical overhaul of social policy and the introduction of universal state benefits. The COS had pioneered the development of a new kind of occupation – the social caseworker – who was often a volunteer and often a (middle- or upper-class) woman. 'Social workers', as they gradually came to be known, were responsible for investigating the needs of poor families and for finding out whether they were 'deserving' cases. There was great concern among those who ran charities at the time that no one who was 'undeserving' should receive any help, because undeserved help would compound the character faults that were then thought to cause poverty and unemployment: laziness, ignorance, immoral behaviour and dependence.

While the early roots of social work were arguably more concerned with social control and with trying to make the poor 'respectable' than with helping them on their own terms, the very fact that social casework was thought necessary did succeed in bringing problems of poverty and social inequality to the attention of middle-class volunteers and opinion-formers on a scale that had never been seen before.

At the same time, journalists, radical politicians and other commentators were writing about the appalling conditions in which many British people lived, giving first-hand accounts and vivid descriptions of slum life which were as shocking to 'respectable' society as reports of other cultures and ways of life among the 'savages' in newly conquered parts of the Empire.

As a result of both social casework investigation and journalistic reports, philanthropists began to provide funds for *research* on poverty and social problems as well as for schemes to help the poor directly. One famous example of this was Seebohm Rowntree's survey of poverty in York in 1901, *Poverty: a Study of Town Life* (discussed by Fraser 1984: 136–7), which showed that an alarmingly high proportion (28 per cent) of York's population were then living below subsistence level. Rowntree's survey, which was followed by other Rowntree investigations after the First World War, is a prime example of the way in which the social conscience of leading manufacturing families (in this case, the well known chocolate and cocoa-processing firm) was translated into social research.

Rowntree's study was more progressive and less moralistic about the poor than a preceding study by Charles Booth, an extremely lengthy and exhaustive study of poverty carried out between 1889 and 1903 and titled *The Life and Labour of the People in London*. Nevertheless, these and other studies of social conditions at the time were marked by an overriding concern to discover the 'facts' of poverty. Providing statistics of poverty and evidence about social problems would make a conclusive case for urgent social reform and a new approach to social policy, it was thought.

Therefore, the key to understanding these early, problem-focused pieces of research is to realize that they were strongly motivated by a desire to be *scientific*. Rather than an appeal for social reform and action based solely upon grounds of conscience or morality, the case put forward by Booth, Rowntree and others was to be based on irrefutable evidence and an objective approach to social problems.

It is at about this time – the beginning of the twentieth century – that the term 'sociology' began to gain currency as a way of summing up this scientific, statistical approach to understanding social problems. Early sociology, reflecting as it did the passion for collecting facts and statistics, came to be known as 'blue book sociology', because it was based so heavily on official reports and population censuses (in blue covers).

All this rapidly accumulating knowledge about social conditions and social problems fostered the development of new kinds of training courses and university degrees in social work. Thus, in the relatively new municipal 'redbrick' universities of the time, such as Birmingham, and in the newly established London School of Economics, three important strands of learning and training were fused together: social work, sociology and '**social administration**', the last being the study of local and central government institutions, and of the framework in which services to the poor and needy were to be delivered.

The early roots of the subject of social policy (or its forerunner, social administration) were therefore inextricably entwined with practical action (social work) and research (sociology). Later, as sociology developed a more independent identity, sociologists began to deplore the idea of their subject being a problem-focused or policy-oriented discipline. Sociology became more theoretical in its concerns, though some sociologists retain an interest in 'real world' and policy issues.

So while the main aim of sociology is to discover knowledge about society for its own sake, the key question for social policy observers is: what difference does a policy/policies make? The object is to focus upon how policies develop, why certain policies are chosen over others and what the economic, political and social implications of policies are.

Coming of age: the welfare state and social administration

In 1950, Richard Titmuss was appointed as the first professor of social administration at the London School of Economics (see Box 1.3). The subject had 'come of age' and was fast becoming recognized as a university discipline in many other British universities.

Titmuss's department at the London School of Economics (LSE) became a central influence on the subject in the 1950s and 1960s. The LSE itself had been set up in the early years of the twentieth century, largely as a result of the efforts of energetic and pioneering socialist thinkers such as Sidney and Beatrice Webb. It was envisaged as a power house of progressive ideas and education. Its chief aims were, first, to provide a route into higher education for able students from working-class backgrounds and, second, to build a solid base of research studies on economic and social problems that would be vital for developing the planned society that the Webbs and other socialists believed in at the time.

Under the directorship of William Beveridge (see Chapter 3, Box 3.4) in the 1920s and 1930s, the LSE became an internationally renowned centre of learning. Among the scholars who joined the LSE during Beveridge's time was von Hayek, an exponent of right-wing ideas on economics and politics who was to have a profound effect on future leaders such as Margaret Thatcher.

Thus the early development of social administration and social policy as university subjects took place in an environment in which a variety of

Box 1.3   Richard Titmuss, 1907–1973

When Richard Titmuss became Professor of Social Administration at the LSE at the age of 43, he was one of the few non-graduates to have ever become professors. Titmuss had had to leave school at the age of 14. His father, who had been thrown out of work on a small farm and became heavily indebted, died before Richard was 20. As a result, Titmuss had experienced first-hand the shock of financial insecurity.

After leaving school, Titmuss worked as a clerk, then as a more senior inspector, for an insurance company. This work deepened his knowledge of both social welfare and inequality. As Kincaid explains, 'During the 1930s Titmuss lived a double life. In working hours, the insurance office – but in the evenings and at the weekends, the actuarial skills learned in the insurance office were brought to bear on data about birth-rates, poverty and ill-health' (Kincaid 1984: 115).

By this time Richard Titmuss had married, and his wife, Kay Titmuss, further encouraged his social conscience and his drive to write on policy and welfare matters. During the Second World War, Titmuss was appointed as an official war historian, and subsequently wrote a masterpiece on the civilian experience of wartime, called *Problems of Social Policy* (1950). Of many later works, among the more important are *Essays on the Welfare State* (1958), *Commitment to Welfare* (1968) and *The Gift Relationship* (1970), the last being a study of blood donation and the significance of this as a model of altruism for the provision of welfare generally.

Richard Titmuss died of cancer in an NHS hospital and, at the time, his daughter Ann Oakley (well known for her feminist analyses of family life and housework) wrote a moving tribute to his life and work.

views and a commitment to scholarly research were highly valued. Richard Titmuss's teaching and research activities ably met these standards. Not only was he highly prolific as a writer and researcher (see suggestions for further reading at the end of this chapter) but, like those who had worked in the early poverty research tradition of Booth, Rowntree and other important reformers, his aim was not simply to do factual research for its own sake. It was also to engage in research which, while still based on **empirical studies** (i.e. observation of factual evidence and real life experience), would be directed by the aims of exposing unmet need, social inequality and the ways in which policies seemed to be failing to bring social justice.

Why was Titmuss so committed to such values as equality and social justice, and what were the implications of this commitment for the development of social policy as a subject? See, first, the brief summary of his life and work in Box 1.3. As the thumbnail sketch of Titmuss's life indicates, the twin strands in his approach to writing about social welfare go back to his own experience.

First, there was the dispassionate critic of social inequalities and of 'who gets what' in a market-based society (see Chapter 4). Titmuss succeeded in elevating the subject of social administration from the tedious study of how the welfare system is administered into a much deeper and more questioning analysis of why inequalities persist, even in a welfare state such as the one developed in Britain after 1945. It was Titmuss who first pointed out that there were two welfare states: the obvious welfare system which provided education, health services and social security, and a less obvious system which particularly benefited the middle classes, and which included hidden subsidies to better-off social groups in the form of tax advantages, public support for higher education (a near monopoly of students from middle-class families when Titmuss was writing) and mortgage interest tax relief (also benefiting better-off households much more extensively at that time).

Second, though, there was the Titmuss who celebrated the welfare state that had been built in Britain after 1945 (see Chapter 4). He strongly defended not only the actual services provided 'free' at the point of use, but also the *values* that underpinned the welfare state: the values of altruism, of community and of the collective will to improve people's lives. By contrast, the values which underpinned the market – individualism and competition – seemed to Titmuss to be destructive of human welfare.

Not surprisingly, therefore, many have seen marked inconsistencies in Titmuss's ideas: how could there be a unified subject of social policy based on Titmuss's approach if it included on the one hand a strong defence of the existing welfare system, and on the other a devastating critique of the inequalities and injustices that it masked?

In retrospect, it is not too difficult to see how both of these views can be reconciled, even though there is some tension between them. It is quite possible to point out the weaknesses and injustices of the present welfare system while at the same time drawing attention to the possibility of greater inequalities and problems if the system were to be scrapped. For instance, the NHS, despite being largely a 'free at the point of use' service in Britain, has not succeeded in eradicating inequalities in health and use of health services (see Chapter 7). But Titmuss argued that the replacement of the NHS with a completely privatized health system, as in the USA, would lead to even greater inequalities than already exist.

Crisis and change: the development of social policy as a subject

During the 1970s, the Titmussian approach to the study of the welfare state was challenged from a number of directions. This was partly because, despite Titmuss's lively criticisms of the flaws in the welfare state, much of the subject of social administration seemed to have developed into a rather complacent and technical description of existing social services and how they were to be delivered.

What criticisms there were of existing social problems, unmet need and inequality seemed to be dominated by the Titmussian assumption that all would be well if a left-of-centre, planned and rather paternalistic approach to providing state welfare was followed. But what if there was

something more fundamentally wrong with the whole approach to providing welfare through state institutions?

It was this latter question that provoked much interest in the 1970s,
when 'social policy' began to replace 'social administration' as the heading or title for university courses in the subject. Students of social policy
were increasingly exposed to a range of **critiques** of the welfare state and
of the traditional welfare values that had been contained in the old subject of social administration.

These critiques (critical discussions) may be divided into *culturalist* criticisms and *materialist* criticisms of state welfare. Culturalist critiques are
those which challenge the *way* in which welfare services are designed and
provided, and the cultural assumptions (e.g. about men's and women's
roles in society) that underpin the manner in which services are delivered.
For instance, in the 1970s a growing feminist and women's studies literature raised questions about the sexist assumptions behind many health,
education and social services, and the ways in which those services could
reinforce gender inequality (see Chapter 5). Similarly, growing awareness
of racism and studies of racial discrimination pinpointed the inappropri-
ateness of many social services to the needs of minority ethnic groups,
and the paternalistic, 'culture-blind' attitudes of those who ran them.

Materialist critiques, on the other hand, focused on material factors and
the economic crisis apparently facing the welfare state. On the political
left, Marxists and other kinds of socialists concentrated on the material
inequalities which seemed to be inherent in the welfare state: for instance, in the provision of housing, schools and hospitals. This kind of
critique (as an example, see Gough 1979) paid less attention to the way in
which welfare services were run, and was more concerned that *not enough*
welfare was being provided to poorer and working-class groups in society.
At the same time, though, Marxists pointed to what they saw as an
uncontainable and rising demand from the working classes for more welfare services and higher social security benefits – a demand that would spiral
out of control and lead to a fundamental crisis in the capitalist system.

For entirely different reasons, commentators on the political right shared
with Marxists a view of the welfare state as an unmanageable economic
burden upon the capitalist economy. Therefore, they too were putting
forward materialist criticisms of the welfare state. However, unlike the
Marxists, right-wing commentators based their criticisms on the belief
that *too much* state welfare was being provided.

CONCLUSIONS: THE SUBJECT TODAY

From today's vantage point (following the landslide general election result of 1997 and the coming to power of the first Labour government
since 1979), many of the debates about social policy that used to take
place in the 1970s and 1980s seem out of date. In those days, debates
were rather polarized: on the one hand, Marxist and left-wing critics of
the welfare state were combining dreams of a socialist future with dire
predictions of the end of capitalism; on the other, the so-called 'New
Right' called for the privatization of the entire welfare system.

Neither school of thought proved to be much good at forecasting the actual development of social policy. As will be shown elsewhere in this book, Conservative government in the 1980s and 1990s did not lead to the full-scale implementation of right-wing ideas and to the scrapping of the welfare state (though there were many significant changes); nor did the massive rise in unemployment during the 1980s and large increases in social security spending result, as many Marxists foresaw, in the break-down of the capitalist system.

The writings of Titmuss about the social policy dilemmas of the 1950s and 1960s seem in some ways to be more useful and pertinent than the theories of the 1970s and 1980s for an understanding of today's social policy questions and the approach of government to solving these ques-tions. In considering how the activities of the state and the market could best be combined to bring the greatest benefit to the greatest number, Titmuss's pragmatic approach seems particularly well fitted to understand-ing the rather modest aims of the Labour government that will shape social policy up to at least the beginning of the new century. For example, Titmuss, in a 1959 Fabian Society lecture, warned of growing inequality in an 'irresponsible society' (Titmuss 1987: 80). In a debate which has strong echoes today, he pointed to the increasing pressures in an affluent society to develop separate and market-based provision for the better-off and inferior or stigmatized services for the poor.

By contrast, the ideas of the 'New Right', which put the market before all else, now have a discredited and tired appearance after almost twenty years of government in which *some* of these ideas were put to the test and found wanting. Equally, the radical left-wing ideas of the 1970s and 1980s, preoccupied as they were with over-abstract theories about class conflict, alienation and the end of capitalism, also seem archaic.

However, this is not to say that these points of view and debates did not have their uses in the development of social policy as a subject. As pointed out above, Titmuss's influence on the subject led to the domin-ance of a rather cosy view of the world, in which the British approach to welfare was thought to be the best and in which a planned, state-run welfare system was seen as inevitably superior to anything the market or voluntary sector could do.

In Britain, this was largely a result of the way the subject developed as an independent discipline. In other European countries, social policy as a subject in university courses is often subsumed under politics, sociology or **public administration** (the study of government), while in the United States, 'social welfare' and social policy studies are often associated with social work education. British social policy and social administration grew rather more separately as a university discipline in the 1950s and 1960s.

Thus the traditional approach to the subject in Britain did establish a strong foundation of social policy studies, but it had its limitations. The explosion of debate about social policy and the welfare state in the 1970s blew fresh air into the subjects and established the fundamental point that there are many ways of providing welfare: in other words, there is a range of competing '**models**' or types of welfare system to discuss, a point that is further explored at the end of Chapter 3, where Britain's welfare system or the 'British model' is compared with other models.

Plan of the book

In this chapter we have begun to explore how social policy has developed in recent times, both as a subject and as a programme of action 'out there' in the 'real' world. In Chapter 10 we will return to these themes. The likely impact of the change of government in 1997 will be assessed, together with broader questions about the interrelationship between social policy, economic change and social trends: for instance, the concept of a 'post-modern' or 'late modern' world and its value in understanding current social policy.

As for the filling in the sandwich – that is, all the intervening chapters – the choices that had to be made were difficult ones. For instance, there is a fundamental choice to be made between writing a book which is all 'isms and ologies' – that is, concerned primarily with theories of welfare, discrimination and so on – or another kind of book which provides a 'Cook's tour' of the welfare system. The drawback with the first kind is that it can easily become a semi-sociological or philosophical discussion, relatively abstract and without much relevance to the world beyond the university. This kind of book would not tell you much about the content of actual policies or how they were decided upon. The drawback with the second kind of book is that, after a few months, it begins to look like last summer's travel brochure. Time moves on, policies change and new Acts of Parliament are passed.

The plan of this book represents an attempt to bridge the gap between the two basic choices outlined above. The next four chapters deal with 'the big picture' and with some important general themes in social policy, as follows:

- Chapter 2: the key ideas and principles upon which social policies are based.
- Chapter 3: the historical development of social policy.
- Chapter 4: 'who gets what? The questions of social and economic inequality raised by social policy.
- Chapter 5: the connections between social policy, social control and liberation.

Although these chapters focus on general themes, however, they also refer to specific policy areas and examples. Chapters 4 and 5, for instance, discuss *social security* policy as an illustration of both the 'who gets what?' question and the question of how far, or in what ways, the welfare system is a controlling influence.

The remaining chapters (before the concluding Chapter 10) also try to marry thematic approaches with specific policy areas, though the emphasis is more upon the latter than the former.

- Chapter 6 discusses education policy, using the example of the 1988 Education Act to reflect upon how policies are made in Britain.
- Chapter 7 defines and explores health policy, focusing on ethical dilemmas as examples of the way professional groups shape the design and provision of services.
- Chapter 8 takes the example of housing policy to examine how rival ideologies, values and utopian dreams influence policy.

■ Chapter 9   gives an account of recent community care, exploring at the same time the fundamental question of 'who cares?' in today's welfare system.

A final point, assuming that you have decided to launch into the rest of the book, is that the term 'welfare *system*' is preferred throughout the book to that of 'welfare *state*'. Interestingly, William Beveridge – a key founder of Britain's welfare system (see Chapter 3) – strongly disliked the 'welfare state' tag. As a supporter of insurance and the principle of saving for a rainy day, he disapproved of any term which seemed to encourage the idea of welfare being a bottomless pit of resources, or an institution which would unquestioningly look after people however 'undeserving' of help they were.

However, avoiding 'the welfare state' term in this book has nothing to do with Beveridge's preferences. Rather, it is to signal some sort of recognition that we have now moved out of the era of 'big government' and have gone beyond the twentieth century's 'post-war' period, in which the state was expected to play the leading role as provider and funder of every major welfare service.

At the same time, there is still a 'system' of welfare. Though inadequate and badly coordinated in parts (see Chapter 9 on community care for examples), there is a connected set of agencies making decisions about, paying for or providing services: central and local government; **quangos** or quasi-autonomous non-governmental organizations (see Chapter 6 for examples in education); the voluntary (non profit-making) sector; the private (for-profit) sector; and the informal sector of the family and community. This book is about the system, why it is run according to certain principles and not others and – in the next chapter – what these principles mean.

KEY TERMS AND CONCEPTS

critique
disciplines
empirical research
hypothesis
implementation
models (of welfare or social policy)
objectivity
public administration

quangos
social administration
theory
values
welfare
welfare system
welfarism

SUGGESTIONS FOR FURTHER READING

The book written by Nicholas Deakin, *Politics of Welfare* (1994) represents a good start in reading about social policy. The introduction and Chapters 1 and 2 of his book provide a helpful historical framework which discusses the development of social policy in Britain.

Another authentic taste of social policy can be obtained by dipping into one or more of the books written by Richard Titmuss. *Problems of Social Policy* (1950), for instance, is a huge work and contains a lot of detail, but here are some genuinely moving and extremely well written passages on Britain's response to wartime problems. Any of Titmuss's later books, such as *Essays on the Welfare State* (1958), *Commitment to Welfare* (1968) and *The Gift Relationship* (1970), give an impression of social policy's roots.

Finally, as another 'period piece', Ian Gough's *The Political Economy of the Welfare State* (1979) provides a readable example of late 1970s radicalism.

2 IDEAS AND CONCEPTS IN

SOCIAL POLICY

INTRODUCTION

The **principles** of social policy are the guiding ideas which underlie policies for social welfare, education, health services and the like. For instance, one policy might make the principle of **equality** a priority, while another might stress choice or **freedom**. This chapter is about such principles – equality, **equity**, **need**, freedom and rights – and how these words can be interpreted in different ways.

While the term 'principle' is both useful and widely used, it has a very general meaning and is potentially rather confusing. In fact it has several different but *interconnected* meanings.

First, a principle might be said to have a *moral* or ethical meaning. If someone takes 'a principled stand', he or she will be standing up for certain beliefs in what is right and wrong and upholding certain moral standards. A moral standard in social policy could be represented, for

Figure 2.1 Family man
(Reproduced by kind permission of Robert Thompson ©.)

instance, by the principle that no individual in need, no matter how poor, should be left without access to health care. Another, more contentious, example might be the principle, advocated by some, that housing and social benefits should either be withheld from single parents or granted only on certain conditions: for example, that the single parent must find work or employment training.

As can be seen from these examples, the moralistic side of a welfare principle contains a vision of how things ought or ought not to be. Social policy reflects the *norms* and *values* of society. All major social policies have a **normative** element, and are drafted with the intent of influencing society or the behaviour of individuals in line with deeply held convictions and values. Thus, there are left-wing normative principles (which would include, among other things, the idea of equalizing outcomes for people) and conservative normative views: for example, the view that social policies should uphold 'traditional family values', a stance which sometimes backfires when politicians' private lives are held up for scrutiny (see Figure 2.1).

A second way of defining principles is to see them as *rules*. To take an example from the physical world, the human body – or any part of it, such as the heart – operates according to certain physical principles: for instance, the physical laws governing pressure and tension.

However, the principles of social policy are not the same as the principles of human biology or the laws of nature. We cannot predict scientifically how social policies will be applied, or what the effects of social policies will be, in the way that a scientist or doctor can predict what w˙ happen if a certain medical operation or treatment is carried out (the even here we must be careful not to expect too much certainty).

On the other hand, there is an important sense in which principles do convey the idea of the rules of social policy. Each welfare system develops a welfare bureaucracy: government departments with thousands of staff and a framework of rules and laws to regulate the work. Users of services will be affected by the rules: for example, in relation to eligibility for a service or a grant.

Third, 'principles of social policy' refer to the *ideas* and theories which underpin social policy. This definition very much overlaps with the first: principles as morals, norms or value judgements.

However, there is a valid and useful distinction between a principle as a moral statement and a principle as an idea or theory. It is possible, as we saw in Chapter 1, to have theories about social policy which are not *primarily* based on morals or value judgements, even though such ideas might be *partly* coloured by political opinions or other biases.

For example, we may seek to define, in as objective a way as possible, what such ideas as 'freedom' or 'liberty', **'justice'** and 'equality' mean in social policy terms. Another example of a leading idea in social policy, which was developed in the early nineteenth century, is **utilitarianism**: a set of principles outlined by Jeremy Bentham (1748–1832) to offer what he saw as a rational alternative to governing on the basis of values or religious morals.

Box 2.1   An early principle still relevant? The example of Bentham and utilitarianism

Jeremy Bentham was born in 1748 into a prosperous middle-class family. At the age of seven he was sent to Westminster school and, at the tender age of twelve, he entered Queen's College Oxford, which 'he hated even more' than school (Warnock 1966: 7). By the age of twenty he had received five years of training in London as a lawyer, but his brilliant mind and wide-ranging interests led him into the world of publishing and discourse on philosophy.

Between early adulthood and middle age, Bentham established himself as a radical thinker on social, political and moral issues. Together with a circle of friends, writers and publishers, he became an influential figure, challenging government inefficiency and abuse and recommending radical and rational solutions to social problems. His influences on policy were especially noticeable in the field of poverty and 'poor relief' (see Chapter 3), though he also put forward an ambitious scheme to reform and redesign prisons, as well as many other constitutional and administrative proposals.

In 1788, he published his *Introduction to the Principles of Morals and Legislation* (see Bentham 1982), which contains all the main elements of what became known as 'utilitarianism' or 'Benthamism'. Though not a socialist (socialism was in its infancy), Jeremy Bentham did advocate changes which were revolutionary in their time: the vote for all adult men and women, annual parliaments, open and accountable government based on rational or scientific principles. Above all, he firmly believed that the value of any policy should be decided on its objective merits, not whether it fitted in with custom and practice or appeared to support any particular religious values.

In this way, Bentham's philosophy could be summarized as 'radical and ruthless'. There is no room for sentiment, or tradition, or for policies which support unearned privilege. The basic question, according to Bentham, is whether any government policy or institution served any valuable purpose or had any *utility* (use) – hence 'utilitarianism'.

But how do we decide whether a policy has a useful function or not? Bentham's answer – and the principle he is perhaps most famous for – was to suggest that we find out what would bring 'the greatest happiness of the greatest number'. The best policy is one which minimizes the harm or discomfort to the greatest possible number of individuals, or which brings 'happiness' to the majority, even if there is a cost to the minority.

Bentham's method or 'calculus' for working this out was based on the degree of pleasure or pain involved in any course of action. Not surprisingly, he was denounced by leading religious authorities of the day because he appeared to be advancing a godless doctrine which appealed to primitive or basic human instincts. In defence, Bentham's calculus of pleasures included the 'higher' things – for example, education and artistic achievement – and he suggested that policies which promoted these have the greatest utility.

How does utilitarianism apply to modern dilemmas of rationing services or calculating who should benefit from welfare? The utilitarian approach to these dilemmas is to apply 'the greatest happiness of the greatest number' principle. It therefore questions whether all human life is of equal value, and whether it is immoral to weigh some people's happiness or continued life against that of others – questions which are still very much with us, as illustrated by moral dilemmas in the provision of scarce health care resources (see Chapter 8). When health service professionals make judgements about patients on other than medical criteria, they may stray into making utilitarian judgements: for example, whether a patient is young or old, is married or has dependants. Consciously or not, they may be asking themselves, 'What use does saving or prolonging this life have, and how far would medical help add to the sum of human happiness?'

On the one hand, utilitarianism can be seen as realistic: in this world, hard choices have to be made and it is better to be clear-headed about the relative costs and gains of a policy so that welfare can be maximized. On the other, utilitarianism can be seen as one element in an overarching Victorian philosophy of self-interest and a penny-pinching approach to public services. While it would be unfair to portray Bentham as someone who advocated pure self-interest – after all, he believed in the idea of expanding public education and other services to benefit the majority – it was the case that a cruder kind of utilitarian ideas gained ground in the nineteenth century and helped to justify the harsh treatment of the poor.

EQUALITY, EQUITY AND JUSTICE

Equality and politics

The principle of equality occupies a central place in debates about social policy. For those on the left of the political spectrum, social policies are ideally the tools or mechanisms with which to create a fairer society by equalizing benefits from health, education and other services.

But from a centrist or right-wing perspective, social policies which attempt to equalize outcomes for people do so at considerable cost: not only do they impose a burden of high taxation on people with average and higher incomes, with the suggested effect of dampening incentives and economic growth, but they also require a highly interventionist state and an army of bureaucrats and professionals.

Nozick, a philosopher who published an influential book, *Anarchy, State and Utopia*, in 1974, powerfully attacked the goal of using social policies and other forms of government intervention to increase equality. He based his argument on a distinction between 'patterned' and 'non-patterned' forms of justice. To summarize Nozick's complex and interesting argument, his fundamental point is that patterned justice involves the idea of continual interference in people's lives in order to bring about a particular pattern in the way property, goods and other things of value (for instance, employment opportunities) are distributed. The pattern would be based upon a particular goal. For instance, there might be a particularly strong attachment to the idea of rewarding merit and of distributing resources and rewards on that basis; conversely, another society might stress the goal of equality between individuals irrespective of merit or performance.

However, according to Nozick, any attempt to enforce patterns of justice will tend to undermine the supremely important value of liberty – hence Nozick's philosophy is an example of 'libertarian' principles. It is wrong and unjust, according to these principles, for any government to take away the individual's property or income in order to redistribute it in the attempt to create patterned justice: for instance, by taxing individuals to fund social welfare. Nozick's approach therefore emphasizes the idea that there is justice in wealth and property being owned in 'non-patterned' ways (for instance, according to historical factors and chance). For him, the only moral form of government is one which is minimal in its interventions and actions; any 'more extensive state would (will) violate the rights of individuals' (Nozick 1974: 333).

Note how perspectives of the 'right', including libertarian principles such as Nozick's, often suggest that the principle of *freedom* is threatened if social policies are too concerned with equality, while a 'left' perspective defends the idea of promoting equality by reference to principles of *need*. Thus, equality cannot be fully understood in isolation from either of these concepts.

However, it is rather misleading to package all ideas about equality and policy neatly into either a left-wing or right-wing perspective. To begin with, there are considerable differences *among* fellow socialists, liberals and conservatives on the question of how much equality is desirable and how far social policies should attempt to 'correct' the inequalities and injustices of society.

For instance, a liberal thinker on equality, John Rawls, argues that a basic goal of every policy should be one of equality. As far as possible, the 'good things' of life should be shared equally: education and career opportunities, welfare services, leisure etc. Further, Rawls regards the right to liberty as fundamental in a just society: everyone should be treated equally in this respect.

However, Rawls also argues that a certain amount of inequality – just enough to create rewards and incentives for the better-off people in society – will benefit not only the advantaged *but also the least advantaged*. With the right amount of incentive, the better-off groups in society will work at an optimum level of efficiency. This will mean that everyone will benefit from well run public services and business organizations. But if rewards for the better-off exceed the optimum level, the poorer groups begin to lose out. The better-off contribute less than they should in the form of taxes (wealth and income which can be redistributed) and have fewer incentives to be efficient, because their incomes are high irrespective of their work efforts. Rawls termed this idea of achieving just about the right amount of inequality the 'difference principle' (see Rawls 1972).

It has always been the case that some on the left have believed that certain inequalities are unavoidable and are even to be encouraged if they are based on merit, while on the right some have subscribed to the idea that there should be certain basic equalities.

In Britain, the old left–right battle lines between Labour and Conservative parties have been redrawn in recent times. Partly, this is a reflection of international events – in particular, the downfall of communism in the former Soviet Union and its satellite states in Eastern and Central Europe. Though almost all Western European socialists had already distanced themselves from repressive, corrupt and highly unequal communist regimes, the end of communism nevertheless removed an important reference point.

In short, socialism may live on as an idea but, if we define it as a set of policies to redistribute resources and to make society substantially more equal than it was, it is dead. No major political party in Britain – including the Labour Party – now supports principles of equality in the traditional socialist sense.

There is another strong reason for this. In the first half of the twentieth century, policies to redistribute wealth and to make society more equal than before could potentially appeal to a majority of the British population. Approximately one-third of the population enjoyed relatively high incomes and considerable wealth, while the remaining two-thirds lived either on moderate and static incomes or in poverty. Most people could agree with the idea of redistribution, knowing that it would be likely to benefit them.

In more recent decades, however, the pattern of income and wealth has shifted. Although inequalities have widened, living standards for a two-thirds majority have steadily improved at the same time. A political party which stands for equality and a substantial redistribution of resources therefore no longer has the appeal it may have had. The Labour

Party in Britain painfully discovered this in its election defeats from 1979 to 1992. Its victory in 1997 is largely attributable to its ability to distance itself from the idea that it will be a high tax party, with policies to help the poorer one-third at the expense of the majority. Any emphasis on equality, redistribution or higher taxes to fund an expanding welfare state has been removed from its policies.

Justifying policies for equality

Given these changes in the political context and the lack of support for full-blooded socialism, can equality still be defended as an important principle of social policy? As with every principle, the answer to this question depends on how equality is interpreted. Three basically different views can be identified: egalitarianism and the goal of near-equality; equity; and equality of opportunity. Attached to each of these definitions are somewhat different justifications for equality.

Egalitarianism

Egalitarianism is an ideal, an expression of equality in its 'purest' or most utopian form (Drabble 1988). It is about finding ways of ensuring that people enjoy the same results or *outcomes* in life: the same incomes, the same life span, similar levels of education and health and so on.

What would be the justification for policies to bring about a state of near-equality? Again, much would depend on the egalitarian's values or morality. The example of communism has already been mentioned. There has also been a thread of ethical or Christian socialism in British egalitarianism, and this has been a recurrent influence on thinking about social policy (see, for example, Tawney 1964). In communism or Marxism, the ultimate objective was a society in which no one unfairly exploited the labour of anyone else. Ethical socialists, however, stressed the *moral* dimension: gross inequalities are morally wrong, whereas a society of near-equals is one in which community, brotherhood and sisterhood will flourish. Note the normative or moral ideas underlying this principle of equality.

For Tawney, a Christian socialist and a leading figure in debates about equality in a welfare society, equality amounted to much more than 'distributive justice' or making sure that incomes and the benefits of the welfare system were equalized among individuals and classes (see the discussion of Le Grand's *Strategy of Equality* in Chapter 4 for an example of a study of distributive justice and an attempt to measure 'who gets what' from the welfare system). Tawney held to a wider socialistic vision of equality, in which the goal of social policy was to help to create a society in which people felt that they belonged to a common community – a society in which they would feel free to participate in making political decisions about their own futures, and in which everyone was valued equally.

In a similar vein, Marshall – another founder of the principles of an egalitarian welfare society – argued that:

> The extension of the social services is not primarily a means of equal-
> ising incomes ... What matters is that there is a general enrichment
> of the concrete substance of civilized life, a general reduction of risk
> and insecurity, an equalisation between the more and less fortunate
> at all levels ... Equality of status is more important than equality of
> income.
>
> (Marshall 1963: 107)

However, *inequality* of income is important to egalitarians in one important respect: large inequalities, it is argued, lead to social division and are,
in themselves, morally wrong. For instance, under the Conservative administration before 1997, public concern was expressed about the enormous
annual pay increases (of over 30 per cent and totalling thousands of pounds)
awarded to the heads of government agencies. This was at a time when the
great majority of public sector employees, working in the same agencies,
were being expected to accept annual pay increases below 2 per cent.

Thus the egalitarian's argument against *inequality* is relatively easy to
invoke, as did Charles Dickens in his scathing attacks on the greed and
selfishness of Victorian businessmen and corrupt public servants. However, a critique of gross inequality is not the same as making a case for
near-*equality*. Here the egalitarians' arguments are harder to sustain, for a
number of reasons.

First, *individuals differ*. Whether as a result of nature or nurture, every
individual has a unique combination of talents, abilities, temperament
and motivation. Policies trying to bring about absolute or near-equality
would work against these differences, rewarding the lazy, the incompet-
ent and the dishonest as well as the innovative, intelligent or honest.

There is also a lack of *justice* in policies which try to ensure equal
outcomes for all. Would it be just, for example, to ensure that all 16-year-
olds 'achieved' the same number of GCSE results with the same grades,
even though everyone knew that a proportion of the 'successful' candid-
ates were being rewarded for either mediocre efforts or none at all? Such
a policy would immediately devalue the GCSE qualification but, more
importantly, would be unjust to those who had worked hard or had the
ability to achieve the better results.

The second factor is *coercion and loss of freedom*. In order for a state of
near-equality to be maintained, very strong regulatory authorities would
be needed to survey constantly individuals' incomes, redistribute wealth
and monitor access to employment. Not only would this cost a great deal
to implement, it would also bring about a very invasive state. Everyone's
private life would have to be closely and regularly scrutinized to make
sure that no one was becoming better off than anyone else. So while
inequality spells lack of freedom for some, because the better-off may gain
at the expense of the poor, *imposed equality* would reduce everyone's
freedom.

However, these criticisms of equality may only be valid where policies
are taken to extremes. It is relatively easy to put up a 'straw man' of
absolute equality and then knock it down, as gurus of the 'New Right'
such as Hayek (1944), Worsthorne (1971) and Scruton (1984) have done.
In arguing that the goal of equality is unattainable, they have always told

cautionary tales of the horrors of repressive state socialist regimes such as the former Soviet Union. But they have never carefully considered the achievements of countries which successfully applied social democratic principles in the past. Countries such as Sweden and Denmark have not sought to abolish inequality, but have acted to reduce the extremes which arise in more market-oriented societies.

So while almost everyone agrees that near-equality is an impossible dream, perhaps even a nightmare, this does not mean that the equality principle need be rejected altogether. In policy terms, a more acceptable and practical principle might be that of *making society more equal than it was*, rather than bringing about absolute equality. This is in one way a *utilitarian* consideration, increasing equality not so much for the sake of it but more to maintain social order and to ensure 'the greatest happiness of the greatest number'. But, more importantly, there is also the justification of fairness – making sure that the less well-off and the disadvantaged are treated with justice.

A policy to bring about near-equality might look more justifiable if we think about it in relation to *groups* rather than individuals. For example, while accepting that *individual* men and women differ – the more and the less intelligent, able, rich and poor – there is a strong argument that men and women *as groups* should be near-equal. This would mean that approximately equal proportions of women and men would occupy each occupational or income level. Sweden, for instance, has set policy targets to do just this, and aims to achieve a balance of no more than 60 per cent or less than 40 per cent of either men or women in a comprehensive list of occupations (see Blakemore and Drake 1995).

Equity

Equity is a useful idea which extends the concept of equality. The notion of near-equality tends to make us focus on an end-state of sameness or similarity: thus, when neighbours X and Y are near-equal, we tend to think of them having similar incomes, houses, size of car, number of children and so on. But if such an end-state is to be brought about by social and taxation policies, what would be required?

This is where the principle of equity is useful, because, to reach a similar end-state or outcome, it is usually necessary to treat individuals, families or groups *equitably* rather than *equally*. An equitable approach means treating people fairly, but *differently*, in order to ensure that there is some equality between them at the end.

Dividing a cake gives a homely example to illustrate equity. Assuming that one guest feels full, two are not very hungry and a fourth is ravenous, equitable slicing would mean no cake for the first, two thin slices and one large wedge. After this, all guests should be in an equal state – full – but they have been treated unequally to achieve this. Treating them all equally, on the other hand, would have resulted in unequal or undesirable outcomes.

In social policy terms, and returning to our neighbouring families X and Y, equitable social policies would treat each household differently depending on its needs and circumstances. For example, if X's son is disabled or had special educational needs, there might be targeted grants, benefits or school facilities which would have the object of compensating the X family for additional expenditure and bringing them back to a state of near-equality with the Y family.

The problem with equitable social policies is that sometimes they do not *look* fair. This might be a result of faults in the policies: they are not really equitable. But as likely as not, it is because treating people in the same way is seen as fair, whereas treating them differently seems to smack of injustice or special favours. For example, equitable cake slicing might work with adults, but try it with small children who expect *equal* slices of a birthday cake. In this situation equity will almost certainly end in tears.

A more serious example is provided by public reaction to Beveridge's wartime proposals for social security reform, which might be regarded as the cornerstone of Britain's post-war welfare state (see Chapter 3). Above all, it was the fairness and equality of the scheme which gripped the public imagination and which resulted in the 'Beveridge Report' becoming a best-seller. The proposal that all contributors be treated equally, paying the same (flat-rate) National Insurance contributions and being able to draw the same flat-rate benefits when in need, seemed to tune in perfectly with the wartime collective spirit of equality.

Yet, in essence, Beveridge's plan owed more to liberal principles of equality than to socialist ones. Treating people 'equally' meant that the scheme did not substantially redistribute resources from the better-off social classes to the less well-off, although of course it did redistribute from the healthy to the temporarily sick and from the employed to the temporarily unemployed. A more equitable social security policy, it could be argued, would have asked the better-off to pay a little more into the scheme in return for the same benefits as everyone else – but would this have looked fair?

Applying the equity principle can also raise problems because fairness demands an accurate and accepted definition of people's *needs*. Suppose that you are again faced with a table of squabbling children at mealtime and that you have determined to distribute food in unequal, equitable portions. If you are both a parent and a student of social policy, perhaps the children will already have grudgingly learned to put up with the principle of equity. However, there may be vociferous objections to the *grounds* upon which the size of each child's portion has been decided: 'That's not fair, he had a big slice yesterday', 'She said she'd be sick if you give her that much' and so on. At the same time, you may yourself be unsure of each child's 'real' needs: is Matthew clamouring for more simply because he is showing off; is Alison hungrier than she is prepared to say, and should she be encouraged to eat more? Faced with all this, it is not surprising that parents, like welfare systems, resort to giving out equal, but inequitable, benefits.

Equality of opportunity

Equality of opportunity is another useful refinement of the meaning equality. The equal opportunity concept may be applied first to em* ment (through policies to remove barriers of discrimination, impr access to jobs, education and training). In an age of temporary work and part-time jobs, this can be important in a welfare sense. Work, despite its drawbacks, raises incomes, and usually provides social contact and reduces social exclusion. Second, equal opportunity principles can be applied to improving access to, and use of, welfare services and benefits: social security, education, health services etc.

However, as with other equality principles, equal opportunity means different things to different people. Conservatives, as well as those on the left, subscribe to 'equality of opportunity'. Views from the political right stress equality of *opportunity*, while those from the left stress the *equality* element in equality of opportunity. These differences of emphasis can result in substantial practical differences in the ways in which equal opportunity policies are applied. Distinctions can be made between (a) relatively limited or modest definitions of equal opportunity, and (b) more ambitious and 'tougher' approaches. These distinctions are summarized in Box 2.2.

Under British law – for example, the Race Relations Act 1976 – policy and practice are much closer to (a) than to (b). But it is better to think of equal opportunity policies on a spectrum from 'modest' to 'tough'. Particular examples do not necessarily fit neatly into either category. In the United Kingdom, for example, not all equal opportunity policies can be pigeonholed as weak. A certain amount of 'positive action' to correct gender and 'race' discrimination is allowed under British law, and in Northern Ireland a Fair Employment Act and other government action has endorsed the principle of 'proportionality' – which in this case means a more equal sharing of job opportunities between the religious communities than before. Although a strict policy of reserving jobs for the underrepresented Catholic minority has not been introduced, it is in Northern Ireland that the UK has moved closest to the principle of a 'tougher' approach to equal opportunities.

The summarized distinctions between **minimalist** and **maximalist**, or 'weak' and 'tough', **equal opportunity policies**, suggest sharp differences, but it is worth re-emphasizing that in reality these distinctions are blurred. If policies favour **positive action** rather than positive discrimination, for instance, we might prefer to see them as being midway between 'weak' and 'tough'.

Positive action refers to policies which stop short of positive discrimination. Under Britain's Race Relations Act, for example, it is permissible to take positive steps to encourage members of underrepresented groups to apply for work in an organization (for example, in the way that job advertisements are worded). Other forms of positive action include additional training courses to meet the needs of underrepresented groups, career breaks for women or improvements in facilities in the workplace for disabled people.

All these measures are designed to develop a workforce which is more representative of the population, but which does not rely on a quota system of reserving jobs for each underrepresented group. Similar principles apply to the distribution of benefits, or access to the services of a welfare system. Positive action here would entail taking steps to encourage access or to enable disadvantaged groups to make use of services.

Box 2.2   Equal opportunity strategies

'Minimalist' principles

Equality policies aim to ensure that people are *treated* fairly or on an equal basis. Discrimination on grounds of gender, 'race', disability or other irrelevant criteria is unjust and illegal in most cases.

'Fair competition' on a 'level playing field' is the hallmark of this approach. The end-result or outcome (e.g. being employed or receiving a benefit) must be decided on *merit* or according to *need*.

Individuals must be treated 'in like fashion'. The end result is unequal, but fair. *Any* discrimination, positive or negative, is wrong.

Quotas, or reserving a certain number of jobs, educational places or services for members of minority and disadvantaged groups, are unjust.

'Minimalist' principles fit best with liberal or conservative principles and values.

'Maximalist' principles

Equality policies aim to create *equal outcomes*. Policies and the law must go further than banning unfair or negative discrimination; they must also positively encourage or discriminate so that minorities and other disadvantaged groups benefit equally from employment opportunities or the welfare system.

There is no 'level playing field'. Historic advantages enjoyed by those now in control mean that they decide how 'merit' and 'need' are defined. Though merit is important, it may have to be redefined to avoid in-built bias against women, the disabled etc.

Individuals may be treated differently according to the social group or category they belong to. 'Positive action' or 'positive discrimination' may be necessary to make sure that underrepresented groups obtain benefits or employment they have previously been excluded from.

Quotas, or at least targets, to bring the *proportions* of people in various groups (women, disabled people etc.) in line with the proportions receiving employment, education and welfare are necessary because without them little will change.

'Maximalist' principles fit best with social democratic or egalitarian principles, though 'tough' equal opportunities policies are found in the right-of-centre dominated USA.

However, positive action does not mean that people will automatically qualify for a service or a benefit *because* they are members of a minority or a disadvantaged group. Need remains the basic criterion. The object of positive action is therefore to equalize access and to ensure that everyone with needs is heard: for instance, by providing translation services to hospital patients whose first language is other than English.

However, the distinction between providing services strictly according to need, as opposed to positive discrimination in favour of a certain group, is not as clear-cut as it may first appear. Some social benefits already combine 'need' criteria with a kind of positive discrimination: for example, child benefit is distibuted to all mothers (or the father, if he is the main carer) on grounds of 'need' – to offset partly the expenses incurred in bringing up children. Yet among this parent category are many who receive but do not need the benefit: for instance, members of the aristocracy. Similar observations may be made about need and the state retirement pension, or various disability benefits.

None of these benefits is strictly speaking an example of positive discrimination, but the fact that they are given to everyone in a certain category means that they are not targeted or restricted to only those individuals wholly dependent on state help. The arguments about whether benefits should be *universal* – available to everyone in a certain category – or whether they should be *selective* or targeted benefits is discussed further, in Chapter 4.

NEED

This brings us to the important concept of need. We have already seen that 'need' is a *problematic* concept (by 'problematic', we mean a term that is not easy to define and where there is a lack of consensus about what it means). This causes difficulties when, for example, we try to decide whether one person's or one group's needs are greater than another's.

Before you read any further, it may help at this point to write down a list of what you think are important human needs. Try to list at least ten. Now ask yourself these questions. Is there any pattern or logic in the list you have drawn up? For example, do some needs come before others? Are some more basic or fundamental? (If you do not see a pattern, add some more needs and then try to prioritize the needs in some way.)

Are your definitions of need culture-free, or do they relate only to a particular country or social group? To test this, think about whether your list would be as applicable in India or Mali, say, as in Britain or another economically developed country. Try constructing a list as if *you* were living in a village in the African Sahel, or on the streets of an Indian city. How does your list compare with that of Doyal and Gough (1991), which is presented a little further on in the text?

The above exercise and the questions it poses should help to identify two fundamental points about need which have been at the centre of social policy ever since the state began to take on certain basic responsibilities for people's welfare. First, there is the question of objectivity. Is it possible to establish a commonly accepted or objective definition of need and to distinguish clearly between those who are in need and those who are not? The second question relates to questions of responsibility and duty. How far is the state responsible for meeting certain needs? Does the citizen have *rights* to have his or her needs met, and does the community have a *duty* to meet them?

These questions are not only of great interest today. They also vexed the conscience of nineteenth-century Britain. In Britain, the 'new' Poor Law of 1834 showed official acceptance of a very basic responsibility of the state towards the poorest citizens. Workhouses and 'parish relief' were organized into a system which was designed to provide for only the absolutely destitute (see Chapter 3). In return for their freedom and loss of **civil rights**, paupers could obtain just enough from the public purse to survive. In this early example of social policy we have a definition of **basic needs**: shelter, food and perhaps some very limited medical care.

Doyal and Gough (1991: 56–9) point out that survival is too limited a definition even of basic need. As they suggest, the victim of a serious accident who is in a coma may be surviving but is not able to achieve anything or to satisfy any other needs. Similarly, the example of severely malnourished famine victims shows that people may be surviving – just – but are hardly having their basic needs met. Another problem with 'survival' as a definition of basic need is that it is rather circular: it is rather like saying that human beings 'need to live'.

For these reasons, Doyal and Gough suggest that *physical health* is a better definition of basic need, because 'to complete a range of practical tasks in daily life requires manual, mental and emotional abilities with which poor physical health usually interferes' (Doyal and Gough 1991: 56).

The advantage of using physical health as a criterion of basic need is that it suggests certain *goals*. Note that Doyal and Gough talk of 'good' physical health, which takes us away from mere survival to a goal which people can aim for. However, the concept of 'physical health' also opens up problems of definition: how healthy do people have to be before we can say that their needs have been met?

Thus, it may not be possible to find completely objective definitions even of basic needs. This is more apparent when we include Doyal and Gough's second criterion of basic needs, **autonomy**. Without autonomy, or the freedom to be able to decide and choose, human beings are arguably deprived of a need as basic as physical health. It is no use being healthy without the ability to realize the aspirations or objectives which make us human: secondary needs such as being able to develop oneself in various ways, to communicate and to become engaged with other human beings. As with physical health, however, autonomy is a matter of degree. There is bound to be debate about how much autonomy human beings need or, more negatively, how much they can do without.

Sadly, loss or lack of autonomy is not difficult to find in the field of welfare and social policy. Older people, for example, are particularly vulnerable in this respect, because they may have been judged to be incapable of exercising autonomy. The very old are often written off as too mentally confused or frail to exercise any autonomy. Studies of confused older people in residential care suggest that the staff or 'carers' may

Box 2.3   Universal human needs?

Doyal and Gough (1991) argue that it is relatively easy to make up a list of needs – social policy research abounds with them. However, it is more difficult to decide which needs are *universal* and which definitions would permit us to compare need satisfaction in different countries or cultures.

Their list (below) has been drawn up according to one main criterion: to be included, each item must contribute towards satisfying the two most *basic* needs (physical health and autonomy). For example, they suggest that sexual relationships need not be included because 'some people manage to live healthy and autonomous lives without sex with others' (Doyal and Gough 1991: 158). What do you think of their scheme and list of needs?

- nutritional food and clean water;
- protective housing;
- a non-hazardous work environment;
- a non-hazardous physical environment;
- appropriate health care;
- security in childhood;
- significant primary relationships;
- physical security;
- economic security;
- appropriate education;
- safe birth control and child-bearing.

exaggerate these infirmities and may actually increase them (Kitwood 1997). Such residents are not even allowed to exercise choice or autonomy in matters which they can still comprehend.

To sum up, physical health and autonomy can be seen as basic needs which, if denied, will result in human beings being unable to achieve other, secondary needs. Putting it another way, *being deprived of basic needs will lead to serious harm*. But what secondary or intermediate needs can be identified? This is the point at which to compare your own list of needs with that of Doyal and Gough (see Box 2.3).

Needs, wants and satisfaction

So far, our discussion of need has highlighted some of the problems encountered in trying objectively to define 'real' needs. But while difficult, this is not an impossible task as long as we remember that there has to be some argument. In fact, debate about needs is a healthy phenomenon. For instance, it may be prompted by attempts to improve standards of welfare or to expose the hidden needs of disadvantaged groups.

Bradshaw (1972), in a pioneering discussion, suggested that there are four main ways in which people define needs.

- **Felt need**, according to Bradshaw, occurs when individuals are conscious of their needs. However, this leaves open the question of whether they decide to express their felt needs or whether they are able to do so. Not all felt need is expressed, because inequalities of power and status may prevent oppressed or less powerful groups from voicing their needs. For example, older Asian women's needs may be neglected in the provision of community services because of the subordinate position of many of these women (see Blakemore and Boneham 1994).
- **Expressed needs** are those which are publicized and known about; they become *demands*, as opposed to the hidden needs of those who are too powerless or otherwise unable to express what they need (for example, people with learning difficulties in sub-standard institutions).
- **Normative needs** are those which are defined according to professional norms or standards; they are the needs defined by outside observers or experts. For example, a professional counsellor may identify a need in a client, which the client may accept, reject or fail to comprehend.
- **Comparative need** introduces the concept of relative judgement: that is, the needs of a group are defined in relation to what other groups have or do not have. There is an element of justice here: if there are two similar groups, but only one is receiving a benefit or service, the group not receiving welfare could be unjustly deprived and in comparative need.

The first definition – felt need – introduces a subjective element into the discussion. On the one hand, there are some needs which can be defined objectively (albeit with some disagreement among observers) and, on the other, wants which are apparently more to do with subjective or personal states of mind and desires. For example, a person may need a certain medical treatment which is invasive and painful, but not want it. Or a hypochondriac will be obsessed with medical treatments even though objectively these are not needed.

Remember that one way of defining need is to say that being deprived of something one *needs* causes serious harm, whereas this is not the case with things that are purely *wants*. A child may desperately want the latest computer game, but arguably being deprived of it will not cause harm and may even do some good.

However, these distinctions between wants and needs are not clear-cut. The very idea of 'felt needs' suggests that a strongly subjective element *can* enter into definitions of need. For example, a pensioner on a low income may decide that keeping in touch with her grandchildren and other relatives is a basic requirement (and a need to sustain primary relationships). She may decide that it is vitally important to buy comparatively expensive cards and gifts, especially on relatives' birthdays or seasonal holidays such as Christmas. But in refusing to compromise on this, she may well have to economize on heating or food costs. In this case, what appear to be unnecessary wants (cards, gifts) take the place of things that safeguard a basic need, such as physical health: for instance, her heating may have to be switched off for lengthy periods, possibly risking death from hypothermia.

Therefore, although being deprived of needs can be said to cause serious harm, so in some ways can being deprived of wants. If the teenager who is deprived of the latest computer games takes this want so seriously that he becomes depressed, feels that he is a social outcast and that his whole life has been blighted, then we may have to take the consequences seriously: for example, shoplifting or other forms of offending.

The value of bringing the subjective element into any discussion of needs and wants is that it helps to answer the question of why *satisfaction* levels are not markedly rising in industrialized countries, when, according to many objective economic criteria, needs are being met more fully than ever before.

For instance, if economic indicators of well-being are anything to go by, great progress has been made in the past few decades: British incomes rose by 230 per cent in real terms between 1950 and 1990 (Vidal 1994: 4), life expectancy has increased and ordinary people now own many more consumer goods – television sets, computers, cars and refrigerators – than could have been dreamt of in the 1950s. But whether there has been progress in meeting the full range of human needs is a much more debatable point.

This is where the subjective element is important, for as Vidal (1994) notes,

> many people feel intuitively that growth has not necessarily made people better off. Evidence that quality of life is declining is all around. The British now work the longest average weekly hours in the European Union ... We appear to have invented new illnesses – from chronic fatigue syndrome to anorexia – and we have increased our vulnerability to older ones, such as asthma, ulcers and diabetes ... Job stress may cost the UK ten per cent of GNP annually. And so on, through jammed-up cities, loss of greenbelt, more noise, increasing need for the car ... the abuse of natural resources ... pollution, and inner city blight.

We do not have to accept the whole of this negative message. For instance, there are objective grounds for saying that health is better now than it was forty years ago (see Chapter 7). However, an equally important factor is whether people *feel* that their needs are being met and whether their quality of life is failing to improve. As societies with welfare systems become more affluent than before, perhaps they can increasingly 'afford' to be disenchanted with the costs of progress (pollution, erosion of public amenities and loss of community life) in a way that poorer, less industrialized countries cannot.

FREEDOM AND RIGHTS

If we are coerced or told what to do throughout our lives and are deprived of rights, we cannot realize our potential to become fully human beings. However, as with equality, 'freedom' and 'rights' can easily become slogans. Difficulties begin when policy-makers or those who deliver welfare services have to decide what 'freedom' and 'rights' mean in practical terms, and on what grounds some people's freedoms may have to be removed or curtailed.

For instance, there may be a need to suspend the driving licence of a driver whose seriously failing vision and hearing pose grave dangers to other road users and pedestrians. However, difficulties arise in defining safety limits for the majority of older drivers, most of whom are safe drivers and enjoy lower insurance premiums as a result. What if a driver's vision is poor but just about adequate to drive a car along familiar routes? Or what if the driver and her partner live in a rural area, where without the use of the car it would be very difficult to obtain services? Should such drivers have the freedom or the right to take moderate risks with their own and others' safety?

Disability throws up a range of even deeper questions about freedoms and rights. The right to vote, for example, signifies an individual's full membership of society as a citizen. But do people with severe learning difficulties have the right to vote and, if not, how can their voices be heard and rights as citizens be respected?

Those who champion the rights of disabled people (for example, Oliver 1990) argue that most, if not all, of the problems they face have been created by the society around them rather than directly by their disabilities. This is a 'social' model of disability, as opposed to a 'charity' or 'victim' model. It suggests that rather than pitying disabled people as victims of their own physical or mental states, society is responsible for improving their freedoms and guaranteeing their rights. For instance, considerable investment in redesigning work, transport and housing facilities is needed in order to remove the barriers to freedom experienced by disabled people.

Whether it is fair or just to expect society to make such a full commitment to the rights of disabled people is an open question, and is likely to cause continuing arguments about how to balance the rights and freedoms of non-disabled and disabled people. However, any discussion of freedom and rights will be unproductive unless these principles are broken down into different elements.

One way of doing this is to follow Marshall's (1950) classic distinction between **civil**, **political** and **social** rights. It is possible for individuals and groups to enjoy one or more of these types of rights, and the freedoms that are associated with them.

- *Civil rights* include basic freedoms under the law: for instance, freedom from discrimination, arbitrary arrest and detention, freedom to meet in groups and to have open discussion, freedom of the press and of expression.
- *Political rights* extend these freedoms to include the right to vote, to join and participate in political parties and to hold government accountable to democratic opinion.
- *Social rights*, according to Marshall, are of a rather different order: they involve a greater commitment of resources and are represented by right to education, social welfare and social security; in short, rights to t' benefits of a welfare system.

Viewed historically, in Britain, the three categories of rights can be seen to have developed gradually, with civil rights being established first, then political rights (for men first, and for women substantially later) and finally social rights. However, Marshall stressed that there is not necessarily an inevitable process of evolution at work here, involving automatic or continued progress towards social rights.

In some countries, such as present-day Singapore, it is possible to observe substantial social rights and a well organized welfare system, but rather limited political rights (see Chapter 5). Thus one kind of freedom and one set of rights does not necessarily lead to another. In fact, social welfare can bolster paternalistic governments by making them appear fair and reasonable, thus reducing basic political freedoms.

To return to particular groups in society, such as disabled people or older people, we may apply Marshall's distinctions to questions about the rights of each. For example, with regard to children, electoral democracies have nowhere extended them *political* rights – they cannot vote or send their own representatives to parliament. However, this does not mean that they cannot have their *civil* rights improved and, under the Children Act and many other pieces of legislation, children have legal rights to education and welfare services: *social* rights.

If one considers people with learning difficulties, it may well be that they enjoy social protection and certain social rights, but they may never be granted civil and political rights even though, in some cases, they are capable of exercising political preferences or participating in decisions made about their welfare.

Another way of looking at both rights and freedoms is to think of them either as *negative* principles ('freedom *from*' certain things that endanger liberty) or as *positive* principles ('freedom *to*' do certain things).

A negative definition of freedom would give every citizen the right to be protected from harm by others: for example, from physical assault, burglary or discrimination. Negative definitions of freedom are very much part of a classical liberal or *laissez-faire* philosophy. In this view, people should be allowed as many freedoms as possible. However, complete freedom, or free-for-all anarchy, would not bring genuine liberty. *Laissez-faire* must be coupled with strong laws to restrain those who would intentionally seek to harm or reduce the freedoms of others. Thus a liberal society such as the USA has always had relatively strong laws to limit the power of both the state and private monopolies (which form to fix prices unfairly and exploit consumers).

A strong belief among those on the political right who subscribe to the 'negative' view of freedom (for example, Joseph and Sumption 1979) is that *to be poor is not to be unfree*. In other words, the poor and the rich alike enjoy political and civil rights, and it is not up to society or to a government to bring about a state of affairs in which everyone has equal freedom of action.

According to this view, a market is vital in ensuring both economic efficiency and freedom. But by their very nature, markets lead to differences and inequalities: people are bound to have differing amounts of spending power. In a 'free' market, there cannot be an equal freedom for everyone to have tea at the Ritz.

Why do defenders of this view, such as Hayek (1944), argue that the poor – the losers in a market-based society – are not deprived of freedom? First, civil and political freedoms are still protected. For example, even though a family on income support probably could not afford a tea at the Ritz, they would have as much (civil) right to enter as anyone else (in contrast to societies in which discrimination against certain social groups was legal, as in the former South Africa, where a black person could legally be denied entry to a hotel). They would also have the political right to meet with others on the street outside to demonstrate about poverty, if they wished.

Second, the argument runs, loss of freedom involves coercion or the *intention* of someone to deprive others of freedom. In a true market, though, there is no conscious or planned intention to reduce anyone's freedom. The market operates impersonally, and its outcomes (for example, rising or falling house prices, booming demand in one industry, decline and lay-offs in another) are apparently unknowable in advance.

Does this argument ring true, especially to anyone who happens to be in the poorer position in a market society? First, we may question the suggestion that the outcomes of living in a market-based society are unknowable. There *is* clear evidence that, if unchecked, inequalities tend to widen. The social gap increases between wealthy elites and a more or less permanent group of disadvantaged people, while those in the middle feel increasingly insecure about their own position. Rather than an increase in freedom and the generation of a mobile society in which enterprise and individuality are rewarded, increasing numbers of people begin to feel unfree and the better-off tend to monopolize positions of power and influence.

Second, there is an assumption that because market forces are blind, nothing should be done to 'tinker' with them, apart from ensuring that there are rules to guarantee fair competition. But it is on this point that many, including some conservatives as well as those in the political centre and on the left, agree that it is both unethical and unwise to allow the market full rein. A more positive view of freedom involves policies to make sure that it is possible for those who are disadvantaged by a market society to have or to do certain things: for instance, to be able to purchase adequate food or housing, or to be educated.

In one sense, the whole of social policy and its history revolves around this question: *how far* should the state step in to mitigate the effects of a market-based society? How far should it guarantee the freedoms and rights of every citizen to enjoy not only 'freedom from' discrimination or harm, but also 'freedom to' have a certain standard of living and welfare?

As we have seen, there are limitations to the pro-market, negative concept of freedom. On the other hand, there is also growing acceptance in social policy of the limits of positive views of freedom. Partly because of the spiralling costs of welfare systems and also because of worries about the creation of welfare dependency, politicians and policy-makers are beginning to rephrase the aims of social policy. It is no coincidence, for example, that in Britain the Labour government's plan for a 'welfare to work' policy emphasizes the *responsibilities* of the young unemployed as much as their *rights*.

CONCLUSIONS

From this chapter you should have gained an insight into some basic principles of social policy: equality, need and freedom. But before leaving this discussion, a word of warning: any debate about concepts is bound to exaggerate their importance. It is easy to elevate them to a position of influence over social policy that in reality they do not always have. Therefore, to end the chapter, it might be worth thinking about the following points in order to put the principles of social policy into perspective.

1 There is rarely, if ever, a clear and unambiguous set of principles underlying any single policy or welfare system. In reality, social policies are usually based on conflicting principles. They may even be supported by rival groups, each with its own set of principles. The Child Support Agency, for example, was in the beginning supported by both feminist opinion (because it seemed as though more absent fathers than before would have to recognize their responsibilities) and conservatives who subscribe to 'traditional family values' and responsibilities. Similarly, feminists and conservatives may combine to support a policy to restrict or ban the use of pornography. When a new policy comes to be implemented, though, these temporary alliances of principles and groups easily shatter.

2 Principles are an important influence on social policy, but it would be wrong to think that the *stated* principles and ideas of a government, or of those who administer welfare systems, actually determine policy. For instance, looking back to the 1980s, it would be misleading to draw up a checklist of 'Thatcherite principles' (such as introducing business principles into welfare provision) and then try to show how British social policy changed course in the space of a few years *as a direct result* of changed ideas in government. Even reforming governments such as those of Mrs Thatcher could not rip up every existing principle and start afresh the next day. The British welfare system today continues to operate on a mix of 'radical right', conservative and social democratic principles, even though there has now been a change to 'Blairite' principles in a 'New Labour' government.

3 It is sometimes the case that so-called principles are *rationalizations* for things that would have happened anyway. For instance, Britain's relatively poor economic performance would have led to attempts to slow down the growth of the welfare system, whichever political party had come to power. According to this argument, Thatcherism and its descendants are but one of several possible ways in which the British political system would have tried to justify to the electorate what was inevitable: tougher limits to welfare expenditure. The popularity of the Conservative message in some quarters during the 1980s may have derived from the way it attempted to make a virtue of the 'tough' approach to welfare (whereas previous governments had been defensive and apologetic about reducing expenditure).

Despite these three points, principles are important, even if they do not always play a strongly decisive role in shaping policy. For one thing, they act as signposts towards new developments in social policy and they can be invoked as goals or targets by those who wish to move policies in a new direction. Mrs Thatcher's drive to inject market and business principles into the welfare system is a case in point.

This chapter has examined principles, such as equality and need, that were once the bedrock of social policy. As mentioned in Chapter 1, students of social policy were traditionally tutored in a framework of mainly social democratic principles. The merits of the welfare state would have largely been taken for granted, just as there would have been trust in the idea of improving large-scale, state-provided welfare services to meet needs.

However, as a result of profound economic and social change, including the splintering of former class divisions and allegiances, we can no longer take for granted all the old aims and principles of the British welfare state. This does not mean that principles or concepts of equality and inequality are irrelevant, but it does mean that such principles have to be rethought and reconsidered to understand better the role of social policy in a more uncertain world.

KEY TERMS AND CONCEPTS

autonomy	minimalist and maximalist policies
basic needs	(of equal opportunity)
civil rights	need
comparative need	normative needs
egalitarianism	normative policies
equality	political rights
equality of opportunity	positive action
equity	principles
expressed needs	social rights
felt need	utilitarianism
freedom	wants
justice	

SUGGESTIONS FOR FURTHER READING

For a specialized discussion of Bentham and utilitarianism, consult Steintrager's (1977) book, *Bentham*. For more general purposes, though, concise and readable introductions to utilitarianism can be found in Eric Midwinter's *The Development of Social Welfare in Britain* (1994) and Derek Fraser's *The Evolution of the British Welfare State* (1984).

To get a flavour of the stirring yet scholarly and well reasoned debates about equality that used to permeate British social policy, try any book by R.H. Tawney, but especially *Equality* (the 1964 edition has an introduction by Richard Titmuss, which is interesting itself as a commentary on ideas about equality in the post-war period). T. H. Marshall's *Sociology at the Crossroads* (1963) or *Citizenship and Social Class* (1950) provide essentia' historical background to the development of welfare principles.

At the other end of the political spectrum, Hayek's *The Road to Serfdom* (1944), written before the end of the Second World War and the beginning of the Cold War, offers a passionate defence of freedom and the principles of a property-owning, market society. And for an overview of both 'old' and 'new' right thinking on concepts of equality and inequality, freedom, justice etc., see Scruton's collection of short articles, *The Meaning of Conservatism* (1984).

For more contemporary reading, my book with Robert Drake, *Understanding Equal Opportunity Policies* (1995, especially Chapter 2), offers discussion of the principles of, and justifications for, equality policies, while Doyal and Gough's *A Theory of Human Needs* (1991) provides a thorough exploration of concepts of need and the policy dilemmas that arise in trying to meet them.

3   THE DEVELOPMENT OF SOCIAL

POLICY IN BRITAIN

INTRODUCTION

In the previous chapter we looked at social policy in a general way, focusing on key principles which are not specific to any particular time or place. However, in this chapter we will focus on welfare development in the United Kingdom for two key reasons.

1 To provide some historical background to particular social policy areas discussed elsewhere in the book: notably, education (Chapter 6) and health policy (Chapter 7). There will also be some discussion of the history of the Poor Law and nineteenth-century attempts to deal with the problem of poverty; this will have relevance to both social security (Chapter 4) and social control and social policy (Chapter 5).
2 To put Britain's overall approach to social policy in its historical context. Any country's social policy can be seen as part of what Jones

(1985) calls a '**whole system**': that is, its economy and level of development, political system and social structure.

As Jones warns, it is easy to make 'shallow' and easy generalizations about a whole system, and there is always the danger of jumping to conclusions about the way British social policy developed and what this means for us today. To understand fully a particular area of policy, there is no substitute for careful study of the history books. Reading suggestions on the history and development of the British welfare state are given at the end of this chapter.

However, as Jones also points out, looking at the big picture of social policy development helps to put the issues of today in perspective. Present-day policy changes can be attributed with earth-shattering importance when, in the broader context of the past fifty or a hundred years, they are relatively minor adjustments. The second part of this chapter will therefore provide you with a sketch of Britain's social policy development, concentrating on how the welfare state was affected by the turning point of the Second World War and by William Beveridge's plan for a new welfare system. We will then be in a better position to compare Britain's current state of welfare with that of other countries.

Before we consider recent and current social policy, though, the next section will explore some of the key developments in social policy which occurred before the welfare state was born. Though these are influences from much further back in time, they have a relevance to modern social policy, partly because nineteenth-century policies towards poverty, for instance, left a deep and lasting impression on British culture and on attitudes to the state and welfare, and also because each example is connected to an important *theme* in social policy, as indicated in Box 3.1.

Box 3.1   Themes in present-day and historical social policy

Key issues in present-day social policy	Historical examples and comparisons
Welfare dependency; 'workfare'; dealing with problems of social exclusion and the possible formation of an underclass	The reform of the Poor Law; the 'workhouse test' and distinctions between the 'deserving' and 'undeserving' poor
Renewed interest in public health and preventive policies; health promotion	Public health reforms: government regulation of sanitation, housing and working conditions
Centralized control of the curriculum and assessment in schools, coupled with more local management of schools; tighter inspection procedures; publishing school league tables	Developing a system of state education; deciding the appropriate roles of central government, local authorities and churches; 'payment by results'

EXAMPLE 1: FROM WORKHOUSE TO WORKFARE?

The significance of the revised Poor Law of 1834 and the development of a system of workhouses to deal with problems of poverty lies in a number of important issues which are still central to debates about *how much* welfare should be provided, and *what kind* of welfare.

Those who framed the Poor Law legislation were above all concerned to prevent the 'undeserving' poor from gaining benefit from the public. The undeserving – as they saw them, lazy able-bodied scoundrels who refused to work – were thought to be morally corruptible by dependence on the state or by any policy of open-handed generosity.

From the earliest days, and including the original 1601 Poor Law brought in at the end of Elizabeth I's reign, Poor Laws had always emphasized this distinction between the **'deserving' and 'undeserving' poor**. However, critics of the old system for helping the poor pointed out that it did not have a sufficient *deterrent* effect. Under the 'new' Poor Law, individuals would have to be prepared to submit to degrading and shameful proced- ures to receive any benefit. Thus only the truly deserving, those worthy of help, would be likely to come forward for help. It is for this reason that we link the Poor Laws with **stigmatization**, for to be seen to be a pauper or – in the old language – to 'go on the parish', was a permanent scar or blight upon one's reputation and that of one's family.

The last remnants of the Poor Law system were scrapped in 1948 (see Chapter 9), and the original scars and deterrent effects of the system have faded, except perhaps in the minds of people in their late sixties or older. However, it is still possible to show how the tougher attitudes towards the poor evident in the 1834 Act had a long-lasting and deeply transforming effect on British social policy and public attitudes towards poverty. It increased the shame and stigma associated with being dependent on pub- lic welfare and it cemented the connection between work and respectabil- ity. Just as the Poor Law Commission eventually devised a 'labour test' (see Fraser 1984: 51) to allow paupers to receive outdoor relief – money or food received from the parish while the recipient remained at large or at home – tacitly accepting that not all could be institutionalized, so is the government today experimenting with policies which use willingness to work as a test of eligibility for benefits.

The concept of *eligibility* is highly important to an understanding of the historical preoccupation with how to distinguish between 'deserving' and 'undeserving' poor people. To be eligible for assistance under the nineteenth-century Poor Law, a person in poverty not only had to be willing to forgo certain liberties and to experience degrading conditions, but also had to fit into one of several tightly defined categories of 'deservingness': not only destitute, for example, but also abandoned or orphaned, wid- owed and with no family support, or disabled or chronically ill.

Throwing greater responsibility for welfare upon individuals and their fam- ilies is bound to increase the role and significance of **means tests**, or assess- ments of people's incomes, savings and ability to draw upon family help. The example of the Poor Law helps us to review the history of the means test and to appreciate its significance in the development of British social policy.

The 1834 Poor Law: a step backwards

Today we live in a period in which the former scale of welfare provision is being questioned. These contemporary questions echo fierce debates about the public relief of poverty *before* 1834.

From a present-day standpoint (and from the point of view of the poor in the nineteenth century), the new Poor Law of 1834 represented a step backwards – a removal of traditional 'rights' to assistance, however limited, and a challenge to the idea that social policies tend to evolve towards a more progressive and generous treatment of the disadvantaged.

However, to many in the 'respectable' and better-off classes, Poor Law reform would have been supported as an improvement. In the early nineteenth century, there was growing concern among the propertied classes about the rising cost of supporting the poor. These were times of immense change in certain ways and in certain parts of Britain, but also of slow change and conservatism in others. Britain was at once a society of rip-roaring frontiers – especially in the free-for-all, rapidly expanding industries of engineering, railways and textiles – and of rural conservatism, strong resistance to change and a desire to protect agricultural interests. Add to this mix of contradictory forces fear of revolution (increased by the example of France), a seething ferment of discontent about lack of parliamentary representation and little-understood economic changes, such as alarming rises in food prices, and it is perhaps not so surprising that the poor came to be scapegoated by 'respectable' society as one of the least desirable results of rapid social change.

The tendency to blame the poor for what are perceived to be negative aspects of social change – for instance, crime and declining moral standards – is still with us, as contemporary discussion of social order and poverty shows (see Chapter 5). But nor was this kind of scapegoating new in the 1820s and 1830s. Since Tudor times, when an organized and parish-based system for dealing with paupers was introduced, there had always been a punitive approach towards the poor, and above all towards 'sturdy' (able-bodied) beggars and vagrants.

The **workhouse**, then, was a central element in the earliest Poor Laws, aiming to make those who received public assistance contribute to their keep. However, there was always a moral aim too. The workhouse was to be an institution to correct laziness and to reform the character. Despite the harsh approach to poverty in earlier times, however, treatment of the poor was demonstrably more punitive and less open-handed *after* the 1834 Poor Law than before. Historically, harsh treatment of the 'undeserving' had been accompanied by traditions of providing charitable support to the needy and deserving. And to supplement this there had developed a widespread informal practice of giving a **dole** of bread, the staple food, or an equivalent weekly payment in money, to low-paid labourers and their families who would otherwise starve.

This latter form of help, an early form of income support, was tagged with the name of the parish said to exemplify the practice: Speenhamland. But although the **Speenhamland system** was widespread, it was not based on law or formal rights. Nevertheless it represented an expectation that the working poor would be helped, and that they could receive such help while continuing to work from and live in their own homes.

The Poor Law of 1834 represented a new body of thought which sought to challenge all this. Not only did it seem to reformers that relief of poverty was leading to ever-rising and unmanageable public expenditure, but the rising *laissez-faire* orthodoxy in economics suggested that it would be wrong to interfere in the labour market by subsidizing poorer workers' wages. Such subsidies were encouraging employers to pay their workers a lower wage because they knew that the parish would make up each labourer's income to subsistence level. In a free market, it was held that supply and demand should determine the price of labour, as it does any other commodity.

Utilitarian ideas (see Chapter 2) also played a leading part in both pressure for reform of the earlier Poor Laws and the design of the new legislation itself. In this case, achieving 'the greatest happiness of the greatest number' meant reducing the burden or 'pain' of public taxation, the local rates levied to pay for poor relief, while at the same time taking a tough but reforming approach towards the poor.

Edwin Chadwick, an influential follower of Bentham, was a leading member of the Royal Commission of Inquiry into the Poor Law set up to investigate existing systems of poor relief; subsequently he was secretary of the commission which implemented the Poor Law reforms of 1834.

The case that Chadwick and the other leading commissioners set out to prove was that the existing Poor Laws needed a radical overhaul and that the community was being too generous towards the poor. Three aspects of their report stood out.

First, the distinction between *poverty* and **pauperism** or 'indigence' was redrawn and reaffirmed. The law accepted no responsibility for trying to reduce inequality and poverty in the broader sense. The 'Poor' Laws were only to assist the completely destitute – the paupers.

Second, the *'workhouse test'* was to replace other kinds of means tests, or assessments, of the able-bodied as to whether they needed assistance. Therefore, although the nineteenth-century Poor Law is seen as the foundation of means testing and all its humiliating and stigmatizing effects, the 1834 Poor Law reforms – if they had been fully implemented – would actually have done away with bureaucratic means testing, visits to the home to assess a person's assets and the like – at least as far as the able-bodied were concerned.

This is because the workhouse test was a chillingly simple one. To be able to receive assistance, the individual would have to lose his or her freedoms and civil rights, and enter a Poor Law institution. Families would be split up, mothers separated from their children and husbands separated from their wives. According to the legislation, outdoor relief would no longer be an option.

Reformed workhouses and other institutions were proposed, to be run according to centrally defined principles and rules, so that no paupers would be treated better in some workhouses than in others. The rationale for this was the principle of **less eligibility**, the idea that no one receiving public assistance should be in a more 'eligible' (satisfactory) position than any wage earner. To have paupers in a better financial position than workers would undermine the wage economy.

Less eligibility and the uniformly harsh conditions of the workhouse were introduced to prevent the poor from seeking out the more generous or liberal institutions, but more importantly to deter the 'roving beggar'. The main assumption contained in the less eligibility principle was that employment was available for everyone able-bodied enough to work. Making workhouses uniformly discouraging was a device to make work more appealing than 'going on the parish'.

As an example of the regulated uniformity of the workhouse, there is the famous scene in Dickens's *Oliver Twist*, when Oliver asks for more gruel. This scene was a criticism not simply of individual cruelty but also of the tight bureaucratic regulations which governed workhouses. The diets of inmates, and the weights and quantities of every ingredient, were carefully controlled down to the tiniest quantity.

Third, the legislation proposed sweeping *administrative* reforms. In this it represents the first of many subsequent nineteenth-century reforms of government and attempts to strengthen the regulatory powers of the state. As Fraser puts it, to Chadwick's 'orderly Benthamite mind the 15,000 separate parishes administering the Poor Law were anathema ... [and] ... Chadwick preferred a centralised, uniform system' (Fraser 1984: 47–8).

Thus the 1834 Act approved the setting up of a central government agency, the Poor Law Commission. This was to oversee the development of new Poor Law unions across the country (parishes were to amalgamate to make more effective providers of relief) and to regulate conditions in the workhouses.

Gradually, Poor Law institutions took on more specialized functions, some becoming infirmaries or hospitals where people without any means could obtain medical treatment, many becoming mental asylums, others institutions for older people and so on. Eventually, as local government was reformed and expanded, it took over Poor Law institutions: for example, there were municipal or local authority run hospitals before the NHS was introduced in 1948.

As it turned out, the great majority of 'paupers' receiving assistance continued to do so outside workhouses and other institutions. Fraser, for example, quotes evidence to show that approximately five out of six received 'outdoor' relief in the middle of the nineteenth century (Fraser 1984: 51). Chadwick's workhouse test was never applied comprehensively because many local authorities did not comply with the Poor Law Commission's requirements, refusing to build the number of workhouses envisaged in the original policy.

Thus the results of the 1834 legislation represent one of social policy's classic examples of the gap between a stated policy and outcomes. Not only did the policy raise questions about the cost and practicability of workhouses, but it also appeared to be designed for a rural and parish-based world rather than the new industrial age. In the large and rapidly growing urban centres of industrial Britain, it was not uncommon to find that many thousands of workers could be thrown out of employment overnight as one or more industries collapsed. To expect masses of labourers to submit to the workhouse test, with possibly permanent effects on workers' family stability, earning power and respectability, was simply unrealistic.

EXAMPLE 2: PUBLIC HEALTH REFORM

One of the leading policy issues today is about the balance of resources devoted on the one hand to **public health** and preventive strategies, and on the other to individual care and curative strategies in medicine. Everyone agrees that it is much better to prevent illness in the first place than to have to deal with its consequences. However, a certain amount of illness cannot be prevented. Moreover, success in reducing heart disease, for example, will only mean that increasing numbers of older people will live to 'enjoy' other illnesses, and ultimately death itself is not optional.

A preoccupation with prevention can lead in some circumstances, if not all, to blaming the victim. For instance, it may be assumed that individuals are responsible for their own fates (smoking too much, eating fatty foods) and therefore for preventing their own illnesses, when a significant amount of illness is caused by genetic or environmental factors outside the individual's control (see Chapter 7).

The history of public health in Britain illustrates both the latter point about the connections between environment and health and the wider question of how far there may be a conflict of interests between public needs (public health, preventive strategies) and individual needs or sectional interests.

The nineteenth century was *the* age of public health and environmental improvement. This is not to say that progress in health was smoothly achieved or always centrally planned. Public health reforms were brought about after protracted struggles between progressives and reactionaries, between central government and local authorities, and between the mean-spirited and those who championed public spending on unglamorous sewer-building, better water supplies and health inspectors.

By the end of the century, Britain had developed a comprehensive system of laws governing health standards (see Box 3.2).

 Why did the Victorians put so much effort into improving public health? First, there was an increasing threat of infectious disease in the squalid conditions of Britain's rapidly expanding towns and cities. The populations of Birmingham and Manchester doubled between 1801 and 1831, while those of Glasgow tripled and of Leeds more than quadrupled in the same period (Fraser 1984: 57).

Historians are uncertain about how much the death rate went up in the first quarter of the nineteenth century, but it is certain that there was a marked increase. Overcrowding and inadequate housing, poor or non-existent sanitation and infected water supplies all contributed to a high death toll and worsening health.

With the benefit of hindsight and scientific knowledge, it is easy to deplore the initial inaction of public authorities in the face of such appalling

> **Box 3.2   Nineteenth-century health reforms**
>
> - *1831: a Central Board of Health* was set up by government to deal with a major outbreak of cholera.
> - *1842: Report on the Sanitary Condition of the Labouring Population of Great Britain*. A pioneering and scathing report on the environmental causes of disease led by Edwin Chadwick.
> - *1846: Liverpool Sanitary Act*. This was an example of how all the major cities required specific parliamentary legislation to permit them to bring about public health improvements. Liverpool's was a model for the times: a local medical officer and staff were appointed to oversee water supply and sewerage improvements.
> - *1848 Public Health Act* set up a national General Health Board. Local authorities were permitted, but not obliged, to set up Local Boards to improve sanitation, build waterworks etc.
> - *1858 Medical Act* established a General Medical Council to control a register of qualified doctors and to regulate training.
> - *1865 Sewage Utilization Act* laid down national standards for safe sewage disposal.
> - *1866 Sanitary Act* for the first time *obliged* local authorities to comply with previous legislation, as under the 1848 Act.
> - *1872 and 1875 Public Health Acts* were two pieces of legislation which consolidated and clarified all earlier regulations. Together, they laid down the duties of local authorities with regard to environmental health (for example, duties to inspect housing and maintain sanitary standards) up to 1936.

problems. Yet urbanization on such a vast scale and at such a pace was unprecedented. Further, in a profoundly unequal society, most members of the privileged classes had little or no idea of the changing circumstances of the mass of the working population, or of the impact of death and disease upon them. Fear, however, filled the vacuum left by lack of knowledge and public awareness: fear of cholera and other deadly diseases, and fear of the contaminating mob. By preventing infectious disease in the general population, the middle and upper classes were protecting themselves.

More than narrow self-interest was involved, however, because concern with public health was inextricably bound up with a mission to control and 'civilize' the masses. The Victorians often mixed together images of the poor, of slums and of contamination. Moral improvement of the masses came to be seen as part and parcel of improving health, communicated in the motto 'cleanliness is next to godliness'.

No one illustrates the public health mission more aptly than Edwin Chadwick, whose zeal and energy were stimulated by a desire to bring order where disorder, squalor and filth coexisted. He had been a leading architect of the new Poor Law (see above), but his later studies of the costs of illness to the poor relief system (caused by the need to support the sick) led him in a new direction. Chadwick's crusade soon 'embraced whole-heartedly the environmental theory of disease prevention, brushing aside the claims of curative medicine' (Klein 1984: 13).

Basing his conclusions on varying rates of disease and death in different localities, Chadwick traced the connection between poor social condi-tions, inadequate sanitation and illness. But he was by no means the first or the only person to conduct research on the social causes of disease. From the late eighteenth century onwards, a number of studies on the connections between urban living conditions and disease were carried out by doctors. Though the scientific causes of infection were not fully under-stood, the medical profession had therefore played a leading part in estab-lishing the evidence for *public* health reform.

As medicine developed in the nineteenth century, this early link be-tween medical research and public health began to wane. Gradually, doc-tors for a variety of reasons began to focus less on public health and more on individualized and curative care.

Historical evidence shows that the commonest illnesses of the nine-teenth century were acute infectious diseases such as typhoid, influenza, tuberculosis and pneumonia, which had little or no medical remedy at the time (McKeown 1979). From the late nineteenth century and through the first half of the twentieth, the terrible toll of the acute killing diseases, which were particularly prevalent among children, was gradually reduced. But this was *not* achieved by medical discoveries or by improvements in individual medical treatment such as immunization. Social policies on public health and sanitation, housing and the working environment, and the regulation of food storage and hygiene, all reduced the opportunities for infectious diseases to spread. As McKeown has demonstrated, much if not all the improvement in death rates in the twentieth century came *before* the introduction of effective medical treatments (for example, immunization against tuberculosis and diptheria; the introduction of antibiotics to counter respiratory infections).

Thus, while there is no doubt that curative medical care remains a highly popular and much demanded form of welfare, modern medicine has its limitations and has not single-handedly reduced the *death* rate – though this does not mean that we should devalue its contribution to the management of *illness* and pain. As long as individualized medical care retains the lion's share of the resources devoted to health, though, there is likely to be a continuing conflict of interests between what individuals want and public health interests.

EXAMPLE 3: EDUCATION, THE ROLE OF CENTRAL AND LOCAL GOVERNMENT, AND THE CONCEPT OF THE 'CONTRACT STATE'

'Must welfare be provided by the state?' is a leading question in social policy. At a time when the role of the state is being questioned, it makes sense to review what happened *before* the era of 'big government' and the twentieth-century extension of welfare systems, when people asked whether it was right for central government to provide any services at all.

Education is a good example of this debate because, in Britain, arguments about the proper role of central government have continued uninterruptedly from the nineteenth to the twentieth centuries. Compared with other educational systems, Britain's has always been relatively uncentralized (Rust and Blakemore 1990). For example, it has only been since 1988 that we have had a national curriculum defined by central government. In this and in other ways, British educational policy has been rather different from the French, German and other European systems.

The development of a 'contract state' in education

Before 1870, the responsibilities for providing, funding and running schools lay largely in the hands of the voluntary sector (churches and charitable institutions) and the private sector (of 'public' schools, many of which were then of inferior quality but some of which were to become exclusive elite institutions). As Best explains,

> Readers . . . will perhaps be astonished to learn that there were few primary schools . . . for which the state had full responsibility in 1850, very many for which it had no responsibility at all, and that its responsibility for the rest lay with a variety of religious organisations.
> (Best 1979: 173)

In a slow process of educational reform from about 1850, the state did come to accept growing responsibility. But the idea that government should actually *provide* education continued to be resisted strongly. Government's first duty, it was thought, was to *regulate* providers: to ensure that education of a sufficient standard was being provided, but by other providers than government itself.

The **contract state**, though, is a term which implies more than regulation. It also includes the idea of government (central or local) paying for services and entering into contracts with non-governmental organizations to provide services rather than providing them itself. The authorities lay down standard definitions of quality (for example, mastering the 'three Rs') and try to enforce those standards in contracts with providers. For instance, in the nineteenth century, churches agreed to have their schools regulated and inspected in return for religious freedom, grants from government and the right to run the schools.

Why did not central government play a more active role in providing state education? A number of reasons have been advanced. The prevailing ideology of *laissez-faire* and individualism militated against spending public money on education. The *nature* and *timing* of industrialization in Britain also played a part: as the first country to industrialize on a large scale, Britain enjoyed fifty or more years of dominance in world markets with little apparent need for education. There was a disdain for applied, scientific and technical education among the elite. Classics and the arts became by far the more prestigious and valued part of the curriculum in elite public schools, while science was neglected.

Thus there are very conservative influences on British education. Britain is still renowned for its class-bound attitudes towards education and the social divisions apparent in its school system. Science and technology are still rather undervalued and undersubscribed and, in comparison with leading European economies, significantly fewer British young people (over 16) stay in some form of education (see Chapter 6).

But this account stresses only the negative side of educational development. Even in the nineteenth century, progressive voices were strongly advocating much greater government commitment to the provision of schools. For instance, John Stuart Mill, a leading writer and liberal – someone who had initially been much influenced by utilitarianism (through his father James Mill's close connection with Jeremy Bentham) – championed the cause of public education. Lord Shaftesbury, an aristocrat who (in modern language) became a 'born again' evangelical Christian, was passionately committed to education as part of the cause of factory reform, the abolition of child exploitation and the provision of factory schools. And Charles Dickens, a tremendously popular figure (who, it might be said, had a direct interest in expanding his readership), both celebrated the importance of good education and highlighted the scandal of child abuse in existing boarding institutions (see, for instance, *Nicholas Nickleby*).

There was also concern about Britain's international competitors, and the fact that other industrializing nations were demonstrating greater public commitment to education. At the same time, changes were taking place in the nature of industrial work. Demand for child labour began to decline. Consequently, gangs of children on the streets were seen more often than before, concern about offending grew and school was increasingly seen as a solution. Regular schooling would keep troublesome young people off the streets and help to inculcate them with industrial disciplines such as timekeeping and 'knowing your place'.

Despite these pressures for change, government policy continued to be one of delay. In the words of Best, the period up to 1870 can be seen as 'thirty and more years of dithering' in education policy (Best 1979: 177). The main stumbling blocks turned out to be the system of voluntary or church provision of education that had already evolved, together with *laissez-faire* attitudes which put market principles before government intervention.

A comprehensive review of education policy published in 1861 (the Newcastle Commission) advised that the voluntary, largely church-run system should remain, but should be improved in efficiency by a system of **payment by results**. This policy not only delayed direct state involvement in providing education but also perpetuated rivalries in the voluntary sector of churches. However, the effect of the efficiency drive after 1861 had a dramatic effect on the classroom. Individual schools' grants, and thus teachers' salaries, were dependent upon how many children attended the school regularly and whether performance in standard tests of numeracy, literacy and basic factual knowledge was satisfactory.

Less efficient schools would get less support, while the schools which boosted attendance and successfully drilled children in the 'three Rs' would be rewarded. As might be expected, rote-learning and strict discipline

overshadowed interest or broader education in the classroom, and payment by results did not reduce the huge class sizes that were prevalent at
the time. Sometimes, a single teacher would be responsible for over a
hundred pupils, aided by monitors or pupil-teachers.

At this stage, British education policy illustrates clearly the meaning of
a contract state: regulation from the centre, a 'purchaser' role for a government department and competition between providers. It is valuable to
compare Lowe's payment by results scheme of the nineteenth century
with the education reforms of the previous Conservative administration,
which introduced a competitive market into the school system, standard
assessment and the publication of schools' performance in the form of
student attainment 'league tables' (see Chapter 6).

Eventually, as the nineteenth century drew to a close, the contract state
principle of funding and providing education was supplemented by
another principle: that of direct provision of schools by local authorities.
In the twentieth century, the state (in the form of local education authorities and a central Department for Education) became the main provider
of education.

THE DEVELOPMENT OF A WELFARE STATE

In the first four decades of the twentieth century, a different set of principles and a different model of social policy gradually replaced the classic,
laissez-faire ideas of the nineteenth century (see Chapter 5 for further
discussion of the development of social policy from the beginning of the
twentieth century).

In health, income maintenance, housing and other important policy
areas, as well as education, government began to act according to more
strongly interventionist principles. These principles have been summed
up as *social* liberalism (to distinguish them from classical, nineteenth-
century liberalism) and, in health care and income maintenance, were
based on the idea of individuals protecting themselves with *insurance*
from the risks of illness, unemployment and other losses of income.

However, to see the early decades of the twentieth century as a complete change from nineteenth-century *laissez-faire* would be wrong because, despite a growing willingness to provide for the individual and to
build up a system of social support, *economic* policies were still largely
constrained by the thinking of classical liberalism. In the face of economic slumps in the 1920s and 1930s, governments could think of little
else to do but reduce public expenditure, balance the books and try to
alleviate the worst effects of economic depression – unemployment and
poverty – by providing meagre and strictly means-tested benefits.

Nevertheless, and despite these limitations, the landmarks of social policy
in the 1920s and 1930s represent some achievements in the face of economic adversity, as the list in Box 3.3 indicates.

The inter-war period of social policy demonstrated that there were
severe limitations to the insurance principle as a way of providing security
of income and health care to everyone. Though government schemes for

Box 3.3   Landmarks of social policy in the 1920s and 1930s

1919   *Housing Act* launched an ambitious post-war house-building programme (see Chapter 8).

1920   *Unemployment Insurance Act* extended insurance cover under the state insurance scheme (introduced in 1911) to almost all workers, except those in agriculture, earning up to £250 per year.

1925   *Contributory Pensions Act* replaced the original 1908 (non-contributory) old age pension scheme and extended benefits to widows and orphans.

1926   The *Hadow Report* on the future of education firmly established the notion of 'primary' and 'secondary' stages and paved the way for later reform in 1944.

1927   *Unemployment Insurance Act* provided help for long-term unemployed people who had insufficient contributions to benefit from the scheme, but it also toughened benefit rules and the 'seeking work' test of eligibility.

1929   *Local Government Act* transferred many of the functions of the Poor Law guardians (officials), to local authority committees (public assistance committees), including responsibility for administering means tests. It also exhorted local authorities to reorganize services according to function (for instance, a health services committee for all in the local area) rather than a public assistance committee to deal with the health needs of 'ex-paupers'.

1934   *Unemployment Act* restored cuts to dole payments which had been made in 1931; it also clearly separated poverty relief from unemployment insurance.

pensions, health and unemployment insurance were extended and improved in the 1920s and 1930s, mass unemployment and the persistence of poverty meant that millions of people could not adequately insure themselves. The poor were forced to rely on the dole and, as in the nineteenth century, had to submit themselves to degrading and humiliating means tests to obtain assistance.

Beveridge: the man and the plan

It is against this historical background that the contribution of one man, William Beveridge (see Box 3.4), should be judged. Beveridge, perhaps more than anyone else, can be seen as the main architect of Britain's welfare system.

Beveridge's plan for a complete overhaul of Britain's social policies was written in the middle of the Second World War, in 1942. Full-scale war

Box 3.4   William Beveridge, 1879–1963

William Beveridge came from a well-off, upper middle-class background. His father was a prominent judge who worked for the colonial service in India. After a public school education, followed by a classics degree at Oxford University and law in London, William Beveridge decided not to follow his father into a career in law, but went to live in a university settlement house, Toynbee Hall.

In doing this, William Beveridge demonstrated that he had both a social conscience and an interest in social questions. University settlements were charitable institutions for graduates with reforming ideas to engage in social work with the poor. Although Beveridge's work at Toynbee Hall, as a warden, was more like that of a university tutor than a community worker, and did not involve him in very much contact with local people, he began to establish himself as an influential commentator on social issues, and especially on problems of unemployment and poverty.

In 1906, Beveridge left Toynbee Hall to work as a journalist, reporting mainly on social policy issues for the *Morning Post*. Then, in 1908, he became a civil servant and an important government adviser (to Winston Churchill at the Board of Trade), helping to frame legislation on labour exchanges (job centres) and advocating the introduction of compulsory insurance of workers against loss of income from unemployment.

Thus William Beveridge's formative years were very much tied up with the social reforms of the Liberal government of 1906–14, and it was this commitment to both Liberal ideas and social insurance which shaped his later, and much greater, impact upon social policy in the 1940s. Between the wars, however, Beveridge took an academic post as Director of the London School of Economics, successfully building it up from a relatively small workers' education college to a leading university institution (see Chapter 1).

Though concentrating on academic affairs at this time, William Beveridge maintained a strong interest in practical action and in devising more efficient and comprehensive approaches to social insurance than the piecemeal system that developed in the 1920s and 1930s. For instance, he was in close communication with Seebohm Rowntree, the social reformer and investigator of poverty, whose 1937 book, *The Human Needs of Labour*, was very influential in shaping Beveridge's ideas on minimum incomes and the levels of benefit necessary to maintain subsistence.

In the early years of the Second World War the government cold-shouldered his earnest desire to help with the emergencies of wartime planning and, as has often been reported, he rather unwillingly (and with tears in his eyes) accepted what seemed to be the rather mundane task of tidying up workers' insurance schemes.

The government report that emerged from this effort in 1942, *Social Insurance and Allied Services*, was a triumph. It was a tribute not only to Beveridge's outstanding ability to bring order and simplicity to complex administrative matters, but also to his imaginative and bold use of language: his scheme promised to vanquish the evils of Want, Ignorance, Squalor, Disease and Idleness and, for the first time in British history, presented both a vision of a community in which everyone would be cared for and the practical means for attaining that vision.

The Beveridge Report became a huge best-seller. People formed long queues to obtain copies and a quarter of a million were sold in the first year. It had caught the mood for welfare reform and became an important element in wartime propaganda.

As a result, Beveridge's plan became the most significant part of the blueprint for the welfare state created by the post-war Labour government of 1945–51. However, it is important to remember that although Beveridge's plan became part of a Labour programme, neither Beveridge himself nor the underlying principles of the social security system he devised were particularly socialistic. William Beveridge had always resisted the idea of joining left-wing groups such as the Fabian Society or the Labour Party and, in 1944, he became a Liberal MP (losing the seat in the 1945 election). Similarly, his blueprint for social security, though comprehensive and universal in its coverage, did not involve redistribution of money from richer to poorer sections of society. Rather, it was intended to provide a basic foundation of support for everyone, and Beveridge assumed that many would turn to the private sector of insurance to add to the coverage provided by state schemes.

had dramatic effects on social policy, just as it did upon the role of government in all areas of life. This war was a particularly distinctive experience for Britain because the country successfully resisted invasion, but, in the early years of the war, was brought to the brink of defeat. It was also a war which involved the whole population. In these extreme times, and as a result of the blitz, food rationing and other common adversities, British people discovered a new sense of equality and purpose. The significance of this mood of collectivism – the so-called 'wartime spirit' – can be overemphasized, but there is no doubt that the popularity of Beveridge's proposals on welfare was largely because they chimed in with wartime hopes and goals: the idea that, if the war was to be won, it had to be won for the purpose of creating a better society than that of the 1930s.

The Beveridge Report was a revolutionary step forward in British social policy in the sense that it revised the social security system completely. Implementation of the report was carried out by the Labour government elected after the war (though legislation on family allowances was passed by the coalition government in 1945). Clement Attlee's Labour government introduced the following social security schemes in the National Insurance Act of 1946 and the National Assistance Act of 1948:

- sickness and unemployment benefits;
- retirement pensions (for men at 65 and women at 60);

- maternity benefits, widows' benefits and a death grant;
- a National Assistance Board to replace the Poor Law.

The Beveridge Report had also established the need for policies of full employment and a national health service. Without these two supporting planks, Beveridge argued, his proposals for children's and family allowances, pensions and unemployment insurance would not work. Beveridge's plan was also revolutionary in that it suggested *universal* coverage of the whole population (wage-earners, the self-employed, people not employed, dependants) and provision of a wide range of benefits *without having to submit to a means test*.

On the other hand, Beveridge's plan contained less revolutionary elements and in some ways it looked back to the problems of the 1930s rather than forward to a post-war world. First, it was based on a principle of **flat-rate** contributions and benefits: that is, everyone paid in the same amounts of National Insurance and received the same benefits. This appealed to people's sense of equality and fairness, but it meant that contributions had to be geared to what the lowest earners could afford. As a result, the National Insurance scheme could only gather in relatively modest sums and – if the system had continued to run according to the strict insurance principles advocated by Beveridge – only inadequate benefits could have been paid out.

Second, Beveridge's idea of a *national minimum* standard of living, though a radical breakthrough in one respect, was based on three less radical assumptions: the first was that people who were dependent on government benefit and had no savings would be helped by 'voluntary action' (the voluntary sector, together with family and community support); the second was that individuals would be likely to top up the national minimum by making their own insurance arrangements for periods of unemployment or illness, and for old age; and the third was that Beveridge's scheme assumed a very meagre definition of basic necessities for survival.

Beveridge's calculations of benefit levels were derived in part from the 1930s surveys of poverty conducted by Seebohm Rowntree and others, and what these researchers had suggested the poor could survive upon. Thus the retirement pension introduced in 1946, for instance, amounted to less than £25 per week for a single person in *today's* (1998) money.

After the war, therefore, Britain's Beveridgean welfare system did bring a comprehensive range of benefits to all and successfully established the notion of care 'from the cradle to the grave'. For a time, and certainly up to the end of the 1950s, Britain's welfare state was about the most advanced in the world, with the possible exception of New Zealand's and Sweden's.

However, the Beveridge plan incorporated three main flaws. First, poverty persisted because benefits for older people, disabled people and the long-term unemployed were set at low levels. Increasingly, people on low incomes had to turn to means-tested National Assistance benefits. Beveridge had intended means-tested benefits to be a little-used safety net, but for a growing number of people on low incomes, they became an indispensable and long-term support. Thus Beveridge's vision of a welfare system based on insurance, and with little or no use of means tests, was never realized.

As demands upon the benefit system grew in the post-war period, the government soon found that it was impossible to find the money for benefits from National Insurance contributions alone. The social security coffers had to be topped up from tax revenues. Thus, today, the idea that benefits are paid from an insurance fund – a pot of gold to which people have contributed over the years – is a fiction. Britain's benefits are paid mainly from current contributions to the system through taxation and National Insurance contributions, not from contributions made in the past, and the entire system runs with only a few months' money in hand.

Third, Beveridge's plan, as adopted and revised by the Labour government in its 1946 Social Security Act, contained the old-fashioned assumption that married women would be treated mainly as dependants, not as bread-winners or wage-earners. These gender inequalities and their long-term impact are discussed in Chapter 5.

CONCLUSIONS: BRITAIN'S WELFARE HISTORY IN COMPARATIVE CONTEXT

The years 1945–51 can be seen as the period in which the main structure of Britain's welfare system was built. From 1951 to 1964, a period of Conservative administration, Beveridge's system was continued, but earnings-related contributions and benefits were introduced. As mentioned, there were difficulties in funding the system from flat-rate contributions.

In the 1960s and early 1970s, a wider range of benefits and support for families, the unemployed, disabled people and the chronically ill extended the Beveridgean welfare system. Against a background of economic growth and rising prosperity for the majority, coupled with the 'rediscovery' of poverty among a minority, expectations of the welfare system grew.

Although there were differences of emphasis in social policy between the two main political parties, the period up to 1979 can be seen as one of basic consensus or agreement about welfare. In other words, as Conservative and Labour governments succeeded one another, they were unlikely to rip up the social policies of the previous government and were predisposed to expand the role of the state as a provider of welfare.

Mrs Thatcher's period of office as Conservative Prime Minister from 1979 to 1990 is often presented as a radical break with the past and as the period in which Britain turned its back upon the Beveridgean welfare state (see Chapter 5). In the following chapters on social security, education, health and housing you will be able to make your own judgements about how far this actually was the case. However, radical and across-the-board change in social policy certainly did not occur in the first two governments led by Mrs Thatcher (1979–87), when economic policy and political items dominated the agenda (Deakin 1994). It was during Mrs Thatcher's third term that the handbag began to rain down with increasing force upon important sectors of social welfare, with major reforms in education, health and community care, and additional reforms in housing.

However, as far as social security is concerned – the cornerstone of the Beveridgean welfare system – there is a case for concluding that, although the 1985 Social Security Act introduced some important and contentious changes (for instance, the Social Fund, which replaced certain rights to benefits with a more discretionary relief system), the fundamental structure of the old Beveridge system was left untouched. The names of the various schemes and benefits were changed, but the underlying system of benefits established in the 1940s could still be discerned.

Change to the 'British model' or the basic Beveridgean welfare state is therefore proving to be more evolutionary than revolutionary. However, evolutionary change can be fundamental in the long run. There are already signs that within one or two decades some of the key elements in the original Beveridge scheme could disappear into the sands. For instance, though the state retirement pension was maintained at a value of about a fifth of average male earnings between 1980 and 1989, since then it has dipped to less than 16 per cent (as a result of being uprated in line with prices rather than wages). If the present policy continues, by the year 2010 the state retirement pension will shrink to only 10 per cent of average earnings and, in the years which follow, will become an insignificant element in financial support for older people.

How then can the British experience of the development of a welfare system be summed up? What sort of welfare system has Britain developed, and how does it compare with others? For purposes of comparison it is worth considering three main types or clusters of welfare states or 'welfare regimes' in Europe, which have been identified by Esping-Andersen (1990).

Liberal welfare states are those in which government provides only a minimum level of welfare services. Examples are Southern European countries such as Portugal, Spain and Greece. Health and welfare services are typically rather basic. As state-provided services are **'residual'** – that is, mainly for the poor – it is expected in liberal welfare states that the family and religious or charitable institutions will play a major part in providing health and social welfare services. However, the state may organize and subsidize social insurance schemes which protect the better-off and those in middle-class occupations.

Corporatist welfare states, exemplified by Germany, Belgium and France, are less dependent on the market and a *laissez-faire* approach than liberal welfare states. They are highly developed welfare states in which the government takes a leading role in organizing and providing health, welfare and education services. These services are often of high quality and are typically funded by a mixture of private and social (state) insurance schemes. However, other non-government institutions or corporate bodies, such as the churches, trade unions and employers, are also important in welfare provision. Hence corporatist welfare states are often rather conservative in their approach to welfare issues: for instance, with regard to the family and the role of women in the labour force.

Social democratic welfare states place more emphasis on social equality than either of the other two types. The Scandinavian countries, especially Sweden, can be seen as representatives of this type. These countries lead the world in terms of the amount of public money spent on welfare services and social security. Consequently, services are comprehensive, available to all and of a very high standard. Social security benefits are also high (along with the taxes to fund them). However, social democratic welfare states such as Sweden place a lot of emphasis on the work ethic and the importance of keeping people in work. For example, one of the main reasons for Sweden's extensive system of parental benefits and nursery care is to facilitate women's return to work after they have had children. The aim, then, is to reduce welfare dependency by a joint policy of full employment and of benefits which are geared to employment.

It is very important to note that classifications such as these are oversimplifications. Any attempt to look at the broader picture, as Esping-Andersen has done with these three models, is bound to mean that particular countries do not fit a particular model exactly, and that countries contain elements of more than one type of welfare system. Sweden, for instance, has been portrayed as a corporatist welfare state (Mishra 1990). Further, recent change and an economic crisis means that the social democratic model is under threat in Sweden. On the other hand, economic growth and policy reforms in the Southern European countries mean that they are adopting elements of the corporatist and social democratic models.

Interestingly, Britain does not easily fit any of these models. This could mean that Britain genuinely differs from all of Europe in its approach to social policy and is better compared with countries outside Europe, such as Canada or the United States, or that Britain is a 'one-off' and very distinctive example unlike any other welfare system. However, it could also mean that the models themselves are flawed and must be adapted in some way to incorporate the British case.

Britain's history of welfare development has shown that, along with Sweden (which interestingly did not, as a neutral country, share the impact of war on welfare), Britain led Europe in introducing a comprehensive and universal welfare system. In that sense, the early emphasis on equality and citizenship, rights to a wide range of benefits and 'free' health care all point to Britain being a prototype of the social democratic model. However, as the above summary of Beveridge's plan and its underlying philosophy has shown, Britain was given a welfare system which was founded upon liberal principles and a rather basic or minimal idea of how much help people should receive in times of need.

Although the welfare state of the 1940s represented a tremendous leap forward, once the system was in place the British approach has been to expand it cautiously. Britain is not easily portrayed as a 'liberal' type of welfare system (as in Southern Europe) but, as a medium spender on welfare, neither has it kept up with social democratic regimes to develop as comprehensive and advanced a welfare state as in Denmark, Norway and Sweden. Nor has the corporatist system of joint provision of welfare by the government, employers and unions – as in Germany – ever been developed in Britain.

In conclusion, Britain's welfare system today represents an interesting mix of principles and influences from the past. There is still a relatively strong foundation of welfare state principles and a commitment to provision of universal benefits. As will be shown in the next chapter, the proportion of the nation's wealth spent on welfare services and social security has not changed since the 1970s, despite Mrs Thatcher's pledge to cut back the welfare state.

However, a significant change in the direction of policy, especially since the late 1980s, has reintroduced into the 'British model' elements of the pre-1940s or even the nineteenth-century approach to public welfare: for instance, tightening the rules governing eligibility for benefits and making benefit payments conditional upon claimants' 'good behaviour' (such as seeking work or training); stressing individual responsibility for welfare (as in official views of the causes of illness); and reviving the concept of a contract state through the privatization of services or the development of a market system in welfare services. For all these reasons, therefore, the British model combines elements of the liberal or residual type of welfare system with a social democratic approach which, though once dominant, did not develop along Scandinavian lines.

KEY TERMS AND CONCEPTS

contract state
corporatist welfare states
deserving (and undeserving) poor
dole
flat-rate (contributions and benefits)
less eligibility
liberal welfare systems
means tests
pauperism
payment by results (in education)

public health
residual (approach to provision of
    state services)
social democratic welfare states
Speenhamland system
stigmatization
welfare dependency
'whole system' comparisons
workfare
workhouse

SUGGESTIONS FOR FURTHER READING

There is now a wide range of texts which give concise and readable accounts of the history of British social welfare. For instance, at the more accessible and concise end of the spectrum there are Kathleen Jones's *The Making of the Social Policy in Britain 1834–1990* (1994) or Eric Midwinter's *The Development of Social Welfare in Britain* (1994).

For fuller and more detailed historical accounts, try Derek Fraser's *The Evolution of the British Welfare State* (1984) which, though rather dull in places, is still one of the best. Pat Thane's *The Foundations of the Welfare State* (1996) concentrates on the period 1870–1945. It is an extremely thorough and readable history and, like Fraser's book, contains an interesting appendix with examples of historical documents.

There are also books which specialize in the inter-war period: for instance, John Stevenson's *British Society 1914–45* (1984), which provides interesting discussion of the social context as well as detailed coverage of various areas of social policy, such as housing, health services and education. Another discussion of the inter-war period is Anne Crowther's *Social Policy in Britain 1914–1939* (1988), a short and readable specialist book which makes occasional references to policies in Scotland as well as to the situation in Britain as a whole.

Useful general texts which throw light on the post-war history of social policy include Howard Glennerster's *British Social Policy since 1945* (1995) and Rodney Lowe's *The Welfare State in Britain since 1945* (1993), while Nicholas Timmins's *The five Giants – a Biography of the Welfare State* (1995b) offers an outstandingly enjoyable and informative read: it is written in a pacy and readable style which brings the subject fully alive.

For a history which is not specifically focused on social welfare yet which offers valuable background on political, social and economic change, Edward Royle's *Modern Britain – a Social History 1750–1985* (1987) is a good choice. Similarly, Paul Addison's *The Road to 1945* (1994) gives insights into the political context in which the welfare state emerged and includes a chapter (Chapter VIII) on Beveridge and social policy.

Just as future generations watching television serials such as the BBC's *EastEnders* or ITV's *Coronation Street* would not necessarily gain an accurate picture of Britain in the late twentieth century, so must we be cautious about reading too much into Charles Dickens's portrayals of social life in the nineteenth century. His novels were the sentimental pot-boiler serials of their day. However, taken with a pinch of salt, novels such as *Oliver Twist* and *Nicholas Nickleby* do offer interesting insights into Victorian social conditions and attitudes, as well as being an enjoyable read.

For quite different reasons, José Harris's masterly biography of William Beveridge (1977) provides stimulating reading. It is a long and densely detailed book, but worth reading for the way in which it relates the great man's life to the development of social thought and social policy from the early 1900s to the early 1950s. A good companion to this biography would be Peter Hennessy's award-winning book *Never Again* (1992), which expertly captures the spirit and the achievements of the immediate post-war years, 1945–51; the chapter titled 'Building Jerusalem' focuses on the achievements of Beveridge and other architects of the welfare state.

Finally, for comparative perspectives on social policy and discussions which put the British welfare system in context, Catherine Jones's *New Perspectives on the Welfare State in Europe* (1993) provides a stimulating collection of chapters by leading policy specialists.

4   WHO GETS WHAT? SLICING THE

WELFARE CAKE

INTRODUCTION

This chapter will consider certain *economic* aspects of social policy – in particular, how much of the nation's wealth is spent on providing welfare and how the welfare system is funded – and questions of *social division*: how the resources and services of the welfare system are distributed. In short, who gets what?

Directly or indirectly, the costs and benefits of the welfare system affect everyone. How far, and in what ways, people are affected will of course vary according to individual circumstances. Some people are totally dependent on welfare benefits for their incomes, while others receive no social security benefits and may make little or no use of public services.

A career-minded childless couple, for instance, may have little or no interest in a public service such as education. If they plan never to have children they may resent having to pay additional taxes to support services they never intend to use. However, when they go shopping, visit their doctor or work with colleagues, they are indirectly experiencing the results or outcomes of the education system. They are relying on the schools to have taught certain skills to each of the people they come into contact with: reading, writing, numeracy and perhaps some technical skills. The education system may do this well or badly, and its efficiency should be of concern to the childless couple. Are they getting value for money in terms of the educational services provided for their community?

The very rich could also be seen as a category of people who are relatively unconcerned about publicly provided welfare. Their children attend elite private schools; when in need of medical care they use private hospitals; and they are sheltered by company welfare schemes which subsidize pensions and housing.

Such people do not directly use the state system of welfare, and therefore gain little or nothing of direct benefit from it. They pay taxes which contribute to the running of state schools and hospitals, but if they do not use the public services they do not personally regain any of the money they have contributed towards them.

However, the rich do gain substantial *indirect* benefits from an extensive public welfare system. The doctor who treats a rich patient in a (private) hospital will probably have been trained at public expense. The roads upon which affluent people travel are (except where tolls are levied) publicly funded roads. Those who own and control businesses depend on the welfare state being able to pick up the bill for health care for their employees. The public welfare system also helps to maintain the 'social fabric' and to prevent or minimize breakdowns of law and order: this is a function which benefits everyone, but particularly those who have most to lose. These benefits, termed **external benefits** by economists, go beyond individual gains or payoffs.

Nor are the benefits of a fully developed welfare system to the rich necessarily restricted to externalities. The well-off also derive *direct* benefits from the welfare system. Where there are universal benefits (paid to everyone automatically, irrespective of means), the better-off *do* regain some of the money they have paid into the system: for instance, in the form of child benefit and the state retirement pension. The amounts involved may be peanuts to the rich, but they symbolize a principle of citizenship which was put forward when the welfare state was established in the 1940s.

The principle of universal benefits is now increasingly questioned, and there is a counter-argument that they should be phased out in favour of targeting welfare benefits on the poor and those in need. However, as long as universal benefits and 'free' services remain (such as those provided by the NHS), middle-class and affluent people who receive and use them will regain some of the money they have paid to the state in the form of taxes. The main arguments for and against both universalism and selectivism are summarized in Box 4.1.

The main point of these opening remarks is to suggest that the costs and benefits of a welfare system cannot be calculated in purely individual terms. First, there is the argument that welfare can be seen as a community resource. Everyone supposedly benefits from an extensive welfare system: social conditions in general are improved and the social environment becomes less dangerous and threatening than it would otherwise be.

Box 4.1   Arguments for and against selectivism and universalism

Selective benefits	*Universal benefits*
Arguments for	
Income support and benefits only given to those who need them	Inclusive: high take-up among people in eligible groups (e.g. parents)
Efficient: they allow more money to be targeted on low-income families and individuals	Efficient: minimum of bureaucracy and administration costs
Reduce demand for welfare and allow public spending to be reduced or contained	Promote citizenship and sense of social unity
Arguments against	
Means-testing involves complex procedures and claim forms: low take-up likely; high administration costs	Lack fairness. The better-off gain too much from the benefits system and may avoid 'claw-back' taxes
Means-testing may involve social disgrace and stigma: low take-up likely	Encourage welfare dependency and overreliance on the state
If all benefits are related to income (means tested), a rise in income disqualifies people from benefit, acting as a disincentive to work (the poverty trap)	Wasteful: even if people improve their income, they continue to receive universal benefits

GAINERS AND LOSERS: INDIVIDUALS AND GROUPS

Figure 4.1 offers a nightmare vision of a society in which social divisions have polarized and in which the benefits or externalities of a widespread welfare system have been lost. But to suggest that 'everyone benefits' from an extensive and expensive welfare system is to miss the point that some benefit much more than others. In this chapter, we will examine how there are 'gaining' and 'losing' *groups* in terms of how much people gain from, or lose out in paying for, the services and cash benefits of the welfare system.

The groups that have most preoccupied social policy researchers in this respect are income groups or, more broadly, social class groups: for instance, the rich, those on average incomes and the poor (or whatever categories one might wish to create on the basis of class or income). Another distinction, in terms of 'gaining' and 'losing', is that of gender: do women get more out of the welfare system than men, or vice versa?

Figure 4.1 Daddy!
(Reproduced by kind permission of the *Independent* ©.)

A central question to be applied to all these social divisions is whether, or how far, the welfare system **redistributes** resources between groups. There are several possibilities.

1 The welfare system has a neutral role. It does not redistribute resources between groups to any significant degree, and its overall effect is to leave existing inequalities largely untouched.
2 The welfare system has a 'Robin Hood' role, affecting the whole spectrum of society, redistributing from the rich or better-off to those on average incomes and to the poorer.
3 The welfare system acts like the Sheriff of Nottingham, redistributing from the poorer sections of society to the better-off. For instance, poorer and average income groups pay relatively high taxes but may underclaim the benefits they are entitled to, or underuse 'free' services.

4 There is also a possibility that the welfare system *partially* redistributes. Redistribution takes place, but within a limited range of groups. For instance, the poorest groups may take more out of the system than they are able to put into it, but a disproportionate amount of the contributions or taxes are provided by average-income people rather than the rich. If this were the case, redistribution would be from the middle to the bottom, not from the top to the middle and bottom groups.

5 It is also likely that different parts of the welfare system will play different roles. For instance, the education system may play a 'Sheriff of Nottingham' role (if more is spent per head on middle-class children than on those from working- or lower-class backgrounds), while social security may be a 'Robin Hood'. Or, *within* a service such as education, there may be different effects: for instance, primary education may have the effect of transferring resources from the better-off to the less well-off, while higher education may achieve the opposite.

Three further points about the economics of welfare need to be borne in mind. The first two concern the nature of our contributions to the welfare system: *taxation* and *care*; the third relates to the importance of keeping a perspective on the individual as well as the group, as far as 'gaining' and 'losing' from the welfare system is concerned.

Contributions: taxation

It is not enough to focus on what people receive from the welfare system or how much benefit they derive from the services they use. It is also of vital importance to consider how the burden of **taxation** is shared and how welfare is paid for (see Glennerster 1992: Chapter 7, for further helpful discussion of taxation).

First, *tax relief* may be as important as a welfare benefit in protecting the interests of the better-off. For instance, tax relief on occupational and private pension contributions makes a substantial difference to the incomes and spending power of many in the middle classes. It represents a hidden form of welfare benefit and an example of 'fiscal' welfare, as discussed by Titmuss (see Chapter 1).

By and large (and there are exceptions, depending on the rates of tax people have to pay, especially at the lower threshold), income tax and National Insurance contributions are **direct** taxes which are **progressive**. The more someone earns, the more he or she will be paying for commonly used services and benefits. In effect, a person who pays the top rate of tax and uses a 'free' NHS hospital service, for instance, has paid substantially more for that service than someone who has been paying a lower rate of tax; the net effect is to subsidize the hospital care of the lower earner and to transfer resources to that patient.

Indirect taxes, on the other hand, tend to be **regressive** – though again there are exceptions, depending on the items that are taxed. Indirect taxes such as Value Added Tax (VAT) are placed on goods and services. They are regressive because everyone, whether a high or a low earner, must pay the same rate of tax. As a result, the better-off person loses a much lower *proportion* of his or her income through indirect taxes than the average or lower-income person. If the better-off make extensive use of certain public services, such as higher education, we may well find that it is the poorer taxpayers who are subsidizing the better-off.

As well as considering the effects of tax contributions on people's incomes, it is important to think about the way in which taxes *and* benefits (both cash benefits and benefits in kind, such as education and health services) tie together to affect the final income of a household's income (see Figure 4.2).

Contributions: care

A second point about the 'who gets what from welfare?' question relates to the way in which economists define contributions to, and benefits from, the welfare system. Economics focuses on the more easily measurable or 'objective' data: flows of money, goods and services in the so-called formal or wage sector of the economy. But contributions in kind, or in domestic unpaid work, can often be missed in these measures. We have to take into account not only how much *money* people either gain or contribute to the welfare system, but also whether, through caring for relatives, for instance, they are contributing time, physical effort and emotional commitment to meeting welfare needs that otherwise the public welfare system would have to meet.

If the time and effort devoted to informal care are taken into account, the picture of who gains and loses from the current welfare system is changed considerably. As Ungerson (1987) and other researchers on family and community care have noted, women are more frequently expected to care for relatives (other than spouses) than men, and often do so from a sense of duty. The enormous contribution to the welfare system made by family carers and volunteers raises many moral and practical questions about whether, or how much, carers should be paid for their contributions, a point which is mentioned again in relation to community care in Chapter 9.

Keeping a perspective on the individual

Although we have begun by focusing on groups (social classes, men and women, and so on) as 'gainers' or 'losers' in the great welfare distribution game, it is important not to lose sight of the individual.

Thinking about an individual's life course sheds a different light on the distribution of welfare. An individual will switch from one category or group to another during his or her life. Individuals may become seriously ill or may be made redundant, for instance, and thus find that they become net recipients rather than net contributors to the welfare system. This perspective is important, because it shows that although the welfare system may fail to distribute resources or services fairly between various groups, it may nevertheless succeed in redistributing resources from the well to the sick, from those who are employed to the unemployed and from younger to older people.

Figure 4.2   The effects of taxes and benefits on household income

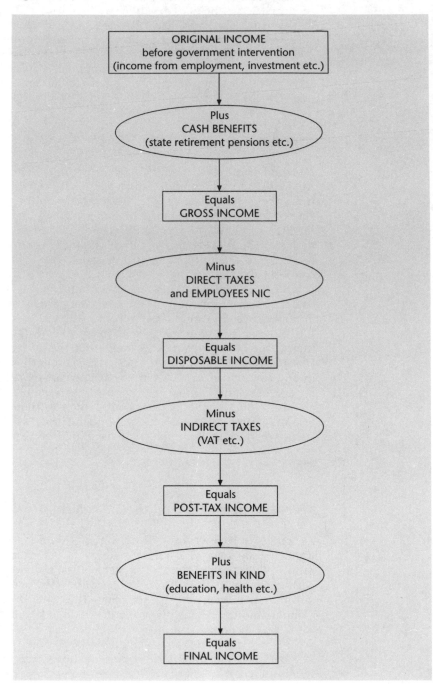

(Reproduced by kind permission of the Office of National Statistics.
Source: Economic Trends No. 494, December 1994: 9. Crown copyright ©.)

This type of thinking lay behind another of the fundamental principles of the 1940s welfare state: the insurance principle. From the individual's point of view, the welfare system was to be thought of as a huge savings bank. For most of a person's working career, the equivalent of perhaps only £60 in services and cash benefits would be regained for every £100 'lost' in taxation and National Insurance contributions. However, in time of need, the balance changes: resources contributed during the 'productive' part of the life are switched to meet needs in a dependent phase of life.

In practice, the funding of the social security system and of welfare services does not work on the strict principles of insurance envisaged by Beveridge, the chief architect of the 1940s welfare system (see Chapter 3). Although the notion of a self-funded insurance scheme is a myth, however, the idea of an individual 'losing' or contributing and 'gaining' or receiving at different points of the life cycle is a valuable one. It helps to explain continued support for a publicly funded welfare state and a willingness to tolerate taxation even when a majority are not net gainers from the system at any one point in time.

HOW LARGE IS THE WELFARE CAKE?

Before we look at the way in which the welfare cake is sliced and at 'who gets what', we need to look briefly at the size of the cake itself and how welfare spending is connected to economic growth.

When an **economy grows** (that is, when the **gross domestic product** (GDP) – all the goods and services produced in the country – is increasing), it is possible for government to spend larger amounts of money each year without raising the burden of taxation. If the economy stops growing or even shrinks, as in the 1991–2 recession in Britain, fewer goods and services are produced, less taxation can be gathered and the government must borrow money to fund the shortfall in its tax revenues, or increase tax rates or reduce public spending.

In the long term, even a relatively slow-growing economy such as Britain's will create a significant increase in the resources available to government. For instance, a growth of 2 per cent per annum will increase the nation's wealth by a quarter over twelve years (that is, a **real increase** of between 24 and 26 per cent). Some industrial economies grow at a much faster rate than this. At 4 per cent growth per annum a country's wealth and income would grow by a half over the same period of time.

If the population grows as quickly as the economy, however, the per capita (per head) wealth of the country will not increase and, if population growth outstrips economic growth, wealth per head will actually decline. In many parts of Africa, for instance, economic growth has been sluggish and population growth rapid, so that standards of living in many African countries have declined to the levels of the 1950s.

In ageing and low birth-rate societies such as those of North-West Europe, on the other hand, economic growth has been relatively steady but there have been increasing demands to fund social security payments and services for an increasing number of people outside the labour force: older

Table 4.1   General government expenditure in the United Kingdom
(excluding privatization proceeds)

	£ billion	£ billion in real terms[a]
1963–4	11.3	123.8
1978–9	75.0	214.9
1988–9	186.9	245.9
1993–4	283.0	283.0

[a] Cash figures adjusted to price levels of 1993–4 by excluding effect of general inflation.
Source: HM Treasury (1995), adapted from Table 1.1, 7.

people, rising numbers of unemployed people and younger people who
remain in the education system for longer periods than before.

Table 4.1 shows how general public expenditure has risen over the past
thirty years, whether we look at this as increases in the actual sums spent
(billions of pounds) or 'in real terms': that is, by translating yesterday's
expenditure into the equivalent value of today's money by allowing for
inflation and devaluation.

The steepest rise in public expenditure took place between 1964 and
1979. From 1979 the rate of increase dropped, but real increases still
continued at a steady rate under Mrs Thatcher's administrations. By 1993–
4, under John Major's Conservative leadership, government was spending,
in real terms, *more than double the amount in 1964*, when Harold Wilson,
the former Labour leader, became Prime Minister.

Largely as a result of economic growth, however, British governments
have managed to fund much of this real increase without devoting a
greater *share* of the nation's wealth to public spending. The economic
cake has grown, but the slice given to government spending has not
changed much in proportional terms. For instance, in 1978–9, government expenditure accounted for 44 per cent of the GDP. In 1982–3, after
an economic crisis in the first years of Mrs Thatcher's administration,
government spending reached a peak of 47.3 per cent. By 1988–9 it had
fallen to a low point of 37.8 per cent, rising again to 43.4 per cent in
1993–4 – almost exactly the same level as in 1979 (HM Treasury 1995:
10). However, to underline the connection between economic growth and
government spending, 44 per cent of the nation's wealth in 1993–4 translated into £283 billion, £68 billion more than in 1979, when 44 per cent
of the national wealth represented £214.9 billion (see Table 4.1).

General government expenditure covers a wide variety of items and
services. Some substantial government priorities lie outside the field of
welfare or social policy, as traditionally defined: for instance, defence,
trade and industry, agriculture, fisheries and food.

Table 4.2 gives an idea of the government's spending priorities and how
the money is divided between 'social' expenditure (social security, health,
education etc.) and other services. These priorities are not set in stone,
and it is important to remember that the *proportions* of public money
devoted to some areas have been declining in recent years (for instance,
defence, housing), while they have been rising in others (for example,
social security).

Table 4.2   Government expenditure by function, as percentage of the national wealth (GDP), United Kingdom

	1978–9 outturn	1986–7 outturn	1993–4 outturn
Social security	10.0	12.1	13.7
Health	4.6	4.9	5.6
Education	5.4	4.8	5.3
Defence	4.5	4.8	3.6
Law and order	1.5	1.9	2.3
Transport	1.8	1.5	1.6
Trade and industry	2.4	2.1	1.4
Environmental services	1.6	1.4	1.4
Personal social services	0.8	0.9	1.2
Housing	2.6	1.0	0.9
Overseas services, including aid	0.6	0.5	0.6
Other non-welfare services	2.6	2.0	2.3
Total expenditure on services	38.3	38.0	39.7
Total welfare expenditure[a]	24.9	25.6	28.1
General government expenditure (including debt interest etc.)	44.0	42.7	43.4

[a] 'Welfare' defined as social security, health, education, law and order, personal social services, housing.
Source: HM Treasury (1995), adapted from Table 1.4, 10.

WHO GETS WHAT? THE LE GRAND THESIS AND ITS CRITICS

In 1982, a specialist on the economics of social policy, Julian Le Grand, published an influential book titled *The Strategy of Equality*. Le Grand studied 'who gets what' from three major social services (health care, education and housing) and a fourth area of services, transport. Transport (including subsidies to public transport) is not conventionally included in social policy discussions, though arguably Le Grand's inclusion of it represents a valuable addition to the social policy literature.

Le Grand's survey did *not* include personal social services. More importantly, in terms of the huge amounts of public money devoted to it, neither did *The Strategy of Equality* deal with social security. As Le Grand himself later put it, 'the book did not set out to deal with Beveridge, social security or indeed the welfare state in general. Rather, it was concerned with specific social services' (Le Grand 1995: 188).

Despite these omissions, Le Grand's 1982 study proved to be highly significant in setting the tone of subsequent social policy debates about the welfare state and its impact on inequality. It challenged the widespread perception that the welfare state primarily benefits the less well-off. The mass media showed great interest in *The Strategy of Equality*, and politicians of both left and right used it to mount criticisms of the 'middle-class welfare state', or a welfare system which seemed to serve the interests of the comfortable majority rather better than the less fortunate.

As Le Grand himself pointed out though, the core message of his study was not particularly new. For instance, Titmuss's 1959 discussion of the post-war welfare state, mentioned in Chapter 1, had already drawn attention to the ways in which the distribution of welfare could favour the middle classes rather than the working classes (see Titmuss 1987). Powell (1995: 164) lists a number of social policy analysts who had begun to identify, before the publication of *The Strategy of Equality*, how the benefits of publicly funded welfare services might be skewed towards the better-off.

As Powell adds, however, Le Grand's book succeeded where others had not in 'assembling a wide range of material within a coherent framework'. As a result, it was widely quoted and established 'a conventional wisdom that the middle class do better out of the welfare state as compared with the working class' (Powell 1995: 164–5).

The leading question, then, is: was Le Grand right? To answer it, we have to remember that Le Grand distinguishes between five different ways of testing the degree of equality or inequality in benefits from the welfare system. It is possible, he suggests, to assess the degree of equality according to each of the five measures separately, or to make some sort of overall judgement of the net effect of all five upon either increasing equality or reducing it. The five dimensions of equality outlined by Le Grand (1982: 14–15) are as follows.

Equality of public expenditure. Is public expenditure organized in such a way as to spread public money equally among social classes, income groups, regions etc.? How much is *spent* per year upon, for instance, each schoolchild in different socio-economic groups? Does the child of an average family in the professional or managerial class have more, less or the same spent upon his or her state education as a child from a family in the unskilled or semi-skilled class?

Equality of final income. Does the way in which benefits and welfare services are distributed have the effect of bringing greater equality between the **final incomes** of the richer and poorer groups? Final incomes represent not only wages or private income less tax but also the value, in money terms, of cash benefits and services in kind (education, health and social services) *received* by each individual or household from the state (see Figure 4.2).

Equality of use. By this measure, we can assess whether the *amounts of service used* by people in different social groups are equal. For instance, do members of working-class groups visit the doctor or use health services as much as, or more than, middle-class groups? Clearly, for reasons of need or ability, some individuals will make greater use of a service than others (for instance, those who are more prone to illness will visit their doctors more frequently, or individuals with academic ability may go on to higher education). However, as Le Grand points out, the question is whether *on average* individuals in different classes use services equally.

Equality of cost. This measure refers to the costs incurred by individuals when they use a service: for instance, transport costs when visiting hospital or a GP, the income forgone when someone leaves employment to undertake education and training, time costs or charges for a service. Le Grand is concerned about this aspect of equality because welfare services can be organized in ways that either reduce costs or even them out be-tween different groups or communities (e.g. by ensuring an even distribu-tion of GP surgeries, or by subsidizing services or transport). Equalizing these costs will increase equality of *access* to services.

Equality of outcome. This is a familiar indicator of equality (see the dis-cussion of equality in Chapter 2) by which we assess the end-result of welfare intervention and service use. As Le Grand reminds us,

> Precisely what is meant by outcome will vary from service to service ... it could be an individual's state of health; for education, the bundle of skills with which an individual emerges from the education system ... for housing, the condition of individuals' dwellings.
>
> (Le Grand 1982: 15)

In *The Strategy of Equality*, Le Grand did not use all five of the above measures in a completely systematic way in his analysis of each major service (education, health, housing and transport). For example, Le Grand took into account that needs for health care vary. In the chapter on the impact of health services he suggests that, *taking need into account*, 'the highest social class group is found to receive over 40 per cent expenditure per person more than the lowest group' (Powell 1995: 179). However, as Powell points out,

> Le Grand examines the issue of equal input for equal need for health care only. For example, he makes no attempt to measure need/demand for education and housing. Le Grand appears to assume that demand for education beyond the compulsory stage is uniform throughout the population, and thus translates class disparities into inequalities.
>
> (Powell 1995: 179)

Since 1982, when *The Strategy of Equality* was published, a number of social policy researchers have urged caution in interpreting its conclu-sions. This does not mean that Le Grand's book is completely misleading. However, there are question marks over:

1 Le Grand's methodology and the way he interpreted the data used: for example, the argument made above by Powell, which is that Le Grand 'moved the goalposts ... in the chapter on health: in none of the other chapters is equality of public expenditure *for equal need* analysed' (Powell 1995: 181).
2 Le Grand's data, much of which were rather dated when *The Strategy of Equality* was published. His study was largely based on research on the General Household Survey (GHS) in a single year (1973).
3 The possibility that Le Grand was not wrong in interpreting his results, but that changes in both the welfare system and society (for instance, rising expectations of better service) have diminished, not increased, class and other inequalities in the amount of use people make of the system.

In relation to the NHS, Powell cites recent research which shows that class advantage in access to, and use of, medical services is not nearly as clear-cut as Le Grand suggested. In the words of one research team (Wilkin

Table 4.3 Mortality ratios and deprivation among people aged under 65 in electoral wards in Northern Region, 1981–3 and 1989–91

	Mortality ratio[a]	
Ranking of wards	1981–3	1989–91
Most deprived fifth	136	150
Second fifth	120	121
Third fifth	109	111
Fourth fifth	100	92
Least deprived fifth	87	84

[a] The mortality ratio means that the death rate is above or below 100, where 100 equals the rate found in the rest of England and Wales in approximately the same years. For example, 50 more people died in the poorest fifth group than one would expect for every 100 deaths in England and Wales as a whole (ratio = 150), while among the least deprived group 16 fewer per 100 died (ratio = 84).
Source: Adapted from Phillimore *et al.* (1994: 1126).

et al. 1987: 158), 'patterns of care depend far more on who your doctor is than on who you are.' Although middle-class patients may be more assertive or questioning in their consultations with GPs than working-class patients, Wilkin *et al.*'s and other studies have shown that these differences do not make much difference to treatment outcomes. Quoting a study by O'Donnell and Propper (1991), Powell concludes that Le Grand 'overestimated the degree of "pro-rich" inequity in the delivery and use of health services.' According to O'Donnell and Propper (1991: 12), who replicated Le Grand's own methodology but used 1985 GHS data, 'there is no evidence of a pro-rich distribution of NHS resources relative to need. Indeed . . . there is some evidence of a pro-poor inequity.'

These studies of health services are based on only some criteria of equality, particularly those of *spending* per head, *use* and *cost* or access. It is not as though the findings contradict or question a trend towards growing inequalities in health itself, which are a measure of final *outcomes* (only one of Le Grand's five indicators).

Although health among the majority has gradually improved over recent decades (whether measured by rates of illness or death rates), the rate of improvement among poorer groups is slow, thus widening the gap between poorer and faster improving better-off groups. An important study of illness and mortality rates in northern England by Phillimore *et al.* (1994) not only confirms this trend but, even more worryingly, showed an actual *increase* in mortality rates in the poorest communities (see Table 4.3), which is mainly accounted for by a rising death rate among middle-aged men.

Such alarming increases in rates of death are unusual in industrial societies with advanced welfare systems. They are happening in Russia, where problems of poverty, poor diet, appalling housing conditions and widespread alcohol abuse are increasing rates of death. To find that death rates are on the increase again in some groups of the British population points to a considerable deterioration in social and environmental conditions.

However, unequal health outcomes are only one test of whether a health service treats people equally. The effect of unequal *use* of 'free' NHS services could still be to transfer resources from the better-off taxpayer or patient to the poorer, and not the other way round, as Le Grand argued.

As far as outcomes such as illness and death rates are concerned, the NHS, or any kind of health service for that matter, can only be expected to take a small share of the responsibility. Health services have only a marginal influence on the overall health of a population. Environmental conditions, including housing and work environments, stress, levels of pollution and diet, play a much larger part (for a helpful review of the evidence, see Taylor and Field 1997: 42–67).

Where Le Grand seems to have made a more convincing case is in relation to other services such as education and housing. Significantly, Powell (1995), in his critical review of *The Strategy of Equality*, is rather silent on these topics.

In 1982, Le Grand found that

> while public expenditure on compulsory education slightly favours the lower social groups, expenditure on the post-compulsory sectors strongly favours the better-off – with the possible exception of student awards . . . The top socio-economic group (employers, professionals and managers) receives nearly three times as much expenditure per household than the poorest fifth.
>
> (Le Grand 1982: 60, 75)

As Le Grand points out, we must make allowances for different kinds of household in making such comparisons. For instance, a disproportionate number of poorer households are composed of older people living alone and with no children; they make little or no use of the education system and therefore have little spent upon them. However, Le Grand argues that even if such differences are taken into account, poorer families – even those with children and younger adults – derive much less benefit from the education system than average and better-off households.

As a result, and despite a dramatic increase in the proportions of younger people going on to higher education (to almost one-third of the 18–20 age group), class inequalities in educational outcome are still marked in Britain (see Chapter 6 for further evidence), whether these are in terms of the number of qualifications gained in different social class groups or the rate of success in obtaining jobs after education. Although the numbers of school pupils attaining five GCSEs at grades A–C has risen impressively since Le Grand wrote *The Strategy of Equality*, a substantial minority still leave school with fewer qualifications and about 10 per cent with no qualifications at all. It is this 'failed' group which still gains relatively little benefit from educational expenditure.

In housing, changes in both policy and outcomes have been more marked than in education since *The Strategy of Equality* was written. Not least among these changes has been a dramatic reduction in the proportion of government expenditure devoted to housing subsidies, rent rebates and housing improvement grants: the nation's wealth spent on housing was more than halved between 1979 and 1994 (see Table 4.2).

The implications of these changes, and of alterations to social security payments such as housing benefit, make it difficult to ascertain who benefits from housing policy. On the one hand, as Le Grand himself notes, the gradual whittling away of mortgage tax relief has withdrawn a pro-rich benefit and has resulted in greater equality (Le Grand 1995: 190). On the other hand, selling off council houses, while it substantially benefited many of the families who bought their own houses from local authorities, severely reduced one of the most important channels of public subsidy to below-average income families. As Le Grand pointed out in *The Strategy of Equality*, 'low income groups have a far higher proportion of council tenants than those with high incomes' (p. 86). In cutting down the size of the council housing sector, while at the same time reducing housing benefit and requiring local authorities to charge more 'economic' rents, the government cut the equalizing supply of public funds to non owner-occupiers in a number of ways (see Chapter 8 for further discussion of housing policy).

In sum, Le Grand's survey of various welfare services still has considerable merits and remains an important insight into the way the welfare system *might* benefit the better-off as much as, or even more than, poorer groups in society. The 'might' is emphasized, however, because both social policy and the nature of social inequality change. 'Who benefits from what' must be kept constantly under review. Recent studies, especially of the health services, show that some scepticism about the Le Grand thesis is justified. The system can be 'pro-poor' in important ways. Perhaps this is not surprising as far as health services are concerned, because the NHS has long been seen as the most 'equal' or socialistic of the welfare services. The education system in Britain, on the other hand, tends to compound class difference and elitism.

Thus we should not jump to overall conclusions about the impact of the welfare system on equality. Many did seize upon *The Strategy of Equality* as evidence that the whole welfare system is against the poor. Not only would this be untrue as far as some aspects of the specific services examined by Le Grand are concerned, but it is especially misleading when we recall that Le Grand did not include the social security system in his survey. Social security spending dwarfs all other items of government welfare expenditure (see Table 4.2), and in 1993–4, for instance, was over thirteen times greater than spending on housing. In 1994–5, social security benefits took a colossal £80 billion of government expenditure (Timmins 1995). Therefore it is to this very sizeable slice of the cake that we must now turn.

SOCIAL SECURITY: THE GREAT EQUALIZER?

Social security benefits may be divided into: (a) **non-contributory** benefits and grants (which recipients qualify for on grounds of need or because they fall into a particular category, such as parents/children); and (b) **contributory** benefits, which are based on the principle of insurance and the recipient being eligible by having paid into the system (or by having credits paid on his or her behalf by the government or employer).

Non-contributory benefits are either **non-income-related** (that is, they are paid irrespective of the recipient's income) or **income-related** and dependent on a means test of some kind. Among the former, the more

Table 4.4 Percentage of benefit expenditure by
recipient group, 1992–3

Older people	46.5
Long-term sick and disabled	20.0
Families	17.4
Unemployed people	12.5
Widows and others	1.9
Short-term sick	1.6

Source: CSO (1994a), adapted from chart 5.7, 70.

important in terms of expenditure are child benefit (£5.8 billion in 1992–
3; see CSO 1994a: 71), attendance allowance (£1.5 billion) and disability
living allowance (£1.1 billion), although other non-income-related benefits
include one-parent benefit, war pension and severe disablement allowance.

By far the biggest item of expenditure of all non-contributory benefits is
the income-related (i.e. means-tested) *income support*, which totalled £14.5
billion in 1992–3. This is the benefit upon which many poorer families
rely, including people who are out of work and have used up their six
months' Jobseeker's Allowance. However, income-related benefits also include housing benefit (£3.5 billion) and council tax benefit (£1.5 billion),
as well as Family Credit, which is a benefit for people at work but on low
incomes (£0.9 billion in 1992–3).

Among contributory benefits, the lion's share goes towards the huge
retirement pensions bill, which was £26.9 billion in 1992–3, for example.
Invalidity benefit took a further £6.1 billion in the same year, unemployment benefit (from 1996, Jobseeker's Allowance) £1.8 billion, and widows'
benefit £1.5 billion (CSO 1994a: 72). Contributory benefits also include
such items as statutory sick pay, statutory maternity pay and industrial
disablement benefit.

Who benefits from all this expenditure on both contributory and non-
contributory benefits, representing a total of £74.1 billion in 1992–3? If
we examine this question in relation to the main recipient groups, we
find that older people form the largest single category. Through payments
on retirement pensions and other benefits for older people, they receive
almost half of all benefit expenditure. Older people and other recipient
groups can be ranked as shown in Table 4.4.

As will be demonstrated below, the net effect of social security is to
redistribute money from the better-off to the less well-off sections of society. In other words, social security is more of a 'Robin Hood' than a 'Sheriff
of Nottingham', and thus offsets some of the 'unequalizing' effects of
other parts of the welfare system observed by Le Grand. But if this is the
case, one may ask: why have social inequalities widened over the past
fifteen years? Why do substantial numbers of people live in poverty, and
appear to struggle to make ends meet on meagre state benefits? (see, for
example, Kempson *et al.* 1994).

To understand how social inequalities can widen when the social security system simultaneously redistributes in favour of poorer groups, it is
necessary to appreciate that inequalities of income have increased partly
as a result of:

- changes in *taxation* policy which have favoured the better-off;
- economic and social trends which have worked to the advantage of the better-off (such as expansion of 'middle-class' jobs and continued decline of 'working-class' jobs in manufacturing);
- changes to social security which have pruned and trimmed the value of benefits, largely by indexing them to price rises rather than to a wage index (wages rose faster than prices between 1979 and 1991).

At the same time, however, the welfare and social security system continues to have a *mildly* redistributive effect, swimming against the tide of increasing inequality, but rather weakly. In the words of Hills, explaining trends in poverty between 1979–85 and 1986–91,

> Over the earlier period, inequality in *market* incomes widened, particularly as unemployment rose. However, the welfare state largely succeeded in blunting the effects of this on the gross incomes of the poorest. In effect, the welfare state was working harder than in the 1970s. Since 1985, however, inequality of market incomes has continued to widen, but the gap in gross incomes has done so faster. In particular, with benefits price-linked, the benefit system has failed to check the rise in inequality.
>
> (Hills 1993: 38)

Hills points out that between 1979 and 1991, average incomes in Britain increased by 36 per cent. In other words, the nation as a whole was better off by over a third in real terms. But over the same period, the real income of the bottom tenth income group '*fell* by 14 per cent. Meanwhile, the incomes of the top tenth rose by 62 per cent' (Hills 1993: 37).

Thus, for a variety of reasons, including government policy, Britain became an increasingly polarized society from the mid-1980s on. Behind the cold statistics presented above, there are millions of examples of individual suffering and disillusion. Many low-income families, and especially the substantial proportion of older people who are solely dependent on the state retirement pension, find it increasingly difficult to make ends meet. According to the government's own figures, the numbers of people living *below* the official 'safety net' level (income support or its predecessor, supplementary benefit) increased by a third between 1979 and 1989 (Hills 1993: 35).

The way in which poverty has been increasing is therefore key to understanding the role of social security. The social security system perpetuates, rather than reduces, poverty. As a result, some people in poverty experience conditions which are not only health-threatening (through inadequate diet, for example) but also life-threatening (for instance, when older people are forced to economize by turning off their heating).

While these are valid points, it is also true to say that benefits, inadequate though they are, nevertheless represent a flow of cash from the better-off to those who are dependent on benefits or are forced to live on them. As a result of their 'Robin Hood' or redistributive effect, taxes and benefits reduce income inequality to an *average* of £7450 per year among the poorest fifth of households, compared to an *average* of £28,250 among the richest fifth. This disparity, a ratio of about 1:4, compares with the ratio of about 1:21 if **original incomes** were left untouched by the tax and benefit system (CSO 1994b: 37).

These comparisons are of course between average households in each income group in the population. There are very rich households with incomes far above the average of their group, just as there is a minority of very poor households whose incomes are lower than the average of the bottom fifth.

Another way of looking at how far incomes are evened out by the tax and benefit system is to consider how much each group's *share* of all the income in the country is modified by it. For instance, before taxes and benefits are taken into account, the richest fifth of households receive just over half of all income, while the poorest fifth receive a meagre 2.3 per cent. After benefits and direct taxes are taken into account, the richest fifth's share falls from over a half to 44 per cent of all income, while the poorest fifth's share rises from 2.3 to 7 per cent (CSO 1994b: 37).

On the other hand, the effect of indirect taxation is to reverse slightly the redistributive effect, resulting in a lessening of the poorer groups' shares of final income. As incomes rise, indirect taxes take a decreasing share of household income, while, as noted in the introduction, poorer households lose a higher proportion of their income through taxes such as VAT. In all, as suggested above, the tax and social security system has a mildly redistributive effect, but it is hardly of an earth-shattering nature.

This is even more apparent if redistribution is looked at from the point of view of *lifetime* earnings and contributions rather than from a single point in time. Reporting on income data for individuals over their complete lives, Hills shows that 'the lifetime poorest' receive 'somewhat more' than the 'lifetime richest' (Hills 1993: 19). These estimates include benefits in kind, such as the NHS and education, as well as social security. However,

> The overall distribution of gross benefits is very flat: almost regardless of income, someone could expect to receive gross benefits over their life totalling around £133,000 (at 1991 prices) . . . *Most* benefits are self-financed over people's lifetimes, rather than being paid for by others. Of the £133,000 average . . . benefits, an average of £98,000 is self-financed. Nearly three-quarters of what the welfare state does, looked at this way, is like a 'savings bank'; only a quarter is 'Robin Hood' redistribution between different people.
>
> (Hills 1993: 19)

Again, this broad picture of 'who benefits' from social security and other forms of welfare provision must be qualified by a number of things: for instance, gender makes a difference, in that, 'on average, women are net lifetime beneficiaries from the system, men net lifetime payers for it' (Hills 1993: 21). The question of how much an individual gains or loses over a lifetime will also be affected by the generation or 'age cohort' he or she was born into.

For instance, individuals who were already of mature age when the welfare state expanded between 1945 and 1975 were more likely to gai in the short term from cash benefits and 'free' services such as N treatment, but without necessarily having had to pay out over a wh working life for them. Conversely, those now in middle age will have to fund existing services and benefits throughout their lives – including, for instance, retirement pensions for those who are now old. But if the welfare system contracts in the future, they may not gain quite as much in their lifetimes as the earlier generation did.

CONCLUSIONS

This chapter has discussed 'who gets what' from the welfare system. In this, the focus has been on *economic* benefits and costs. This is not to deny the importance of the social and political costs and benefits of having a well developed welfare system. For instance, commentators on the right claim that an 'over-generous' or open-handed welfare system creates social costs or problems such as welfare dependency and laziness – or, more politely, 'work disincentives'. Supporters of a comprehensive welfare system, whether on the left or the right, would point to its social benefits: for instance, greater social stability and perhaps less crime.

However, these latter questions, important though they are, were not the main subject of this chapter. Discussion of the *social* effects of the welfare system – especially the connections between social policy, social control and poverty – is continued in the next chapter. Similarly, specific problems such as the poverty trap, which are linked to both economic and social aspects of the welfare system, are also discussed in the next chapter.

Before we sum up the economic side of 'who gains and who loses' from the welfare system, however, it is important to underline the point that restricting our gaze to cash or money benefits (or the equivalent, in money terms, of services in kind, such as NHS treatment) could give a rather narrow view of equality. As mentioned at the outset, conventional economics may miss the important contributions of labour or care provided 'free' by carers or family members.

Second, as Powell reminds us, when earlier social theorists such as Tawney (1964) and Marshall (1970) defined equality in social policy, 'they appear[ed] to be talking about equality of status, entitlement, universality and citizenship rather than the more demanding forms of distributive justice as outlined by Le Grand' (Powell 1995: 170). In other words, it would be a mistake to judge the welfare system solely according to the way in which it distributes cash benefits or other calculable outcomes, such as length and quality of medical treatments, or the number of educational qualifications gained, when the architects of the system did not have these objectives in mind.

There is something over and above these rather narrowly defined outcomes: a principle of equality which transcends class and other inequalities. The politicians and planners who established the welfare system after the Second World War were inspired by this idea of equality. 'Equality of entitlement' is a principle that one will be treated equally as a citizen when in need of a service, whatever one's earnings or station in life.

But do we have to continue to judge the fairness or desirability of the welfare system according to the standards and ideals of its founding parents? Le Grand suggests that we do not, and that 'those who advocated or set up the welfare state do not have a monopoly on the criteria against which it may be judged' (Le Grand 1995: 187). The post-war architects of the welfare state may have been concerned to establish equal access to a basic minimum standard of service or a minimum level of benefit, but that should not prevent us from reckoning who has gained or lost in money terms or services.

Although Le Grand (1982) carefully stated the terms upon which he was measuring equality and the services involved (health, education, housing and transport), one unfortunate consequence of his study was that it helped to establish the idea that the *whole* welfare system is biased against the poor.

As we have seen in this chapter, though, the impact of the welfare system as a whole upon top-, middle- and bottom-income groups is mixed. With regard to services in kind, there is considerable evidence that the NHS gives more to people at the lower end of the income scale than it takes from them – not the other way round, as Le Grand maintained in 1982. As Hills (1993: 16) remarks, 'benefits in kind are less concentrated on the poor than cash benefits, but households at the bottom of the distribution still receive more than those at the top (particularly from the NHS).'

The impact of education (and especially unequal take-up of higher education) and some aspects of housing policy, on the other hand, does appear to be less 'pro-poor'. Hills's survey suggests that, overall, it is households on *middle* incomes which gain most from services in kind such as education and health, whereas top-income households gain relatively little.

Social security, by far the most significant 'gatherer and distributor' of resources in the welfare system, funnels a net flow of money to poorer income groups from the better-off. However, because of wider social and economic inequalities, this vital role of social security may be obscured. For one thing, tax reforms have lightened the burden of those on the highest incomes, while relatively high taxes have been levied on poorer groups, especially through increases in indirect taxation. As a result, British society through the 1980s and 1990s moved decisively towards a 'two-thirds affluent, one-third poor' division.

Ironically, given Mrs Thatcher's negative views of the welfare state, the very existence of a well tried social security system facilitated the 'Thatcher experiment' in economic policy and its effect on the labour market in the early 1980s: namely, a sharp rise in unemployment from around one million to over three million. The welfare system acted as an economic and political shock absorber, preventing social breakdown but permitting economic divisions to widen.

People in poverty – one-parent families, older people, the unemployed – would have been even poorer without the welfare and social security system. Each pruning exercise, or restriction of the rate of increase in benefits (such as the freezing of child benefit levels between 1988 and 1992), makes the poor worse off than they had been before. Paradoxically, it is the gradual restriction and slow-down of real increases in benefit levels which demonstrates how important the welfare system used to be in modestly redistributing resources in favour of the poor.

KEY TERMS AND CONCEPTS

economic growth
external benefits
gross domestic product (GDP)
income
  original income
  gross income
  final income
real increases (e.g. in spending,
  wages or benefits)
redistribution

social security benefits
  contributory
  non-contributory
  income-related
  non-income-related
taxation
  direct
  indirect
  progressive
  regressive

SUGGESTIONS FOR FURTHER READING

Among several textbooks on the economics of welfare, Barr's *The Economics of the Welfare State* (2nd edn, 1993) is perhaps the best in terms of combining in-depth economic analysis with a comprehensive coverage of the welfare system. Howard Glennerster's *Paying for Welfare: the 1990s* (1992) is a readable and also an authoritative introduction.

For an overview of the main themes in social security, Michael Hill's *Social Security Policy in Britain* (1990) and Pete Alcock's *Understanding Poverty* (1993) are very helpful, while a recent study for the Rowntree Trust, John Hills' *The Future of Welfare* (1993), provides a valuable corrective to doom-laden and apocalyptic notions that the ageing society and growing demand for health and welfare services will make the current welfare system unaffordable.

Finally, to follow the debate about Le Grand's book, *Strategy of Equality* (1982), see the 1995 article by Powell in the *Journal of Social Policy* (full reference in Bibliography) and Le Grand's reply to Powell in the same issue.

5   SOCIAL POLICY AND SOCIAL
CONTROL

INTRODUCTION: SOCIAL CONTROL AND THE RISE OF WELFARE

Has the gradual extension of a system of government-organized welfare since the nineteenth century eroded liberty and personal freedom? In return for a certain amount of security, have we lost both self-reliance and willingness to look after others? Or are such ideas misleading, and have we gained freedoms and opportunities as a result of the state provision of social security, 'free' education and health services?

This chapter addresses these central questions and the debate about the connection between social welfare and social control. Such questions might seem odd to anyone who takes it for granted that social welfare is unequivocally 'a good thing'. Surely, if problems are alleviated as a result of the provision of services and benefits, then the more that is provided the better?

There is a case to be answered, however. Sometimes the welfare system does become more concerned with controlling people than with meeting their needs as independent citizens. Commentators on both the political left and the right have suggested that an over-bureaucratic state can, in the name of providing help, become paternalistic and insensitive.

There is a danger, though, that arguments about the growing power of the state and its ability to control people can be put forward in an over-simplified way. Historical experience suggests that the rise of welfare can only be explained by reference to a wide range of other factors, not just 'social control' factors. However, processes of change – while important in their own right – did pose problems of conflict and threatened the social order, and sometimes the expansion of welfare services or benefits was seen by the authorities as a way of dealing with such problems. Among the more important types of pressure for change were:

- the economic effects and demands of *industrialization* in different countries – social and economic conditions affected the ways in which early welfare systems grew, and how far the government was expected to help with organizing or providing welfare services to deal with new kinds of social problems;
- the varying impact of *war* on social policy in different countries;
- the role of *religious conflict* within and between countries, and its impact on attitudes to charity and state welfare;
- the need to increase *economic efficiency* by improving public health and education;
- the development of democracy and *public demand* for better public welfare, sometimes expressed in the form of industrial or civil conflict such as strikes or protest marches.

Welfare systems developed in different ways and for different reasons in European countries and in North America (see Jones 1985: 34–77, for a useful summary of the evidence). Jones concludes that social and political control factors, while by no means the only ones, did play a leading part in prompting some early social reforms:

> there exists no discernable link between the level of economic development (indices of industrialization and urbanization) and the first introduction of social insurance measures designed to meet the needs of ... the sick ... the old, and the unemployed. It [was], if anything, the *less* developed of European societies which [proved] to be the most prompt in introducing social insurance ... [There was] a tendency for traditional, patriarchal regimes to embark promptly – even prematurely – upon preventive social policy measures.
>
> (Jones 1985: 52)

Other observers of the development of welfare also established a strong connection between social control and social policy. For example, a famous study entitled *Regulating the Poor: the Functions of Public Welfare* by Piven and Cloward (1971) showed that federal spending by the United States government on social welfare tended to increase when there were perceived to be dangers of civil unrest and inner city riots (as had occurred widely in the 1960s). On the other hand, Piven and Cloward argued, growing restrictiveness in providing welfare and the introduction of stricter forms of means test can be used by government as ways of (a) gaining electoral support among the comfortable majority and (b) controlling or 'regulating' the poor. Social policies, in their view, have contributed to a process of **marginalization** of the poor.

Hillyard and Percy-Smith (1988) have argued in their book *The Coercive State* that a wide variety of social policies, including social security and health service reform, illustrate a trend in Britain towards a more controlling and less democratic form of government than before. This is taking place, they suggest, despite a 'liberal rhetoric' or widespread assumption that government is based on democracy and that the actions of the state are legitimate. However, they are careful to point out that the growing power of the state is a complex phenomenon. It cannot be reduced to a single trend or example, because government and people's experience of it is multifaceted:

> In short, the state in its various roles may at different times, in different situations and for different people, be seen as benevolent protector or provider, impartial arbiter between competing interests, a minor irritant, or alternatively, as obstructive, intrusive, oppressive and coercive.
> (Hillyard and Percy-Smith 1988: 14)

Too much control – or not enough?

More recently, the connection between **social control** and social policy has been viewed the other way round. Rather than social control being seen as the problem, there is mounting concern that, as welfare systems retract and social inequalities grow, increasing disorder will result. The problem could be a *lack* of social control. Gray, for instance, argues:

> What is less obvious is the role played by the new inequality in weakening the ties of community. Inequality has divided us, most palpably, in cities, where it has enforced a brutal segregation according to income and access to jobs. It has promoted an erosion of relationships of trust affecting most aspects of social life, alongside a precipitous collapse of public trust in institutions.
> (Gray 1995: 12)

This represents an important change in thinking, because it shows that 'social control', though it has many negative connotations, also has a positive side. Social control, represented by the word 'community' in the above quotation, can lead to a social order which enhances welfare, security and trust. The difference between an ordered and disordered society can mean the difference between being free to walk alone at night without fear of intimidation or violence, or not; it will also affect whether or not we have to pay a steep price for individual security (insurance premiums, alarm systems, house security etc.).

Note that these examples illustrate a contradiction. A social order which is rule-bound, in which there is effective law enforcement and where everyone is expected to conform also brings certain freedoms: chiefly, freedom from worries about crime or, more positively, a sense of belonging to a structured community.

One particular welfare system illustrates this contradiction very well: the city state of Singapore. In Singapore, which is virtually a one-party state, the government represses free thought and political opposition. The mass media, the university and any potential sources of dissidence are tightly controlled. There are strict penalties for infringing rules governing everyday life, from personal dress and hairstyles to throwing litter. Yet Singapore is one of the few large modern cities in today's world in which women can walk freely without serious worries about being attacked, and where street crime and burglary are still relatively uncommon.

The key to understanding social control in Singapore is not just an economy in which work is plentiful, or effective law enforcement and political repression, but also social policy. Singapore has a comprehensive system of health and education services which buttresses the social order and enhances **consensus**, making the existing paternalistic system seem more acceptable than a nakedly repressive regime.

Does this mean that, in Western capitalist societies, increasing social disorder and rising rates of crime are attributable to cutbacks in the growth of welfare provision? Unfortunately, the answer may not be straightforward. The role of social policy in either maintaining order or causing change is much debated and, depending on one's political viewpoint, could be summarized in different ways.

- Factors other than changes in social policy or cutbacks in welfare could be causing social upheaval: for instance, social and geographical mobility; the break-up of old neighbourhoods, communities and extended family ties; the decline of stable employment opportunities (especially affecting young men); and changes in culture and social norms which reflect, among other things, more individualistic approaches to life and greater tolerance of self-seeking or violent behaviour.
- There is, on the other hand, an argument that 'over-generous' or open-handed social policies have brought about increasing social disorder. Arguing from the political right, Murray (1994), for instance, suggests that in the period between the 1950s and 1980s social security benefits were both substantially increased in real terms and made easier to obtain. According to this argument, increasingly liberal welfare systems undermined work disciplines and subsidized lifestyles which are socially deviant and rejecting of authority. Family structures were undermined by welfare, which made single parenthood both more financially feasible and more morally acceptable.
- Third, social welfare might be achieving the opposite of what Murray suggests. If the bonds of social control are weakening, it may not be social policies which are bringing this about. Rather, social policies, despite attempts to curb the growth of the welfare system, are doing the opposite. They provide some (crumbling) social cement and some protection from the divisive effects of economic and cultural change.

Bearing these different perspectives in mind, we will examine in this chapter *whether* or *how far* social policies have played, and may continue to play, a central role in buttressing the social order. The relationship between social policy and social control will be discussed in three main ways: (a) at a political level; (b) at an individual level; and (c) at a local or urban community level. This latter, third aspect of social control will be discussed in the concluding section of the chapter.

SOCIAL POLICY AND THE POLITICAL ORDER

Social welfare and political control in historical perspective

To illustrate this aspect of social control, one of the best known historical examples of the connection between politics and social welfare will be outlined first: the introduction of social insurance in Germany by Bismarck, the German Chancellor, in the late nineteenth century.

This example is important because Germany led the field in social insurance at that time, and Germany's insurance scheme had an important influence on social policy thinking in other countries, notably Britain. The leading Liberal politician, Lloyd George, visited Germany and was impressed not only by the social benefits of the scheme but also by the political credit gained by the government. By 1911, the Liberal government had introduced the first social insurance scheme to Britain in the form of a National Insurance Act (Part I dealt with insurance against loss of earnings through sickness, Part II with unemployment insurance).

The German government's reforms brought in compulsory insurance for sickness, industrial injury and old age pensions during the 1880s. These policies were developed before the vote was gained by the working classes and at a time when the government was trying to contain the pressures and demands of a rising trade union and labour movement.

Jones (1985: 50) is not alone in seeing early social insurance in Germany as very much a 'top-down' set of reforms, and 'a means whereby an existing ruling elite endeavours to shore up and legitimize its position in the face of threatened ... upheaval.' But this was not the whole story. As mentioned in the introduction, social welfare development occurred for a variety of reasons. In Germany, social insurance was provided at a comparatively early stage, partly because of long-standing traditions of paternalistically looking after workers and giving them some social protection (Spicker 1993: 136).

This may also be seen as a matter of social control and trying to protect a traditional, semi-feudal order. However, Spicker argues that it represented a genuine recognition of workers' rights and needs. To see the German reforms solely as a matter of veiled repression would be wrong. There were other autocratic regimes in the nineteenth century where nothing like the 'progressive' German model of social insurance was ever on the agenda.

Twentieth-century Britain: social welfare in the political order

Another point to remember is that governments may try to use social policies to establish political control, but this does not mean that the always succeed; sometimes new social policies have an effect which is far from stabilizing.

In Britain, Lloyd George's social insurance reforms of 1911 initially led to more conflict and disorder than consensus and acceptance of government control (Lloyd 1993: 34–5). Opposition came from employers who resented having to pay towards employees' insurance cover. There was also some rather frivolous opposition among well-to-do employers, who played up outrage at the idea of having to lick insurance stamps to record weekly contributions for their domestic servants. More significantly, private insurance companies opposed the government scheme, fearing a loss of business, while even trade unions were sceptical about it. Better-paid manual workers' unions had already set up their own 'sick clubs' or medical insurance schemes, and resented the idea of government take-over or control. Finally, many doctors opposed compulsory health insurance because they feared growing state regulation of the work of the medical profession.

The willingness of Lloyd George and the Liberal government to struggle against all this opposition was significant. Despite the end-result in 1911 being a rather modest and limited insurance scheme, the reform showed that Lloyd George and the Liberal government were motivated to challenge many established interests. No doubt Liberal leaders were partly hoping to steal the thunder of a growing Labour Party movement by pushing forward with social legislation. But there were reasons other than political calculation or trying to retain electoral support. Lloyd George's motives were, at least in part, genuinely to help low-paid workers. There was a challenging, radical side to Lloyd George's campaign, and therefore it is hard to see the social policies of this time simply as a device to maintain political control or the status quo.

However, while social and economic reforms can disrupt the political order rather than cement it, at least in the short term, there is an argument that over a longer period social policies do have the effect of stabilizing society and reducing political conflict. What is the evidence for this?

In Britain, there have been three major 'leaps' in welfare development: the Liberal government reforms of 1906–14, the Labour government welfare state programme from 1946 to 1951 and the Conservative social policy reforms which began in 1979 but accelerated from the mid-1980s to the early 1990s (see Chapter 3).

Mrs Thatcher's new broom approach to social policy – while it was intended to win popular support as well as representing a hard-headed approach to spending – received a very mixed reception and in the short term seemed to provoke conflict rather than to develop a new consensus (Deakin 1994).

Labour's 1940s reforms, which introduced a comprehensive welfare state in the exceptionally consensual and socially disciplined atmosphere of the immediate post-war years, could be seen as an attempt to prevent the 1930s world of economic depression and social division from returning, and was in one sense a response to a (potential) threat of crisis and disorder (Hennessy 1992). However, even these comprehensive and inclusive reforms stimulated as much political conflict and tension as stability.

A consensus on the continuation of a welfare state existed between the two main political parties between 1945 and the mid-1970s. A loose form of **social contract** between government, trade unions and employers emerged in the 1960s and 1970s. But there were always divisions on how social policy should be developed (for instance, with regard to education policy and comprehensive schools).

Marxist or 'political economy' views of the social order (see Chapter 6 for a discussion of these perspectives) suggest that, although governments have proved willing to invest in large-scale welfare systems in order to stabilize the inherent tensions and inequalities of capitalist society, this enterprise will in the end lead to even greater instability, mainly because welfare spending exacts too high a tax on private employers and may begin to make capitalist firms in high welfare-spending countries uncompetitive.

At the same time, **welfare capitalism** cannot really do without an advanced welfare system, which: (a) helps to regulate the labour market by absorbing the shocks of economic restructuring and redundancy; (b) mitigates the effects of political crisis and questioning of 'the system' by giving capitalism a human face or an appearance of fairness and equal opportunity; and (c) meets the needs of a capitalist economy for a labour force which is kept in reasonable health and is sufficiently well educated to keep up with new work technologies.

Although Marxist explanations of the relationship between capitalism, political control and social policy have provided some insight in the past, recent social policy trends in the United Kingdom and elsewhere cast doubt on these theories. A capitalist economy's need for a well maintained traditional welfare state may not be as great as suggested.

The United Kingdom experience shows that governments can dispense with the 'social contract' approach to social welfare which had developed in the 1970s, based on agreements between government, trade unions and employers. When she came to power, Mrs Thatcher made short shrift of anything smacking of Labourite social consensus. The 'Thatcher experiment' also demonstrated that previously unthinkable levels of unemployment could be allowed to occur, together with relatively radical reforms and pruning of the welfare system. Despite these threats to political and social stability, governments could not only survive but prosper electorally.

Britain and other examples

This conclusion could be based on too short term a view. We do not yet know whether the social policy changes introduced by former Conservative administrations have indeed unleashed unmanageable political and social tensions and, if so, whether new forms of social policy will be needed to help to restore the political and social order.

One way of assessing future prospects in Britain is to consider the impact of welfare reforms in other countries, though comparisons are always difficult because distinctive and different political conditions affect outcomes. However, one particularly telling example is provided by New Zealand, a country which had built up an advanced welfare state in many ways the forerunner of the British model.

In New Zealand, family allowances were introduced in 1926, twenty years before Britain's Labour government did so, and 'by 1938, New Zealand had the most comprehensive social security system in the world' (Walker 1994). Over the past decade, however, two governments (first a Labour government, then a National Party (conservative) government from 1990) brought in drastic social policy changes, including: the selling off of the entire public housing stock, together with cuts to housing benefit; a new tax which claws back the retirement pension from all but low-income pensioners; the ending of 'free' health care and the introduction of new means tests for access to health services; and reductions in unemployment, single parent and widows' benefits of between 10 and 25 per cent.

The impact of these and other economic policy changes in New Zealand has been rather like the taxation and social security reforms in Britain (see Chapter 4), only more so. For instance, in New Zealand, a two-parent, two-child family in the poorest fifth of the population will have lost, on average, over 20 per cent of its income, 'a far larger decline, in a far shorter period than anything suffered by similar sections of the population in Britain' (Walker 1994).

Over the same period in New Zealand, crime rates have soared, so that they are now higher than anywhere else in the industrialized world, including the United States, while in the early 1990s the prison population also rose by 10 per cent a year, exceeding Britain's high rate of imprisonment. Suicide rates are among the highest in the world, at 38 per 100,000. The police force is now visibly armed with automatic weapons, mainly to contain a steep rise in violent incidents, social unrest and racial conflict.

However, while these signs of disorder are worrying, they are unlikely to lead to complete social breakdown or the kind of political crisis envisaged by Marxists. Both New Zealand and Britain are traditional welfare states in which the transition to being 'post-welfare' systems is particularly painful. In each country there are long-standing expectations of the role of state as a provider of benefits to rich and poor alike, so that politicians and political parties which challenge these expectations will continue to experience losses of support, as the Conservatives in Britain and the National Party in New Zealand have found.

New Zealand demonstrates that welfare cutbacks and restructuring can go a very long way before there are anything like completely unmanageable political tensions or conflicts. Therefore, the 'cementing' role of social policies in maintaining the political order, though important, may not be absolutely crucial. Other ways of maintaining political order – in particular, a greater reliance on policing and the criminal justice system – may to some extent replace the role of social welfare.

Finally, though, we should remember that the relationship between social policy and the political order varies greatly between countries. In France in 1995–6, for instance, a great deal of political instability (including nationwide strikes and protests) was triggered by proposals to trim the country's huge social security budget and to introduce welfare reforms. The French example of political conflict and disorder *before* welfare cutbacks have taken place is very different from the New Zealand case, in which social disorder and protest emerged after cutbacks began to bite.

SOCIAL CONTROL AND INDIVIDUAL FREEDOM

When we think of social control, the relationship between the individual and a controlling social group or institution springs to mind. But what does 'social control' in this sense mean? Perhaps two definitions could be borne in mind: (a) social control which is *directly* **coercive**, such that an individual's autonomy or freedom is deliberately and obviously suppressed; and (b) social control which is *subtly* **oppressive** and which encourages people to fit into accepted social roles or suppresses their individuality in less obvious ways.

Social welfare and coercion

Those who are in a controlling position – for instance, professionals and practitioners in health and welfare services – may tell service users that what is being done is 'in their own interests'. However, an objective appraisal might reveal that control operates to benefit the service provider or the administrator of a policy more than the user of services.

Not surprisingly, most of the criticisms of directly coercive control occurred when long-stay care in mental hospitals and other kinds of residential institution was much more common than it is today. Ken Kesey's fictional *One Flew Over the Cuckoo's Nest* (1962) – later dramatized and made into a feature film starring Jack Nicholson – and a study by Erving Goffman of institutional care, *Asylums* (1991), had a telling effect upon attitudes among professionals as well as the general public towards 'overcontrol' in long-stay institutions.

Kesey and Goffman both tried to show not only that patients in mental hospitals are restricted in their freedoms, losing civil liberties and their rights as citizens, but that institutional control seeks to change behaviour and identity in a malign way, disabling individuals and making them more dependent than before.

The 'liberal critique' of social control in institutions helped to pave the way for the development of community care policies and the widespread closure of long-stay facilities (see Chapter 9). Despite the move to community care, however, abuses of power and 'overcontrol' in residential settings still occur.

Nor is the directly coercive approach restricted to health services or personal social services. There is renewed interest – for instance, in both the United Kingdom and the United States – in finding new ways to deter undeserving claimants and to prevent social security fraud. Spicker (1993: 108) and Dean (1991: 180) note that this has resulted in a shift towards a more directly controlling approach in benefits policy, resulting, for example, in: greater willingness to suspend benefits where fraud is suspected; a greater likelihood of prosecution in cases of benefit 'fiddles'; policies to lower the value of benefits, to encourage claimants to find work; making receipt of benefits conditional upon taking up employment training; and, in some parts of the United States, the introduction of **workfare** policies (work schemes, organized by the authorities, which are a kind of 'work test': claimants only receive benefits if they are prepared to work for them). As Spicker observes, 'workfare work' therefore becomes a deterrent against claiming.

Social policy in the United States presents some of the more marked examples of the growing use of social security policy to try to effect changes in behaviour and attitude among welfare recipients. For instance, Horowitz (1995), studying an American government-sponsored project to assist teenage mothers and help them move from welfare dependency to becoming 'responsible citizens', found that some professional helpers relied heavily on a coercive approach and demanded submission to authority from the teenage mothers. The effects were that, in some cases, intervention achieved the opposite of what was required: welfare dependency was increased, while self-esteem and independence were reduced. Other professional helpers, however, genuinely fostered a more independent outlook among teenage mothers and helped them to make their own decisions.

The point about Horowitz's study is not just that professional practice varies, affecting the degree or nature of social control in welfare settings, but that *policy* and the underlying aims of a project are a crucial determinant. In the American and British cases, moral concerns about single parenthood and fears about the welfare system creating dependency, strongly voiced by politicians of the centre as well as of the right, have helped to create a climate in which a coercive approach to control is encouraged.

This is not to argue, however, that social security fraud and undeserved claiming should be ignored. There is a substantial amount of unjustified claiming, resulting not only in a loss of resources that could be better spent elsewhere but also in a degree of undesirable welfare dependency among claimants, as well as general cynicism and disillusion with the welfare system. Nor is it sufficiently convincing to make the point that losses from the public purse through dishonest tax evasion are greater than social security fraud, and that therefore the latter is excusable. Two wrongs do not make a right, even if the wrongs are of different sizes.

A more relevant point, perhaps, is that while a degree of control and a fair system for checking eligibility are clearly needed, the recent policy shift towards a tougher stance on social security carries with it dangers of excessive or punitive control: the kind of policing of personal and family life which is unacceptable in a free society.

Related to this is public concern and discussion about the threat posed to social order by the emergence of an **underclass**. However, there is disagreement about whether such a group exists or, if it does, whether the causes are cultural (the work-shy and criminal lifestyle of people who reject society) or structural (people are excluded from the labour force as a result of economic change and unemployment). For commentators and politicians on the political right, though, the idea of the underclass as a chosen way of life represents both an explanation for welfare dependency and a reason for 'getting tough' on social security.

However, the underclass debate is something of a distraction from the point that nearly half of all British households now receive means-tested benefits of one kind or another – this is hardly a small minority or underclass (Pepinster and Castle 1995). Field (1995) argues that the complexity of the means-testing system, with 25 separate kinds of benefit and complicated claim forms of six pages or more, encourages both cheating and passive acceptance of handouts:

> A deadly lesson is being taught: the only way to survive is to cheat. Because means-tested help is reduced as income rises, people on low or no wages have no incentive to improve their lot.
>
> (Field 1995: 27)

According to Field, an extension of anti-fraud measures and new regulations to restrict eligibility for benefit is inevitable unless steps are taken to reform the basic principles of social security. Thus, a large number of claimants will experience increasing restriction and regulation of welfare benefits. Despite government policy to lessen dependence on the state, social policy is steadily increasing the importance of means-testing, resulting in greater need for control.

As well as direct forms of control, as seen in tightening eligibility rules, we also need to consider the ways in which social policies and social welfare might be thought to have *indirectly* controlling effects. To illustrate this aspect of social control, the examples of gender and age divisions will be discussed, focusing especially on the impact of social security policy on these divisions.

Social policies and indirect control: the examples of gender and age

As far as gender roles are concerned, there has been much criticism of the ways in which social security and other forms of social policy have reinforced gender inequality, particularly by assuming that women will be economically dependent on men and that they will play a less important role than men in the job market (see, for example, Lewis 1983; Dale and Foster 1986; Pascall 1986; Hallett 1995).

The Beveridge committee's plan for social security, implemented in 1946, was built upon the insurance principle. But it was assumed at the time that most married women would not continue in paid work. Accordingly, the Beveridge plan allowed married women to opt out of the full-time workers' scheme (single women were on the same footing as men as long as they contributed to the insurance scheme). The married women's option was only phased out in 1978. Up to 1978, therefore, the majority of women did not build up a pension equal to that of men in full-time employment, and they did not have rights to unemployment and sickness benefits. Even after 1978, married women already paying reduced insurance contributions could continue to do so, with the result that in 1989, 20 per cent of married women were still on a lower rate of contribution – and consequently would qualify for lower rates of benefit than men (Callender 1992: 134).

In short, early social security policy assumed that it was right for married women's security to be determined by their husbands' contribution record. As Wyn puts it,

> While the notion of interdependence between wife and husband is a just and worthy cause, Beveridge's model requires that each partner depends on each other for contributions which are inherently unequal. A husband's dependence on his wife to wash his socks, cook his meals, and clean his house is not of the same nature as a wife's dependence on her husband for her source of livelihood . . . as long as she is unable to rely on other sources of financial support, he is in a position to define the terms of the relationship.
>
> (Wyn 1991: 108)

Not only were women to be categorized in terms of 'marriage, motherhood and family', but the status of 'widows, divorced and deserted women, and cohabiting and single women' was to be defined as 'deviant' in terms of social security classification (Colwill 1994: 56).

The social security system has gradually been reformed, so that traditional distinctions like the married women's option have disappeared. However, there is still evidence that the original principle of contributory benefits – which, as Wyn reminds us, is built upon 'a male model of employment patterns requiring full-time and continuous employment' – has the effect of disadvantaging many women, as well as an increasing number of men who are losing permanent jobs.

It is still the case that more women's than men's working careers and employment patterns 'do not typically conform to this [full-time, permanent employment] model' (Wyn 1991: 108). In Britain, well over two-fifths of women in paid employment work part-time, but fewer than a tenth of men do so. The rate of part-time working among British women is the highest in the European Union, next to the Netherlands (Eurostat 1992). Women are also much more likely than men to interrupt their careers in paid work to take on childcare or other family care responsibilities.

Thus the social security system has an *indirectly* disadvantaging and controlling effect on women in a number of ways, and the following are some examples.

For a variety of reasons, women will often have less continuous records of insurance contributions than men, which means that they can be disqualified from *unemployment benefit*. (This benefit was replaced, in April 1996, by the Job Seeker's Allowance (JSA). The JSA integrated the schemes for benefits for unemployed people with the income support scheme, and it also shortened the period in which contributory unemployment benefit/job seeker's allowance can be paid, from twelve months to six months.)

Successive tightening of entitlement rules has meant that women are more likely than before to find it harder to claim unemployment benefit/ JSA, 'increasing women's economic reliance on their partners' (Callender 1992: 135). For example, the 1988 Social Security Act brought in a condition that unemployment benefit could only be received if employment had been continuous for two years prior to claiming. This affects women, with their greater chances of interrupted working careers, more often than men. Another Social Security Act, in 1989, also particularly affected women by tightening requirements for availability for work: unemployment benefit claimants have to demonstrate that they are immediately available for work and that they are willing to accept full-time work offers. Women with family care responsibilities who wish to take on paid, part-time work often find these requirements difficult to meet, resulting in withdrawal of benefit and greater dependence of such women on men or other family members. These are just two examples of the ways in which unemployment benefit reforms have affected women; Callender (1992: 134–7) documents several others.

With regard to *retirement pensions,* the 1986 Social Security Act changed the method of calculating the amount of state earnings-related pension (SERPS) in a way which is more likely to disadvantage women than men. Instead of the pension being based on an average of the best twenty years of earnings, as originally proposed when SERPS was introduced in 1976, the earnings-related pension will now be based on an average of all years in the working life. As a result, many women, who are more likely than men to have experienced years with no pay or low pay, will find that their state earnings-related pension will be considerably lower than their male partner's. This financial or economic inequality will lead to a greater frequency of low income and a greater degree of dependence among many women in later life.

Income Support is a means-tested benefit which assumes that claimants do not have any other income (above a very minimal level) from employment or another source. If one partner works for more than 16 hours a week, however, the other can no longer claim this benefit, or the benefit is reduced according to the earnings entering the household. This rule has the indirect effect of discouraging women in particular from re-entering the labour force or seeking part-time work. If the partner becomes unemployed, income support rules discourage the other from continuing with even a low-paid part-time job (and it is women who are far more likely to be holding down such jobs). If they do stay in work, they find that their partners are disqualified from benefit and that the family will have to survive below the income support level: that is, at a level of poverty which is below even the government's minimal standards.

Despite all the evidence that the social security system can be oppressive, however, there is another side to the story. Income support and benefits of other kinds, though providing only a basic income, may nevertheless give a degree of independence to some women's lives. This 'modicum of independence', suggests Wyn, may 'enable women to get out of dangerous relationships with men' (Wyn 1991: 109). So while life on social security can hardly be said to be liberating in the full sense, it might give a degree of freedom to women wanting to set up their own households or to control their own resources.

Taken to an extreme, this is the argument put forward by Murray and others on the political right: that social security policy has been a key element in weakening traditional family norms and in creating the acceptability of single parenthood. However, the argument does not have to be pushed to the extreme to show that the effects of social security benefits on people's lives are contradictory. They have mixed effects: as we have seen above, social security rules bring disincentives and controlling effects, and the very meagre levels of income on benefit are hardly conducive to a free or liberating lifestyle. But it is also true that without social security, a certain amount of freedom would be lost. If there are proposals to freeze or reduce a benefit – as with the government's recent decision to reduce lone parent benefit by between £5 and £10 per week, for instance – those who defend women's rights and freedoms are often among the first to object.

Another good example of this was the decision of the government to freeze the value of child benefit in 1988: it was no longer to be uprated from year to year. Defenders of child benefit saw in this decision the gradual erosion of a benefit that is particularly helpful to women. After a change of heart (and shortly before a general election), the government decided to 'unfreeze' child benefit. Although the lost uprating from 1988 to 1991 was not restored, this benefit remains for the time being an important part of the social security system.

Child benefit illustrates a central point about social policy, social control and gender. On one side, child benefit helps women as well as children, because it is mainly they who receive and use it (although, of course, a small proportion of fathers who have sole custody of their children also draw child benefit). Child benefit payments are not large, but it is argued that even in some middle-class homes, particularly where mothers are not in paid work, it gives a small but significant degree of independence. But, on the other side, the rationale of child benefit seems to confirm and institutionalize women's traditional domestic role as the main carer of children, as do other schemes such as maternity leave and maternity benefit.

However, Britain's welfare system does not provide a good example of the effects of social security and other policies on gender roles because, by comparison with other European countries, provision in areas such as maternity benefit, child and family policy is limited. Sweden, though it is currently undergoing welfare reforms, is still one of the most generous and comprehensive examples of a welfare system which is supposed to help women, especially in policies which are meant to ease women's re-entry to *work* and to support them in the task of balancing family and paid work responsibilities. Britain's and Sweden's policies in the area of maternity, work and family life (excluding child benefit and similar payments) are compared in Box 5.1.

What have been the main effects of Sweden's policies on work and family support as far as gender roles are concerned? First, women's participation in the labour force is much higher than in Britain. In Sweden, almost 90 per cent of women of working age are in paid employment, compared with just over 60 per cent of British women. In this respect, the policies seem to be successful in helping to liberate Swedish women from the home and from traditional domestic roles.

On the other hand, the apparently liberating family and childcare policies in Sweden seem to have subtly confirmed traditional family roles. A lot of Swedish women continue to work 'long' part-time (over 20 hours per week) precisely because the generosity of the welfare system gives little incentive to work full-time and perhaps pursue a career to higher positions.

The Swedish labour force has become one of the most sex-segregated in the world. Swedish women in paid employment are particularly clustered in the occupations which have expanded with the welfare system: teaching,

Box 5.1   Child and family benefits in Britain and Sweden

Britain

Maternity leave	10 months, of which 11 weeks before childbirth
Maternity benefit	90 per cent of earnings for 6 weeks; low flat rate for 12 weeks; no benefit for remainder

Sweden

Paid parental leave	18 months; may be shared equally between partners; may be taken all at once, or in several separate periods up to age 8 of each child (90 per cent of earnings throughout)
Pregnancy leave	50 days; 90 per cent of earnings
Father's leave	10 days after childbirth; 90 per cent of earnings
Parent's right to work a six-hour day	Up to age 12 of child
Leave from work to care for sick child, or for child if usual care-giver is ill	90 days per year; 90 per cent of earnings
Leave to visit child's school	2 days per year; 90 per cent of earnings

Source: Statistics Sweden (1992: 27).

personal social services, health care and other care services. They are markedly underrepresented in traditionally 'male' occupations such as management in private sector industry, construction or engineering, though recent Swedish legislation on equal opportunities is attempting to reduce these divisions (see Blakemore and Drake 1995).

Arguably, then, the Swedish approach, by protecting women and providing a generous system of state support, has reinforced at least some important gender divisions. This does not mean that the Swedish example proves that support for parents at work should be reduced or that social policies which aim to assist women will inevitably reinforce traditional gender roles. Swedish policies provide many positive outcomes for women. There are opportunities to enjoy a protected standard of living while being involved with child-rearing and paid work.

The point is rather that social policies which try to bridge the worlds of work and family seem to have a mixture of effects, both liberating and controlling. Further, while the emphasis has been upon disadvantages for women, men are also affected by gendered assumptions in social security policy. For instance, Callender (1992: 138) notes how the thrust to reduce welfare dependency and increase the number of checks made upon benefit claimants was targeted upon men more often than women. Men, according to traditional gender norms, are more often expected to be working and less reliant on benefits than women.

The example of retirement pensions and the construction of old age provides another illustration of the indirectly controlling effects of social policy. When the first state pension was introduced in Britain in 1908, it was very popular. Millions of poorer old people saw it as a liberation from worries about the Poor Law or 'going on the parish'. The following quotation (which begins with the reaction of an older person to the pension) illustrates this: '"God bless that Lord [sic] George ... and God bless you, miss!" ... and there were flowers from their gardens and apples from their trees for the girl who merely handed them the money' (from F. Thompson, Lark Rise, 1939: 100; quoted in Lloyd 1993: 14).

The first state pension was not a large amount and was restricted to people over the age of 70. By 1946, however, pensionable ages had been reduced to 60 for women and 65 for men. Not only that, but a more significant condition was introduced: receipt of the pension was from then on dependent upon giving up work. This institutionalized the idea of old age as a 'pensioned off' and workless phase of life (Walker 1990: 59), an idea we have come to accept even though the retirement condition was abolished in 1989. Thus state pensions for older people are a necessary and vital part of their support, but they have also played a part in excluding older people from the workforce. In part, they have been an instrument of social control and are an example of the patterns of ageism discussed by Bytheway (1994).

CONCLUSIONS: CAN SOCIAL POLICIES BRING BENIGN CONTROL?

In this chapter we have concentrated on negative aspects of social order and social control. Social policies have brought benefits to people and even a measure of liberation. Critics of the welfare system have stressed, however, that welfare systems, and especially social security policies, seem more likely to reinforce undesirable aspects of the social order than to challenge them. According to these arguments, the welfare system is shot through with sexist assumptions about the roles of men and women at work and in the family, ageist definitions of a dependent and redundant role for older people and stereotypes of benefit claimants as irresponsible members of an underclass.

As noted at the outset, however, we must be careful to separate what we mean by social control (and whether social control is always a negative or oppressive thing) from the role of social policies in either supporting or challenging social control and the existing order.

First, is it fair to view social control in an entirely negative light? There are rather more positive definitions of social control which deserve exploration. A view of the social order as something which can genuinely help individuals to develop, or which will encourage the social integration of both individuals and minority groups, would suggest that social control can be benign.

In what circumstances could this happen? To answer this question, the educational process could be used as an illustration. Learning to read, for instance, involves mastering the rules and conventions of language in written form: the shapes of different letters, how words are spelt, the rules of grammar and punctuation.

The parent who reads with the child and points out these rules and understandings is in a way exercising 'social control', though usually in an enjoyable and flexible way. Nevertheless, in pointing out where the child has misread a word, or by gently correcting mistakes and guiding the young reader back to the text, the parent is controlling the situation and the child's learning. Of course, this may be done well or badly: with too much control and too little enjoyment, the young child may well reject the parent's help.

Later, at school, the same principles apply. To make progress, the child needs a certain amount of control: the tasks he or she works on must be sufficiently exciting and interesting, but the classroom environment must also be relatively calm and secure. Equally, the school itself will need to be well run. Thus social control exists at a number of levels: individual, group and institutional levels.

Presented in this unproblematic way, social control *can* be seen to be working in the individual's best interests, even though individuals – for instance, young children – may not realize the benefits of being controlled. Control that leads to independence of the individual is genuinely liberating. The child is guided into reading, but eventually becomes an independent reader who is free to explore a wider world of books.

The problem with this definition, however, is that social control is never completely or solely in the best interests of the person being controlled. Control involves varying degrees of paternalism, and in its most paternalistic forms will make it difficult or impossible for individuals to exercise their independence.

Two examples illustrate these problems. One example is provided by the policies which govern how far the staff of residential or care institutions are legally permitted to restrain residents and what means of physical control they are allowed to employ, if any. There is some uncertainty about this. For instance, guidance under the 1989 Children Act seems to be interpreted by some authorities as meaning that young people in residential institutions cannot be prevented from leaving the premises, even if they seem to be likely to put themselves in danger or are likely to go out to break the law. In some cases, staff in such institutions have been told that the most they can do is to stand in front of the young people to inform them that they should not leave. In other areas, however, residential staff have been trained in methods of physical restraint, such as 'safe' arm-locks, and are expected to use them.

Given the ever-present dangers of physical abuse in residential care, the policy of some authorities to forbid the use of physical restraint in certain care homes is understandable. On the other hand, there is a case to be made for physically restraining a girl of 13 or 14 who is prostituting herself, or a boy who has overdosed once before and is leaving to obtain more drugs.

A second example of the difficulty of defining 'benign' social control is provided by policies for care of the mentally disabled. In this area of policy, traditional assumptions about the vulnerability of people with learning difficulties have tipped the balance firmly towards paternalistic approaches to meeting 'special needs' (Stainton 1994). However, as Stainton points out, there are ways of changing policy to meet needs in ways which give more respect, choice and freedom to mentally disabled people: for instance, by developing more flexible ways of funding services for this group and encouraging a system of 'brokerage', so that individual service users and their advisers (for example, social workers) would be more able to reject paternalistic advice or control than at present.

The examples of young people in residential care and mentally disabled people in the community both show that defining citizenship, and who has the right to take decisions for him or herself as a free citizen, is a contentious area. Agreement by the controlled to be controlled is hardly a sufficient justification for apparently benign control. After all, mentally disabled people could be manoeuvred into willingly accepting all kinds of limitations upon their freedom.

We all tend to absorb from the society around us the social rules and the expectations of that society, yet rules and expectations may work to oppress the majority and indirectly benefit those who are privileged or who have a greater say in controlling society.

On the other hand, 'radical' criticisms of the nature of society and social control are not very helpful in deciding what the policy response should be to today's social problems and apparent threats to the stability of the existing social and economic order. The world of work, for instance, is full of oppression and different kinds of social control, but the collapse of work in postmodern economies is having a seriously disruptive effect upon the morale and integration of younger people. People value work, and it is a critically important element in human welfare. As Robertson Elliot (1996: 97) observes, 'unemployment jeopardises orderly progression through the "normal" stages of the life course', prompting either 'rebellious and lawless' responses among young men or 'troubled, but generally conforming' responses.

This suggests that, if we are interested in policy and what can be done to tackle problems, we have to move beyond sociological criticism to an examination of what practical strategies might make a difference to those who are relatively powerless or who are experiencing oppression. In addressing these problems, policies may in one sense be shoring up a system of social control, but they also have the potential to deliver benign effects and to help people to achieve some independence.

To conclude, it is likely that the question of how far social policies are either liberating or oppressive can only be resolved with any certainty by studies of specific policies or the particular social groups or individuals affected by those policies. Horowitz's (1995) study of teen mothers and policies to 'help' them is a case in point.

KEY TERMS AND CONCEPTS

coercion	stigmatization
marginalization	underclass
oppression	welfare capitalism
social consensus	welfare dependency
social contract	workfare
social control	

SUGGESTIONS FOR FURTHER READING

Though written over two decades ago, with the American context in mind, Piven and Cloward's *Regulating the Poor* (1971) is a classic study of the link between welfare and social control. It still deserves to be read, especially with hindsight and the knowledge of what subsequently happened in social policy in the 1980s in both Britain and the United States.

Hillyard and Percy-Smith's *The Coercive State* (1988) is a useful book to complement Piven and Cloward's earlier study, though the main thesis and contents are quite different. Hillyard and Percy-Smith's book surveys a wide range of policy areas (including examples such as the 1988 reform of the NHS) to show that in many respects the welfare state has become much less democratic and accountable over the years.

Hartley Dean's *Social Security and Social Control* (1991) is a rather specialized study of social security tribunals, though there are plenty of general observations and in-depth discussion of some of the themes mentioned in this chapter. As an alternative, Pete Alcock's *Understanding Poverty* (1993) provides a readable and succinct overview of social security policy which also has much to say about the nature of social control. A longer historical view of poverty and social control can be found in Tony Novak's *Poverty and the State* (1988).

A large number of books by feminist authors trace the connection between gender divisions, social policy and social control: see, for instance, Lewis (1983), Dale and Foster (1986), Pascall (1986) or Hallett (1995). Rapid change in social security and other policy legislation means, however, that some of the observations in these books are outdated. However, Caroline Glendinning's and Jane Millar's *Women and Poverty in Britain – the 1990s* (1992) provides a factual and thoughtful account.

6   WHO MAKES POLICY? THE EXAMPLE

OF EDUCATION

INTRODUCTION: POLICY, GOVERNMENT AND STATE

In this chapter, the example of education will be used to explore two questions which are of general significance in social policy: *who* makes social policy; and *how* are policies made?

In education, as with all major public services, government and state play leading roles in shaping the system. However, what is meant by 'government' and 'state' is not always obvious, and first some basic definitions are needed. *Government* involves an intricate web of relationships among:

- A Prime Minister and his or her ministers in Cabinet, who together form the central core of government policy making.
- Senior civil servants and government ministers, who, in their various departments, work out the details of important policy changes.
- Parliament and the government of the day. Government must manage legislation in the House of Commons and the House of Lords. It must deal with challenges to its policies from opposition MPs and sometimes from MPs in the government's own party. Government must also respond to select committees (small cross-party committees of MPs which are appointed for the lifetime of a Parliament to scrutinize government legislation and to investigate important policy questions).

The state includes:

- Public servants: for example, teachers and Department for Education and Employment officials who administer and implement policy.
- Local government (elected councillors and local government officials) and other locally elected bodies (for example, school governing bodies).
- **Quangos** (quasi-autonomous non-governmental organizations), which are set up by central government (for example, by the Department for Education and Employment) to supervise and/or fund a particular function or task. For instance, Ofsted (the Office for Standards in Education) is headed by a Chief Inspector of Schools and is responsible for supervising arrangements for assessing the quality of schools and teachers.

Government shapes policy, but what actually happens on the ground is often determined by the effectiveness of civil servants at the national level, or by the amount of cooperativeness shown by local officials or by professionals such as teachers.

Government and state are sometimes partners and sometimes rivals in creating and implementing policies. However, they are far from being the sole influences on policy. A great many other things constrain the hands of government and state: for instance, the *economic cost* of a policy and the public money available, the *political acceptability* of a policy and the legacy of *previous policy decisions*. Even a government which is strongly committed to change will often find it extremely difficult to alter existing policies or the ways in which policies have been decided in the past.

Key interest groups (for example, business interests or parents' lobby groups) may also have enough power either to block a policy or to amend it, or to put new issues on the **policy agenda**. This last term refers to the way in which some issues gain leading importance in national life while others do not, or slip off the agenda after a period of being in the limelight.

There are differences of opinion as to what is of pressing importance. Therefore, it would be wrong to think of the policy agenda as a single list of priorities that everyone agrees upon. However, it is a useful concept. It helps to understand which issues the government wishes to place at the top of the agenda and which at the bottom, while pressure groups such as parents' representatives may have different priorities.

EDUCATION: A CENTRAL POLICY ISSUE

Education affects almost everyone in ways no other branch of the welfare system does. Only a small minority of people at any one time receive hospital or health care, or are users of personal social services. For most of us, the doctor, nurse, social worker or DSS official are bit-players in life's drama. On the other hand, all but a few of us spend at least eleven formative years in schools and colleges. An increasing proportion of us come back for more.

Not surprisingly, as childhood and adolescence are often the times when we experience heights of success and depths of failure, as well as extremes of boredom and enthusiasm, education can easily become a focus for strong feelings. We might blame a particular school or teacher for lack of success or self-confidence. Conversely, we may associate education with a glow of achievement and adopt rose-tinted memories of the way we were taught. Thus education is much debated because people feel qualified to discuss it. Parental concern also heightens the interest in this policy area. The determination of many to make sure that their children receive 'good' education, or at least the best available, means that a range of policy issues are rarely out of the limelight: for instance, whether and how children should be tested, how the quality of schools and teachers should be evaluated and whether policies governing parental choice of school, and schools' own selection methods, are fair. As the politician Lord Eccles observed, 'British parents are very ready to call for a system of education which offers equal opportunity to all children except their own' (quoted in Andrews 1992: 80).

In 1994, the decision of Tony Blair, the Labour leader, and his wife Cherie Blair to send their son Euan to an 'opted out' state secondary school, the London Oratory, caused considerable public controversy (*The Guardian* 1994). Tony Blair appeared to be endorsing Conservative policy on parental choice and self-governing state schools. The Blair case illustrated deep divisions in Britain about the rights and wrongs of allowing secondary schools to opt out of local authority control, as did a similar controversy about the decision of another leading Labour politician, Harriet Harman, to send her child to a selective school.

A third and equally important set of reasons for education's high profile can be found in broader concerns about the effectiveness of education policy in meeting Britain's economic needs. A survey of the European Community (CSO 1994c: 33) showed that, among the twelve member states at that time, only Spain had a lower percentage of young people aged 14–18 in education than the United Kingdom. In Germany (97 per cent), Belgium (95 per cent) and France (93 per cent), educational participation was appreciably higher than in Britain (81 per cent). The United Kingdom's lag in developing education and training for 16–18-year-olds results in shortfalls in the numbers of trained people. Although unemployment rates remain relatively high among the unskilled, it is quite common to find critical shortages of skilled or trained employees, especially in areas of employment where there are rapid developments in technology or working patterns.

There were worries that government policy in the 1980s did not address these shortfalls by greater investment in education. As Sampson (1992) points out, the proportion of the United Kingdom's national wealth (GDP) devoted to education *declined* from 5.6 to 5.0 per cent between 1980 and 1990, even though the economy grew.

Concerns about under-investment underline two main weaknesses in British education: the first is an apparent failure to develop applied, vocational or work-related training to the levels that are needed for a competitive economy. The second is a tendency towards elitism: the standards of the majority or average students are neglected in favour of cultivating the achievements of a favoured minority.

However, there have been some trends away from elitism. Almost a third of young people were qualifying to enter university by the mid-1990s, compared with only one in eight a decade before, and this can be seen as an achievement, despite university teachers' worries about the way it was achieved and the limited resources available to cope with it. Furthermore, more than two-fifths of the age group were achieving grades A to C at GCSE by 1995, compared with fewer than a quarter achieving equivalent grades in O levels in 1985.

Despite these improvements, though, there is public concern about whether standards of attainment in British schools are keeping up with those in other countries. In such countries as Japan, South Korea and Taiwan, for instance, 'on maths and science tests, children achieve an average score three or four years ahead of our own pupils' (*Independent on Sunday* 1995: 18). According to educational researchers, schools in these East Asian countries achieve better results by trying to develop the talents of all children rather than focusing on the higher achievers, as is the tendency in Britain. Similarly, international comparisons with more successful or faster-growing economies show that, though higher education in Britain has expanded to take in 28 per cent of young people, this is a lagging performance when set against Germany's 43 per cent, Japan's 53 per cent and the USA's 64 per cent (Holtham 1994).

These apparent shortcomings in British education raise questions about the policy-making process. Why have there been difficulties in bringing about progress in education? Does some of the difficulty lie in the way in which decisions are made in Britain? Thus, education policy raises questions about whether there is too much power at the centre and whether decision making is too elitist.

POLICY MAKING AND MODELS OF POWER

In order to make sense of what has been happening in education, it is helpful to compare different views or models of how policies develop. No single model will perfectly account for every policy and its outcome. To understand the policy process satisfactorily we need to combine a number of models.

The democratic pluralist model

The **democratic pluralist model** is probably the closest to popular and 'common sense' views of how government *should* act and of how policies *should* be made in a democratic society (though widespread publicity about politicians' abuses of power and privilege has eroded many people's trust that decisions are actually made this way).

A democracy does not necessarily entail complete equality of power or an equal say in policy making. Clearly, some individuals and groups are more articulate and better resourced than others, and for a variety of reasons will have more say over policy than poorer and marginalized groups. In a **parliamentary democracy** the people's representatives are supposed to be able to speak from their own point of view and according to their own consciences. Representatives (MPs) are not supposed to be delegates who simply report or mirror the opinions of their constituents. In any case, constituents' views are often difficult to summarize, as opinion on many key issues is sharply divided.

In practice, MPs are more constrained by party discipline than by their own consciences or views, and their behaviour in the House of Commons usually reflects the instructions of party leaders. Despite these imperfections, however, the democratic model holds that general elections guarantee the accountability of governments to the public: a government which persistently ignores the wishes of the people will be thrown out of office.

This model suggests that governments are also held in check because power is widely diffused in society among a number (a plurality) of groups: for instance, professional associations and unions (such as the various teachers' unions), business leaders and associations, and pressure groups (such as religious organizations and lobby groups).

A government which ignores powerful sectional interests and pressure groups will quickly lose its authority and be forced to back down on its policy decisions. This suggests a picture of policy making as a partnership between government and major social institutions and groups. Government may initially set the agenda, but must constantly respond to demands from the social groups and economic influences which surround it.

The elite control model

The **elite control model** suggests that elite groups of various kinds combine to run all the major government institutions, with relatively little accountability to anyone outside their own exclusive ranks. 'Democratic' institutions exist: for example, relatively unfettered mass media, elections, parliaments and individual rights to express oneself. However, as a result of a combination of skill, experience and monopolizing key leadership positions, it is always members of elites who have the decisive influence or the authoritative voice in these supposedly democratic institutions.

Elites are rather different from each other in terms of what they do and what their first priorities will be. There may be some conflicts of interest among civil service, political, military, business and professional elites. However, a theory of elite control suggests that top-ranking members of leading professional, governmental and business organizations will tend to be drawn from the same social backgrounds and to share a similar culture. For instance, most will have attended the same kinds of elite schools and universities. Bonds of family and kinship will also tend to tie them together. Even if some have risen into the elite from non-elite backgrounds, they will have been safely incorporated into the exclusive club. Thus, despite their differences, members of elites will tend to pull together to make sure that they retain overall control over policy decisions.

This model would suggest that, in Britain, all the fundamental policy decisions which led to the creation of the welfare state in the 1940s were the work of a male white elite. A tiny influential group worked out what would be in the best interests of the masses and proceeded, in the post-war period, to implement their wartime blueprint. Barnett (1986) contends, for example, that a high-minded and left-leaning Whitehall elite played a major part in this.

Whether or not Barnett is right about the way in which the welfare state was created (for further comment, see Deakin 1994: 36), this example raises the interesting point that elite control need not necessarily result in policies which are fashioned according to the narrow self-interest of the elite itself. The NHS, for instance, is largely the product of conflict and power struggles between a political and a medical elite (see Klein 1995). There was relatively little input from either Parliament, which endorsed the NHS Bill with little amendment, or any other broad-based or democratic institutions. Yet the NHS remains one of the most popular institutions: a socialist-inspired health service planned and implemented by elites.

The political economy model

The **political economy model** rests on rather different assumptions from the first two. Basically, both the democratic pluralist and elite control models pose the question: 'which groups are in control?' Is policy shaped primarily by democratic institutions and groups, or is it determined by elites?

A political economy perspective, on the other hand, draws more attention to the underlying economic system and how the political system interacts with it. Now that state socialism has been dismantled in the former Soviet Union and Eastern Europe, the systems which prevail in almost every country in the world are openly capitalist market economies of one kind or another. Even China, though retaining a communist political structure, is rapidly developing a market economy.

Thus, the basic idea of a political economy perspective is that social policy is shaped by the needs or demands of a *market* economy. This includes education policy. The political economy model asks in what ways government spending on education is influenced by the needs and demands of business and industry: for instance, by the drive to cut employer costs by reducing the burden of taxation or, conversely, to encourage education spending in such areas as the use of new technologies in business. According to this model, types of education which are seen as unproductive in a capitalist economy are likely to be downgraded and underfunded.

Although a political economy perspective emphasizes the needs of the capitalist system as a whole, it also has implications, like the first two models, for the question of who controls or dominates policy.

In many respects, the political economy model comes close to the theory of elite control. As it suggests that most major policy decisions are subject to the backing of 'big business' or capitalist interests, it is a short step to saying that government and civil service elites interlock with business elites (leaders of City and financial institutions, and of manufacturing, retail and other commercial organizations). Evidence of this is provided partly by recent governments' reliance on business leaders to head new policy developments or to manage government agencies (for example, Sir Ron Dearing, chair of the School Curriculum and Assessment Authority from 1994, has held many company directorships).

The political economy model can be equated with Marxist views of a class-structured society in which a ruling class controls policy. The way in which this control is exercised is a matter of debate among Marxists, who disagree with each other about how directly or openly government and state are manipulated by ruling class interests (Ham and Hill 1993: 35).

Some maintain that the ruling class is a cohesive group which will always act collectively to defend its interests and steer state policy towards its ends. Other 'neo-Marxist' thinkers have argued that government and state have a relatively free hand to set the agenda and to shape social policies. This **relative autonomy** of government from capitalist interests is necessary so that the state can hold the ring between competing capitalist interests (for example, conflicts between financial interests and industrial or manufacturing interests). Moreover, the capitalist system as a whole 'looks better' or will have more legitimacy if government acts with some independence than it will in a situation in which government and state could easily be portrayed as puppets of big business.

Despite these differences of emphasis, Marxist perspectives share a common view that it is the underlying political-economic system which shapes policy, rather than particular social groups or leaders. There may be shifts of power within the ruling class, they argue, but the system as a whole will tend to perpetuate gross inequalities of wealth and power. This in turn creates the potential for conflict between haves and have-nots, and between those who control policy and the mass of people who have to deal with the consequences of government decisions.

MODELS OF POWER AND EDUCATION REFORM: THE 1988 EDUCATION REFORM ACT AND ITS AFTERMATH

In this section, recent education policy will be examined, focusing on the 1988 Education Reform Act – an important piece of legislation by the former Conservative government which 'set the agenda' for the incoming Labour government in 1997. The aim, as stated at the beginning of the chapter, is not to summarize every change in education but to analyse the *process* of change: how and why decisions are made, and what the implications are for the democratic nature (or otherwise) of decision making in Britain. The models of power outlined above will be referred to where they help to make sense of what has been happening in British education since 1988.

The impact of the 1988 reforms

There is still some uncertainty about how much of a landmark the 1988 Education Act will prove to be. At one extreme, it could be written off as a package of cosmetic reforms which prompted a deluge of paperwork, with new procedures for testing schoolchildren and introducing curriculum reforms, but very little of substance.

However, it is more likely that the Act has set off a series of fundamental changes in British education. For Deakin, the Act 'is justly compared in its impact to the Butler Education Act of 1944' (Deakin 1994: 162), though he suggests that its architects were not particularly forward-looking or mindful of the consequences of what they had unleashed.

A significant sign of the lasting impact of the 1988 reforms can be seen in recent Labour plans for education. While Labour's plans in opposition sought to modify key aspects of the Conservative policies since 1988, they did not aim for a return to the 1970s policy of developing a common or comprehensive form of secondary education for everyone. This break with the past led to one of the few open and lively debates over policy at the Labour Party conference of 1995, when Roy Hattersley – a former Labour minister and champion of comprehensive schooling – strongly opposed Labour's plans for recategorizing schools into three kinds (community, aided and foundation schools).

He argued that foundation schools will be grant-maintained or 'opted out' schools in disguise (that is, schools which are funded directly by the Department for Education and Employment and which opted out of control by the local education authority). They would continue to gain extra funds and, through careful selection of pupils, would be seen as superior institutions. Thus Hattersley suggested that the 'articulate middle classes' will continue to 'talk their way into an unfair advantage' in gaining access to foundation schools (Hattersley 1995).

Others disagree with this analysis, however, suggesting that Labour's apparent switch in policy towards the Conservative approach was 'far less dramatic than expected' (Judd and Abrams 1995). According to this view, opted out schools will lose much of their independence to local authorities, being unable (as foundation schools) to set their own admissions policies.

However, the Labour government's early plans for education, as revealed in a White Paper in 1997, adopted much of the Conservatives' language of testing, educational standards and parental involvement. For instance, the main points of this White Paper include: new kinds of improvement targets for all schools; early dismissal procedures for failing teachers; greater central control over the curriculum to ensure that at least an hour a day is spent on literacy and numeracy skills with primary schoolchildren; and 'home–school contracts' to involve parents closely with their children's education. In most respects, these policies look more like a continuation of the 1988 reforms than a new approach in education, and therefore they suggest that the 1988 Act had a lasting effect.

The main features of the 1988 reforms were:

1 The introduction of a *national curriculum* and standardized *attainment tests* for all children at the ages of 7, 11 and 14.
2 The removal of certain powers of regulation and planning from local education authorities (for example, local education authorities (LEAs) could no longer set limits on the size of growing or popular schools). This was combined with the handing over of many of the responsibilities for running state schools to their headteachers and governing bodies – a policy of *local management of schools* (LMS). School governers and heads of secondary and larger primary schools were required to manage their own budgets and to plan their own development, including staffing. However, LEAs were left 'with a significant role, albeit redefined, in strategic planning and quality assurance' (Ranson and Travers 1994: 223). Funding of locally managed schools was still to be funnelled through LEAs.
3 The creation of a new category of *grant-maintained* state schools. These were to be funded directly by central government (the Department for Education and Employment), rather than by LEAs. The funding formula gave an incentive to schools to opt out of LEAs. While a neighbouring local authority-funded school might be struggling to repair a leaking roof or pay for a much-needed additional teacher, opted out schools could contemplate building a swimming pool or new classrooms. The Act stipulated that parents had to be balloted about any proposals for a change to grant-maintained status, and that a majority of those who voted had to be in favour for the change to be agreed by the Secretary of State.
4 In addition, the 1988 Education Reform Act sought to strengthen further the voice of education *consumers* (parents and employers) in the running of schools. School governing bodies were to have not only elected parent governors but also local 'worthy citizens' from business and professional backgrounds.
5 Drawing upon an American policy experiment ('magnet schools'), the Act launched proposals for *city technology colleges* (CTCs), which were to be jointly funded by government and business. This new kind of secondary education was to be provided in the best equipped and best staffed environment possible. CTCs were supposed to educate in the broadest sense, while stimulating achievement, entrepreneurial attitudes and industry- and business-relevant skills.

Evaluating the reforms: the power dimension

The reforms could be evaluated solely in terms of their educational merits. At the same time, the changes introduced in 1988 led to significant shifts of *power* from local authorities and the teaching profession to central government and a burgeoning group of education quangos.

However, there is little doubt that the educational case for reform was strong. The case for a national curriculum had been accepted in educational circles well before 1988. Nicholas (1983), for example, described the lack of a national curriculum in Britain as 'anomalous and idiosyncratic' when compared with European education systems. Similarly, concern about the relatively high numbers of British young people leaving school with few or no qualifications had already led to demands from employers and other groups for testing and for setting national standards of school attainment in literacy and numeracy. Within the educational world, there was also pressure for a degree of devolved management from local authorities to schools.

The political context

The significance of the 1988 education reforms therefore lies less in the basic ideas, which were not particularly original, but more in the ways those ideas were interpreted and put into practice. There were two main features of the education reform process: first, the speed with which changes were introduced and the lack of consultation or consideration of alternatives; second, the degree to which the reforms centralized power.

In 1987, a Conservative government was elected to power for a third term in office under the leadership of Mrs Thatcher. Some social policy changes had already been introduced in the period 1979–86 by Mrs Thatcher's previous administrations (for instance, a 1980 Education Act strengthened parents' rights to preferred places for their children in state schools). However, with notable exceptions such as the sale of council housing, Conservative social policy in the first two terms had tried to clip the wings of the welfare state rather than to change it.

Mrs Thatcher's third term presented a long-awaited chance to bring radical organizational changes to the main welfare state services: health, social services and education. Before 1987, Mrs Thatcher had been 'nervous about addressing highly controversial areas' in social policy (Deakin 1994: 152). But the third election victory in a row appeared to give popular assent to a much more ideologically driven programme than before. Right-wing 'think tanks' such as the Centre for Policy Studies and the Institute of Economic Affairs proved to be particularly influential in providing ideas and strategies for policy change.

All three of the major service areas were to taste Mrs Thatcher's patent cure: the introduction of market disciplines into public sector services, strong challenges to the traditional power and status of professional groups such as teachers, a weakening of the role of local government by the setting up of quangos to administer or fund services at 'arm's length' and an emphasis on choice and the rights of individual service users.

There was little warning of the education reforms in the 1987 election campaign. Proposals for change were released by the government shortly beforehand, but not with enough detail to spell out the full implications. Thus the democratic or pluralist model offers little or no insight into the origins of the education reforms of 1988.

Nor is there much evidence to support a 'political economy' interpretation of the reforms. Mrs Thatcher's government may have professed an understanding of the needs of business and enjoyed close attachments with business leaders, but the specific ideas on how to reorganize education came from a small political elite, not from sustained discussions between government and industry or business groups.

If the political economy model has any force at all, it is more as a background explanation of the forces influencing government at the time: on the one hand, capitalist interests lie in economical government and keeping down government expenditure. On the other hand, as Sampson (1992) points out, some business opinion laments the low standards attained by many British school leavers and the way in which this reduces Britain's productivity and competitive edge. According to a political economy interpretation, therefore, any government would be predisposed to look for policies which could raise standards with relatively little increase in expenditure.

The strongest interpretation, however, is that government was motivated first and foremost by ideology. Many of Mrs Thatcher's policies began in this way. There was a tendency to push innovations from the top downwards, although this approach was tempered by political pragmatism and caution in some cases. In the case of education, however, it was the lack of consultation with education representatives outside government which underlines the impression of policy making by a tight circle of top people in government: the Prime Minister and her policy advisory group, and selected Cabinet ministers.

Parliament and the legislative process

The education reforms were very quickly drafted. The late Nicholas Ridley, a former government minister, is quoted as saying that the education reforms were 'hammered out in ... no more than a month' (Gilmour 1992: 167). It was these quickly drafted plans which became law shortly afterwards.

The government at that time enjoyed a large majority in the House of Commons. When a government has a small or non-existent majority, as under John Major's leadership, it is more likely that proposed legislation will be subjected to scrutiny and amendment, especially if the government's own party is divided and if its supporting MPs must be placated with concessions or changes to a Bill. Proposed legislation must go through a series of stages before it becomes law and government policy (see Figure 6.1).

In the case of the Education Reform Bill, however, the government's original plans as set out in the White Paper survived virtually intact. This occurred despite widespread concern that the Education Reform Act gave too many new powers to central government and, in so doing, that it raised serious constitutional issues. However, the British system allows a Prime Minister with a safe majority to push a legislative programme through Parliament, using it more or less as a rubber stamp.

Figure 6.1   How policies turn into legislation

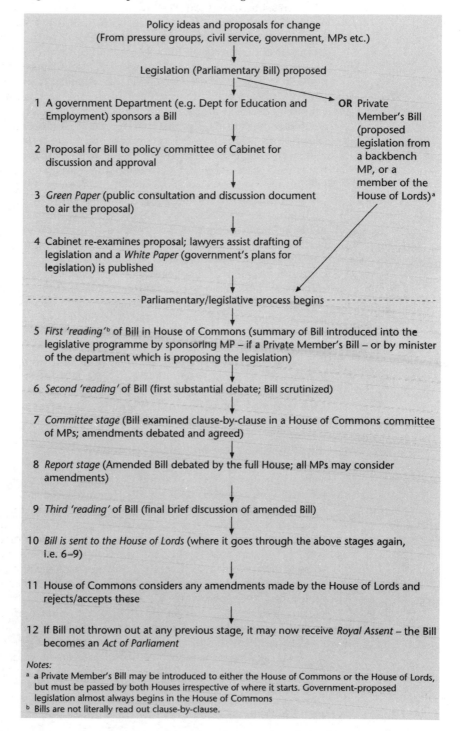

Policy ideas and proposals for change
(From pressure groups, civil service, government, MPs etc.)

↓

Legislation (Parliamentary Bill) proposed

↓

1 A government Department (e.g. Dept for Education and   **OR** Private
Employment) sponsors a Bill   Member's Bill
                                                                                           (proposed
↓   legislation from
                                                                                           a backbench
2 Proposal for Bill to policy committee of Cabinet for   MP, or a
discussion and approval   member of the
                                                                                           House of Lords)ᵃ
↓

3 *Green Paper* (public consultation and discussion document
to air the proposal)

↓

4 Cabinet re-examines proposal; lawyers assist drafting of
legislation and a *White Paper* (government's plans for
legislation) is published

↓

- - - - - - - - - - - - - - - - - - Parliamentary/legislative process begins - - - - - - - - - - - - - - - - - -

↓

5 First *'reading'*ᵇ of Bill in House of Commons (summary of Bill introduced into the
legislative programme by sponsoring MP – if a Private Member's Bill – or by minister
of the department which is proposing the legislation)

↓

6 *Second 'reading'* of Bill (first substantial debate; Bill scrutinized)

↓

7 *Committee stage* (Bill examined clause-by-clause in a House of Commons committee
of MPs; amendments debated and agreed)

↓

8 *Report stage* (Amended Bill debated by the full House; all MPs may consider
amendments)

↓

9 *Third 'reading'* of Bill (final brief discussion of amended Bill)

↓

10 *Bill is sent to the House of Lords* (where it goes through the above stages again,
i.e. 6–9)

↓

11 House of Commons considers any amendments made by the House of Lords and
rejects/accepts these

↓

12 If Bill not thrown out at any previous stage, it may now receive *Royal Assent* – the Bill
becomes an *Act of Parliament*

Notes:
ᵃ a Private Member's Bill may be introduced to either the House of Commons or the House of Lords,
but must be passed by both Houses irrespective of where it starts. Government-proposed
legislation almost always begins in the House of Commons
ᵇ Bills are not literally read out clause-by-clause.

In other democratic systems (for example, in the United States), there are more checks and balances between different legislatures (Senate and Congress). The role of President in both the United States and France is a very powerful one, but unlike a British Prime Minister, an American or French President may be forced to govern with majorities of representatives from opposition parties, as did Democrat President Clinton with a Republican majority in Congress and Gaullist (conservative) President Chirac with a socialist majority in the French parliament.

Both of these examples – and many other Western countries – have written constitutions. In most cases this gives a more significant role than in the United Kingdom to supreme courts, whose role is to test whether a government's actions and policies are lawful within the constitution. In the United States, Supreme Court decisions can effectively amend or block government policies.

In contrast, the 1988 legislation on education in the United Kingdom highlights the way in which policies can be steam-rollered through Parliament, however hotly they are debated by opposition MPs. The House of Lords may also find flaws in proposed legislation and seek amendments, but the second chamber's powers are tightly circumscribed; the Lords cannot permanently veto legislation or insist on changes.

It is for these reasons that Gilmour (1992: 187) argues that the British system is best described as a 'plebiscitary democracy' rather than a parliamentary democracy. A plebiscite is a one-off vote of the people, as in a referendum or a general election. Having made one key decision, the electorate hands all power to a ruling elite.

In education policy, the implementation and results of the Education Reform Act bear out many of Gilmour's criticisms. There have been two main 'problem areas': first, the National Curriculum and testing system and, second, the school 'opt out' policy.

Implementing the National Curriculum

The government's lack of spade-work in preparing for these important reforms soon began to show itself. Having drawn a bold but oversimplified plan of the new curriculum and testing system, the government was forced to turn to the very educational experts and professionals it had earlier cold-shouldered in order to find ways of implementing the policy.

In the educational world, the words 'National Curriculum' soon came to be associated with complexity, educational jargon and time-consuming debates about levels of attainment and content. Successive ministers of education were drawn into questions about whether they were imposing government ideology upon the school curriculum in subjects such as English, history and religious education. Professional advisers tended to broaden and overload the curriculum, while the Department for Education was accused of trying to return education to 'a 19th-century curriculum – the basics plus RE' (Ranson and Travers 1994: 225).

Within a few years, the lack of coherence in implementing the National Curriculum and testing system resulted in a crisis. Teachers, whose morale had already been steadily eroded by a relative decline in their pay and working conditions, began to refuse to set standard attainment tests. The boycott spread widely in 1993 and, as Ranson and Travers (1994: 224) observe, what began as a protest over ill-prepared tests 'became a general dispute about the national curriculum, testing, and . . . using information from the tests to create national league tables of school performance.' This example is particularly illustrative, because it shows that a 'policy' is never a static thing. A policy is much more than the written guidelines or laws which bring it into being. A policy *becomes* what is eventually implemented. The teachers' resistance to curriculum and testing reform is also interesting because it modifies the 'elite control' view of policy making. In this case, the teachers were not able to create a new policy, but they were able as a professional pressure group to challenge and obstruct government power.

Thus, in the case of the National Curriculum and testing, the 1988 Education Reform Act set off at a very fast pace but collided with almost every hurdle, limping to a standstill in 1993. The government then had to recognize this, accepting the findings of a review of National Curriculum and testing by Sir Ron Dearing (1994). Dearing's conclusions referred to such problems as the excessive pace of change, bureaucratic complexity, a failure to provide resources for teachers, curriculum overload and confusion over the purposes of assessment. While it must be accepted that mistakes will always be made and any new policy will need to be 'fine-tuned', the scale of the problems identified by Dearing seems to confirm the point that there was insufficient consultation, debate and clarification of objectives at the initial 'design stage' in 1988.

Implementing the school 'opt out' policy

The idea of allowing secondary schools to opt out of the local system was to have been another major new policy on how schools should be run. When, 'to the surprise of her colleagues', Mrs Thatcher launched the idea in the 1987 general election campaign, 'she predicted opting out would be as successful as council house sales in liberating families from socialism' (Carvel and MacLeod 1995: 15). A stampede of schools wanting to opt out was expected, especially as there were to be financial incentives for schools willing to change status.

However, this policy has met with even slower progress and more resistance than the reforms of the curriculum and of standard tests in schools. In the first few years, only a handful of the 25,000 schools in England and Wales applied to opt out. In Scotland the policy did not take off at all. By 1993, there were still only 693 'grant-maintained' (opted out) schools, and this total fell far short of the government's modest target of 1500 in England and Wales (Ranson and Travers 1994: 227). By 1995, the number of grant-maintained schools was still little over a thousand. Far from quickening, the rate at which schools applied for grant-maintained status or held ballots on the issue declined sharply after 1993. This is despite the fact that a 1993 Education Act introduced several measures to encourage opting out: governing bodies of all state secondary schools were to be required every year to consider opting out; local authority publicity against opting out was to be limited; and for the first time special schools and religious schools were to be allowed to opt out.

The story of introducing grant-maintained or opted out schools was, in many ways, one of how *not* to implement a policy. Plans emerged from the top rather than being based on an evident need or demand for such schools. In fact, most parents and teachers have proved to be quite conservative in these matters, in the main preferring local authorities to continue to oversee and run much of the education system (though LMS *has* been relatively successful and may in part account for the reluctance of school heads and governors to opt out, as they now enjoy considerable management autonomy within a local authority framework).

To many parents, voting for grant-maintained status appeared to be a risky educational experiment, and this accounts for some of the reluctance to back the policy at the local level. For instance, parents fear a drift towards selection by examination among opted out schools. Where opting out has occurred, it is more often by schools which face reorganization or closure than in cases where parents and teachers are relatively happy with existing arrangements.

In sum, this example shows that there are limits to a government's ability to impose change from the top, even when a government had a 'radical' agenda and a large parliamentary majority. However, although the school opt out policy progressed at a snail's pace, the Conservative government was successful in quickly pushing through many other administrative reforms, especially in the ways in which education is *funded* and *supervised*.

CENTRALIZING THE EDUCATION SYSTEM

Changes in both the funding and supervision of schools, colleges and universities have greatly strengthened the hand of central government. Now that power has shifted to the centre, it is very unlikely that any government – including the Labour government elected in 1997 – will want to give it back; indeed, the government's first steps in education policy (see introduction) seemed to continue with the centralization trend set in 1988.

Elected local authorities have gradually lost much of their control over education spending: for instance, LMS means that school budgets are devolved to each school's governing body, while the granting of independence to further education colleges meant that local authorities lost control over a whole sector of education spending.

While these changes have brought some *de*centralization of responsibility (to individual schools and colleges), this has been outweighed in many respects by the trend in the opposite direction, towards centralization. Encouraging schools and colleges to behave as independent institutions and to compete with one another may look as though teachers and parents are being given a lot more control over education at the local level, but in practice such reforms demand greater central *regulation*. Teachers, whether in schools, colleges or universities, now spend much more time than in the past filling in forms, preparing for inspections and managing budgets.

The rise of a 'quango state' in education

The proliferation of bureaucracies to oversee quality of services, to check standards and to set performance targets can be observed in other parts of the state-run welfare system (for example, the NHS) or in other areas where public services have been privatized (for example, the water companies). Paradoxically, greater market 'freedoms' usually demand more, not less, government control and interference in the form of regulatory bodies and quangos.

In education, funding through central government agencies is now much more important than it used to be (whether funding is for grant-maintained schools, independent further education or sixth-form colleges). The 1944 Education Act had given local authorities the chief responsibility for education spending. But by 1994 in England, a third of this spending (£10 billion) flowed through the channels of central government agencies or quangos (Meikle 1994).

Central government control is strengthened because in many instances funding is conditional upon meeting certain performance targets or standards of quality. For instance, further education colleges in recent years have been funded according to the numbers of students they can enrol. This acted as a direct incentive to put 'bums on seats' irrespective of students' needs or abilities, and some believe that such a strategy led to a dilution of standards and conflicted with the goal of raising quality and student achievement. Universities also saw a rapid expansion of student numbers, but this was followed after 1992 by heavy financial penalties, imposed by central government, for recruiting above limits set by government.

Figure 6.2 gives an overview of the roles of the various supervisory agencies or quangos in education in 1995. It reinforces the impression of a growing centralization of power, though it is important not to confuse a simplified diagram of the *structure* of the education system with the active *processes* of conflict and policy making which have occurred since the system was set up.

In other words, Figure 6.2 gives an impression of control from the top, by central government, but this is not always the case. As we have seen in relation to teachers' qualms about the curriculum and testing reforms, implementation of policy at the local level does not always go entirely the government's way. Policy can also be questioned by the very authorities which seem to represent central government: the funding and regulatory quangos, such as the SCAA. Leaders or senior executives of quangos are ready to challenge government from time to time, as shown by Sir Ron Dearing's review of the introduction of the National Curriculum and testing (see above). Dearing (chairman of the SCAA at the time of writing this book) has been described as a 'tireless reformer' (Macleod 1995) who has demonstrated a willingness to put the interests of education, and especially

Figure 6.2   Governing education: an outline of the system

GOVERNMENT
Prime Minister and Cabinet, including
Secretary of State for Education

Primary and secondary education	Further and higher education
CENTRAL/NATIONAL AGENCIES	
School Curriculum and Assessment Authority (SCAA) (r) (National Curriculum, testing children's attainments)	Committee of Vice-Chancellors and Principals (CVCP) (Autonomous body; tries to protect university interests; usually bends to the government's will but can modify policy)
Office for Standards in Education (Ofsted) (r) (school inspection arrangements)	Higher Education Quality Council (HEQC) (r)
Funding Agency for Schools (FAS) (f) (for grant-maintained schools)	National Council for Vocational Qualifications (NCVQ)
	Higher Education Funding Councils (HEFCs) (f) (for England, Wales etc.) Further Education Funding Councils (f)

LOCAL AGENCIES/INSTITUTIONS	
Local education authorities (mainly f, some a)	Further education colleges
	Universities
School governors (parent, teacher and local representatives) (a)	University colleges
Headteachers (a)	
Local authority schools Grant-maintained schools	

(f) = Funding agency
(r) = Regulating or checking standards
(a) = Administering/operating the system

of vocational education for 16–19-year-olds, before interests of power or allegiance to party.

CONCLUSIONS: EDUCATION, POLICY MAKING AND MODELS OF POWER

Recent education policy provides an intriguing example of how policies are implemented in Britain and of who makes the key decisions in the first place. As we have seen, what sense we make of the education reforms and who we think is responsible for them will depend on which model of power we think is the more persuasive.

First, the *democratic pluralist* model would appear to have little value as an explanation of the *origin* of the education reforms that were introduced. Though there may have been a groundswell of opinion in favour of shaking up the education system and improving standards, all the *specific* proposals for change (for instance, what the National Curriculum would contain, grant-maintained schools and opting out) came from Mrs Thatcher or her closest advisers and ministers (Gilmour 1992; Deakin 1994). Thus, the model of *elite control* seems the more persuasive.

There are, however, two problems with this conclusion. The first is that a pluralist model does not rule out the idea that there is a concentration of power in government. It would be naive to expect every policy to reflect grassroots opinion or consultation with pressure groups. According to Dahl (1961), who wrote a pioneering study of city politics in America, a pluralistic democracy in the real world works on the principle that central and local government control. The point is that, in a democracy, government is accountable to the people at election time, and also (especially in the United States) to the courts.

Thus, a different conclusion would be that Mrs Thatcher's government was only acting as any government does in a parliamentary system. Government may have run ahead of the public will in education matters, but it was open to the electorate to reject a Conservative government and its education policies in 1992 (which it did not) and in 1997 (which it did).

Does this mean that the democratic pluralist model provides an accurate view of policy making in Britain after all? Unfortunately, such a conclusion would also be unsatisfactory.

A democratic model, although it does allow for the idea of government playing a lead role, nevertheless portrays political leaders and institutions as relatively open to 'outside' or pressure group influences *during the process of policy-making*. According to Dahl, interest groups should be able to influence government decisions before they are finalized. However, the education reforms of the 1980s were introduced with little or no consultation. As will be recalled, only the vaguest references to education changes were made in the 1987 election campaign, and when the government put forward its proposals in 1988 it did so without going through a consultative ('Green Paper') stage.

There are also other concerns about the health of democratic institutions in Britain today (see, for instance, Hutton 1995), and these throw additional doubts upon the value of the democratic pluralist model. In education, control by democratically elected local authorities has been eroded in a number of fields, as key functions (funding and regulation) have been taken over by centralized bodies or unelected quangos which meet in private.

Quangos do not necessarily lack competence or commitment to education. The main argument about their role, as Meikle (1994) concludes, is over quango board members, who are 'responsible for either huge budgets or huge powers [and] are there through patronage.'

Thus there is a strong argument that the dominance of one party in Parliament weakens sources of opposition to centralized government power. Despite this, however, it would be wrong to jettison the democratic pluralist explanation of policy development altogether. As we saw at the

implementation stage of policy making, there is evidence that a pluralist (if not fully democratic) model can at least partly explain how recent policies developed.

On balance, then, a reliable or accurate picture of policy making depends upon the simultaneous use of two or three models, rather than exclusive reliance upon one. An emphasis on elite control might be particularly relevant for analysis of 'the corridors of power' and the early stages of policy formation, whereas it might be necessary to incorporate ideas about pluralistic politics and democratic influences when looking at the local level or at how policies are received at the grassroots.

The third *political economy* model is, as we saw, rather different from the first two. It offers more of a background explanation of economic and political influences on policy than a way of analysing why particular policies were adopted and others were not.

If we were to rely solely on a political economy view it would not be easy to explain why the Conservative government's education reforms took the shape they did: why, for example, the government felt it necessary to introduce grant-maintained schools or particular kinds of testing or curriculum reform. Many of these policy ideas were the brainchildren of Mrs Thatcher and a close circle of political advisers and ministers, not the products of an economic system which needed those particular changes. While industrialists and business leaders may have put pressure on the government to improve standards of numeracy and literacy in the schools, there are no clear signs that a particular recipe for reform was demanded.

The value of the political economy model lies in the way it can highlight the tension in a capitalist society between the pressure towards keeping down social expenditure (as demonstrated in the tight control of funding for local authorities in 1995) and the pressure towards developing a more productive workforce (through better training and education).

The proportion of Britain's resources devoted to education has changed very little over the past decade. As noted at the outset, the share of national wealth devoted to Britain's education system even fell slightly during the 1980s. And although the incoming Labour government of 1997 promised to find an 'extra' £1.5 billion for education for the year 1998–9, this represented only a small increase over the budget planned by the previous Conservative administration. The Labour government's spending plans were notable for their caution and restraint (see Chapter 10) and, given this strategy, the education service faces almost as tight a financial squeeze as other parts of the welfare system, such as the health service.

We have seen that in more successful or faster-growing capitalist economies than Britain's (Germany, Japan, South Korea, the United States), up to 90 per cent of 18-year-olds gain educational qualifications and much higher proportions of the age group go on to higher education. A purely economic explanation based on 'capitalist interests' cannot, therefore, account for Britain's educational lag: if educational expansion benefits the capitalist economy, then why have British capitalist interests failed to stimulate greater educational development while those in Japan or America have succeeded?

The answer, one suspects, lies in the *political* part of the political economy model. The political elites in Japan and South Korea, for instance, have

pushed in a very determined way for educational expansion and modern-
ization. As Holtham points out, achieving such change

> is not simply a matter of money. Indeed, Japan, for example, does not
> spend a particularly high proportion of its GNP on education . . . But
> it is true that, from where we are at present, greater state expenditure
> overall will almost surely be needed.
>
> With the middle classes unwilling to pay more tax and the Gov-
> ernment already borrowing more than 5 per cent of GDP to finance
> its deficit, where can the necessary resources come from? Clearly some
> brutal choices must be made in the years ahead.
>
> (Holtham 1994: 8)

Recent education policy shows that Britain's political elites are unwilling
to face these choices. The reasons for this are a matter of debate, but it is
likely that Britain's traditional class divisions in education play a large
part. Political elites, whether of the left or right, will be reluctant to bring
fundamental change to a selective and elitist system that suits them well.

It may well be realized that economic success requires a bigger investment in education and a much higher proportion of younger people in
post-16 training, but both Conservative and Labour plans for education
suggest reluctance to risk electoral unpopularity by raising taxes to achieve
these goals.

Thus, of the three models, an elite control model seems to explain best
the formation of education policy in Britain, although the other models
we have considered provide valuable perspectives. Britain is a parliamentary democracy, but the example of education shows that any change of
government at election time largely has the effect of exchanging one
political elite for another; despite differences in matters of detail (for
instance, over the Conservatives' grant-maintained schools and Labour's
foundation schools proposal), the closeness of government and opposition plans bear out the impression that education policy in Britain will
continue to duck the 'brutal choices' mentioned by Holtham.

KEY TERMS AND CONCEPTS

democratic pluralist model of power
elite control model of power
implementation
parliamentary democracy
policy agenda

political economy model of power
quangos (quasi-autonomous
    non-governmental organizations)
relative autonomy

SUGGESTIONS FOR FURTHER READING

Chris Ham and Michael Hill's *The Policy Process in the Modern Capitalist
State* (1993) remains one of the best and more readable texts on the
nature of policy making and models of power.

An elegant and succinct view of the nature of power in modern society has been written by Steven Lukes (*Power: a Radical View*, 1974). Though written primarily for a sociological and political science audience, it has many applications in social policy.

For a wry and insightful view of the exercise of power inside British government, Sir Ian Gilmour's *Dancing with Dogma* (1992) is well worth reading. It is especially interesting as an example of an 'old guard' Tory's view of Mrs Thatcher's politics and policies.

Nicholas Deakin's *The Politics of Welfare* (1994) offers a balanced, academic review of politics and the social policies of the 1980s and early 1990s. This is one of the most readable and widely informed texts on politics and social policy.

Finally, for reading on the 1988 Education Act, see Brian Simon's *Bending the Rules* (1988).

7 ARE PROFESSIONALS GOOD FOR YOU? HEALTH POLICY AND HEALTH PROFESSIONALS

INTRODUCTION

Consider some personal situations in which you have been treated by a 'health professional'. For example, think about reclining in a dentist's chair. The dentist is hovering above, ready to administer a local anaesthetic. Although anticipation of pain might be uppermost in your mind, there may be some other thoughts: how effective will this course of treatment be? How much will it cost, and who will be paying? If you have to bear most of the cost, is this fair and can you afford it?

Although you may be concentrating on how to get through the next fifteen minutes, other thoughts may flit across your mind: what are your impressions of the equipment or 'technology' used by the dentist? Who paid for it? How considerate or friendly is the dentist, and how good is she or he at finding out what you need? When and where did the dentist receive training, and do you have confidence that he or she will not hit a sensitive nerve?

The more we reflect on personal experiences such as this, whether with a dentist, a nurse, a doctor or a therapist, the more we come to realize that what happens – the **outcome** of the course of treatment – is not simply a result of an individual professional treating an individual patient with particular needs. Individual outcomes are also affected by broader factors, such as

1 *Government policy:* for example, how much treatment and what kinds of treatment, if any, will be provided 'free' at the point of use by patients? How does this affect our willingness to use health services?
2 *Technology:* what have advances in the 'tools' available done to change our experience of medical treatment, of going into hospital or going to the dentist's?
3 *The market:* is demand for health care and for particular treatments high or low? Are doctors, nurses, physiotherapists or dentists in short supply, or is the market flooded with too many?
4 *The professions:* are medical professionals and practitioners such as dentists able to dictate the level or quality of treatment given to patients? Are they able to insist on certain professional standards of treatment, or are they sometimes forced to provide cheaper, short-term remedies?

These are just four major examples of influence, and there may be yet others. They show that outcomes are not determined wholly by the professional. Professionals themselves operate in a world of constraints, costs and opportunities. However, this chapter, in addressing the fundamental question 'Are professionals good for you?', will focus on the role of the professional as a key actor in social policy. Although the examples are taken from the field of health, some if not all of the lessons about professional power and influence which we may learn from these examples can be applied to other parts of the welfare system: for example, personal social services, probation, housing and planning, education and training.

WHAT IS HEALTH POLICY?

Thinking about the background social and economic influences on what happens to us in the doctor's surgery or the hospital shows us that government policy itself is decided by a range of factors. What the government can afford by way of health services, the rising cost of drugs, what the public expects from health services, developments in medical technology and many other factors all contribute to the shaping of health policy. This in turn will constrain what an individual doctor, dentist or nurse can offer.

However, it is important not to see health policy solely as something to do with medical experts or health services. Of course, medical treatment may enhance health. Unless a decaying tooth is filled it may be lost, leading to other problems and poorer dental health. Sometimes, however, treatment may actually make no difference or, even worse, may adversely affect health. **Iatrogenic diseases** are those which result from medical intervention or from medical complications following treatment.

In general, health and illness is decided by many factors other than individual treatment. Dental health, for example, is much affected by diet and lifestyle (for example, how much sugary food we eat, and how often) and by **preventive policies** such as fluoridization of water supplies, something which has had a very marked effect on reducing the incidence of tooth decay in children.

In sum, 'health policy' can be defined either narrowly, as (a) government efforts and policy to improve health through the health services and medical treatment, or more broadly, as (b) any government activity which affects health and illness, not just the activities of the Department of Health, the NHS, professionals or other health services. The broader picture (b) shows that 'health policy' is related to many other policies: taxation of tobacco, for instance, or the effectiveness of regulations on air and water pollution, the safety of food and the working environment.

Poorer developing countries illustrate how health and illness are often more influenced by policies in other fields than by health services. Agricultural policies in an African country, for example, may have a much greater impact than a ministry of health on the life expectancy of women and children if they succeed in stimulating the production of nutritious local foods. Conversely, economic or agricultural policies to increase the production of cash crops can have the effect of raising the cost of locally produced foods, and thus threaten balanced diets and the health of children in the poorest families.

However, even if health policy is defined more narrowly as being concerned only with the health services (a), it is important to include under this heading the less visible preventive and environmental services, as well as those which involve curative services or one-to-one relationships between practitioners and patients.

For instance, going back to the dentist's chair, perhaps a more pertinent question to ask than 'Will this treatment work?' would be, 'Why am I here at all?' or 'Why have preventive services not worked in my case?' We may be right in blaming ourselves for at least some of our dental health problems ('Should I really have eaten all those sugary foods?'). But this would neglect the role of preventive measures such as fluoridization or education about diet.

HEALTH, ILLNESS AND MODERN MEDICINE

Seen in this light, the assumption that health services and health professionals play the major part in making people healthy must be seriously

Table 7.1 Selected causes of death, by sex and age, 1989 and 1951 (number of deaths per 1000 deaths)[a]

	Males			Females		
	Under 15	15–64	65+	Under 15	15–64	65+
Infectious diseases	52 (72)	10 (141)	5 (14)	48 (93)	13 (168)	4 (7)
Cancer	79 (30)	224 (182)	258 (141)	80 (31)	441 (259)	212 (134)
Circulatory diseases[b]	29 (7)	279 (203)	478 (420)	31 (10)	157 (176)	495 (425)
Accidents and violence	190 (104)	308 (174)	14 (19)	143 (74)	178 (55)	16 (21)

[a] 1951 rates are in parentheses.
[b] Includes heart attacks and strokes.
Source: Adapted from Table 7.5, *Social Trends 21*, HMSO (1991).

questioned. However, the work of health professionals is not insignificant and can contribute especially to improving quality of life when people have fallen ill.

In relation to more serious illnesses, there have been remarkable improvements in medical treatment. Advances in 'keyhole' surgery and in anaesthesia, to give just two examples, have enabled operations to be performed on very old patients, for whom some treatments (under general anaesthetic) would formerly have been too risky.

Modern health services therefore face a set of priorities and needs which are entirely different from those of 100 or even 50 years ago. **Acute**, life-threatening (mainly infectious) diseases have been replaced by long-term or **chronic** conditions as the more prevalent forms of illness: examples are rheumatoid arthritis, multiple sclerosis, diabetes, asthma and various forms of mental illness. Death is now often preceded by relatively long periods of disability. Medical services and treatments may assist with the management and control of symptoms, but they cannot cure these diseases.

In the past, death rates and the causes of death provided a clear picture of what were then the major diseases of the time. Now, however, the leading causes of death (see Table 7.1) show us only part of the total picture of health and illness. No deaths can be directly attributed to depression, for example, yet this is a serious illness or 'problem of living' for millions. Evidence from the General Household Survey (GHS) shows how long-standing illness is now much more prevalent than acute sickness, which is defined as 'the restriction of normal activities, as a result of illness or injury, in the two weeks before interview' (OPCS 1994: 24).

It is true that impressive medical advances have been made in the treatment of some serious illnesses. Acheson and Hagard (1984), for example, while recognizing a steady rise in the proportion of deaths from some cancers, suggest that the rise would have been even greater but for the introduction of more effective forms of treatment (of cancer of the testes, for instance). However, while modern medicine can help with the management of chronic and degenerative diseases, the **curative** approach can still do *relatively* little to reduce the number of deaths from modern 'killing diseases' such as cancer and heart disease.

The possibility that medical research will one day be able to unlock the mysteries of developing cures for the various forms of cancer must never be discounted, though the track record of medicine with regard to discovering 'miracle' cures is not encouraging. Much more compelling is the evidence which suggests that the causes of many diseases – and therefore the ways of preventing them, or at least delaying their onset – are still closely connected with environmental factors.

Acheson and Hagard (1984) describe heart disease and lung cancer as having reached epidemic proportions in Britain today. Smoking dramatically increases the risk of premature death from both of these diseases, while unhealthy diets, hazardous working environments and 'lifestyle' factors (for example, the amount of exercise) also seem to have important effects. Differences in rates of cancer, heart disease and other diseases among social class or occupational groups confirm the point that environmental factors significantly affect the causes of death and disease in modern society.

To illustrate this point, you may recall the research by Phillimore *et al.* (1994) which shows widening inequality in health from 1981 to 1991 in northern England (see Chapter 4). This study confirms earlier research on Britain as a whole, which also revealed a very marked association between social class position and illness. As Phillimore *et al.* (1994: 1127) conclude, 'These results underline how closely health and wealth are related.' Thus there are very important policy implications: preoccupations with trying to change the eating habits or lifestyle of poorer people will have little impact on health; improving their incomes and housing will.

Not surprisingly, given findings like these, there have been severe criticisms of the health professions, and suggestions that they have either wittingly or unwittingly helped to disguise both the limitations of medicine itself and the basic social and economic causes of disease. But how justified are these criticisms? In the next section we will look at some of the more important critiques of the health professions, before beginning a discussion of what could happen if the 'power of the professionals' over health policy were to be replaced by other interests.

THE HEALTH PROFESSIONS: TOO MUCH POWER?

A number of sociologists and other critics of the medical profession have put forward the idea that the medical profession does indeed have too much power over policy and over patients. But to justify this argument, somewhat different explanations have been put forward. Feminists suggest that the rise of the medical profession has provided a vehicle for medically trained men to exercise power over women. For example, Donnison (1988) shows how professional men began to gain control of midwifery from the eighteenth century onwards.

Another kind of explanation has been put forward by Illich (1990), who argues that modern medicine has actively 'colonized' areas of our lives that formerly were not medicalized or subject to the scrutiny and control of the medical profession. In Illich's eyes, the medical profession has become an exploitative and disabling influence on society. It has sought to capitalize on patients' vulnerability by making them ever more dependent on medical solutions for their ills (in the form of drug-based treatments, surgery and hospitalization), when, according to Illich, the solutions lie in a more basic change to healthier ways of life and patterns of consumption.

One problem with Illich's view is that it puts a lot of emphasis on the medical profession's own actions and its ability to colonize or dominate health policy. But we do not have to put all the blame on the shoulders of doctors to conclude that much of what doctors are expected to do is inappropriate to our needs. As Kennedy puts it,

> We have all been willing participants in the creation of a myth, because it seems to serve our interests to believe that illness can be vanquished and death postponed until further notice . . . Science has destroyed our faith in religion. Reason has challenged our trust in magic. What more appropriate result could there be than the appearance of new magicians and priests wrapped in the cloak of science and reason?
>
> (Kennedy 1980: 641)

Thus the **medicalization** of social problems – the tendency to seek medical solutions to socially created ills such as depression or sadness, unemployment and redundancy, poverty and isolation – could be part of society's response to much deeper or more fundamental changes. To call these a 'breakdown of social order' might be too alarmist, but there is an argument that as communities fragment, as families become smaller and more individuals live alone than ever before, so a growing number of people are left comparatively isolated.

De Swaan (1989) suggests that the medical professions do not so much set out to dominate society as fill a void and respond to a growing demand for the medicalization of people's problems. He gives other examples of the ways in which decisions and policies became increasingly 'medical' in the twentieth century: for instance, decisions about offenders and whether they should be 'treated' rather than punished or simply kept in prison; the role of medical advice in assessing the claims or needs of disabled people; and the increasing use of medical checks in employment, recruitment and the world of mortgage and life insurance (de Swaan 1989: 1167).

Another illustration of the medicalization of the social world is suicide and self harm. Self harm is committed by many thousands of people each year. It includes not only those who end their lives but also those who disable themselves, sometimes permanently, as a result of drug overdoses or other actions. The seriousness of this problem, especially among younger men, has prompted the government in Britain to adopt significant reductions in the suicide rate as one of its main targets in health policy for the year 2000.

However, some think that the government's confidence in the medical profession, and especially in GPs, in helping to achieve this target is misplaced. The record of medical practitioners and nurses in dealing with patients who have harmed themselves is not very good. But more than this, suicide or self harm can all too easily be seen as a 'medical' problem. As Taylor and Field put it,

> Suicide is a particular risk among those suffering from depressive disorders, especially those who are coming out of their depressive state. Yet, despite the association between depressive disorders and suicide, most people who harm themselves do not have a long-standing (clinically defined) mental illness. Most are suffering from an emotional breakdown, often triggered by some (inter-) personal crisis. The tendency of some people to take their emotional problems to their doctors in the hope of a cure for their unhappiness can have disastrous consequences. Three-quarters of those who overdose have seen their doctor in the two weeks before they harm themselves, and the majority overdose on medically prescribed drugs.
>
> (Taylor and Field 1993: 147–8)

Thus, in the case of suicide and self harm, the work of medicine and the professions may be more likely to make the problem worse than better. This is not only because doctors can place in patients' hands the very means with which to harm themselves, but just as importantly because the 'medicalization of sadness' diverts time and resources away from finding out more about the social roots of suicide, and from care which may be more effective (for example, community-based networks of people ready to listen to and help those who are suicidal).

The above example underlines the limitations of modern medicine. However, a balanced view must recognize that the influential role of doctors is partly a product of social demands and pressures, which include consumer demand for medical solutions to problems, and the development of medical technology and new medical treatments.

If the medical profession were all-powerful, the status and role of doctors would be broadly similar in every society. However, as de Swaan (1989) suggests, the position of the medical profession varies considerably in relation to the health services of different countries, together with the amount of power or influence it has over health policy.

This can be demonstrated by considering some key questions raised by medical intervention in people's lives, or what might be called *health policy dilemmas*. When looking at these dilemmas, we often find that there are no clear-cut solutions and that policy is unclear. There may be no consensus on what the appropriate role of the doctor, patient, carer or health worker should be, and in particular there may be uncertainty about how much say the doctor should have in deciding what to do.

Here are some examples of health policy dilemmas which have raised debate about the role of health professionals and the ethical aspects of their work:

- the patient's right to know about his or her condition;
- voluntary euthanasia;
- the value of screening or medical checks;
- terminations, especially of advanced pregnancies;
- *in vitro* fertilization;

- experimentation and patient trials of new therapies or drugs;
- how to ration scarce life-saving treatments;
- complaints and compensation for faulty treatments;
- conflicts of interest raised when health professionals work in the private as well as the public sector of health care.

HEALTH POLICY DILEMMAS AND THE ROLE OF HEALTH PROFESSIONALS

Such is the pace of innovation and change in medical research that new dilemmas arise all the time. For example, the new techniques which make it possible for post-menopausal women to see a pregnancy through to full term raise questions about whether such techniques should be freely available to older women. However, many of the dilemmas listed above have been with us in one form or another for a long time. Perhaps you will be able to think of yet more examples. The above is not a complete list, and is only intended to give an idea of the complex questions raised by medical intervention in our lives.

When we are trying to resolve such issues, the key question is: 'Should we leave it to the professionals?' Should doctors, either as individuals or acting as a professional group, take final responsibility for whether someone lives or dies, or, for example, whether relatives are told about a patient's terminal illness?

If we do decide to allow medical practitioners to resolve these thorny moral dilemmas on their own, as many feel we should, then the result would be an unstated or **inexplicit policy** to do this. For example, to turn a blind eye to the practice of not resuscitating very old and terminally ill patients who have heart failure is to develop an inexplicit policy of **passive euthanasia**. The British Medical Association wishes to make policy on this issue more explicit, as illustrated by the news item shown in Box 7.1.

This example suggests that health professionals themselves may wish to share the burden of responsibility for difficult decisions, and it also shows that there are arguments for having an *explicit* policy on ethical issues. Having an openly stated or explicit policy means that guidelines must be drawn up, legal rights must be considered and more formal procedures for dealing with decisions must be established: for example, an ethics committee might be given the task of deciding how to ration scarce life-saving therapies to a waiting list of patients.

Formalizing the process of how to deal with health dilemmas has its drawbacks as well as advantages. For instance, giving responsibility to a committee rather than to an individual doctor might lead to a situation in which no one is happy with the compromise decisions which are made. And who would sit on such committees: doctors, nurses, a lawyer and a social worker? Would a psychologist be excluded, or a minister of religion? Other problems would arise in the *interpretation* of whatever guidelines or codes had been drawn up. Would doctors, for example, be afraid to take risks or act in a humane way for fear of falling foul of a rigid code of practice?

> **Box 7.1   BMA urges 'right to die' hospital code**
>
> The terminally ill and the very old with little quality of life should have their wishes to die respected if they suffer a heart attack in hospital, rather than have attempts made to resuscitate them, the British Medical Association and the Royal College of Nursing said yesterday.
>   Patients should make their wishes clear to staff and there should be discussions with family and the senior consultant in charge of the case. Then 'do-not-resuscitate' orders should be drawn up.
>
> (Chris Mihill, *The Guardian*, 3 March 1993)

Thus there are arguments on both sides of the question as to whether explicit *policies* and formal machinery should be developed to deal with dilemmas in health care. To illustrate these arguments, three examples from the above list will now be considered: the questions of (a) the patient's right to know; (b) voluntary euthanasia; and (c) health screening.

The aim here is not to provide a comprehensive summary of the rights and wrongs of each issue. Rather, it is to begin to identify the *criteria* that could be used to design a policy: what is important in deciding how a policy should work? Having identified some important criteria, you may then wish to think about the other examples of health dilemmas on the list on pages 127–8. Above all, what role is appropriate for the doctor, the nurse or other health practitioner in resolving these dilemmas?

THE EXAMPLE OF THE PATIENT'S RIGHT TO KNOW

This dilemma is a particularly good illustration of the arguments for and against the idea that 'the doctor always knows best', or, more generally, that all professionals, as experts, are bound to know better than laypeople or clients what is best for them.

The doctor–patient relationship is based on trust as well as confidentiality. There is a strong expectation that patients will be able to tell their doctors about anything that is worrying them, secure in the knowledge that these confidences will not be shared with others, such as relatives. At the same time, trust in the professional's expertise implies that the patient is not expected to cross-question the doctor too much. Traditionally, a rather paternalistic view of the doctor–patient relationship suggested that it was quite in order for doctors not to tell patients everything about their illnesses or treatment plans. Patients were not expected to know 'too much' about their illnesses, or to demand particular treatments from the doctor.

More recently, a more open and equal view of the doctor–patient relationship has developed. There is now strong support for the idea that patients should have ready access to personal health records held by doctors. It is widely believed that patients should be fully informed so that they will be better able to take decisions about their treatment and understand what might be done to help them. Arguably, these attitudes have been encouraged by recent government health reforms (see below), which have fostered a 'consumerist' view of health services, but they have also been strengthened by the Data Protection Act, which gives people the right to see information about themselves which is held in computer files (though, because of the special sensitivity of some health data, this right is qualified).

Although it would seem as though the patient always has a right to know about his or her condition, there are strong reasons for questioning this right. Medical practice throws up sharp dilemmas, and some professionals think that it is not always in the patient's best interests to know everything. But if we are to allow professionals such as doctors to withhold information from patients in certain cases, then on what grounds could this be allowed? How could a policy to guide doctors and other professionals be constructed? Some examples follow of the criteria or yardsticks with which we might consider qualifying the right to know.

Medical uncertainty

In some cases, no one can say what the future course (prognosis) of a disease is. One argument is that there is no point in unnecessarily worrying the patient until the professionals are as sure as they can be of the outlook.

Perhaps a distinction is needed, within this category, between a medical condition which is the result of a number of (as yet unknown) problems, and a medical condition which is clearly known but where the patient's response or chance of survival is unknown. In the first case, information might be withheld pending further tests (and on the understanding that the patient will be told once test results have been obtained); this may be different from the second kind of situation, in which the professional already knows a great deal about the *likely* course of a disease but not exactly how it is going to affect a particular individual's health.

With regard to the latter, a common response might be: 'Surely the patient should be told as much as possible, even in the case of incurable conditions and where the doctor can only guess at how much time the patient has to live?' This is an easier question to ask than to answer, however, as the following account of a doctor dealing with a patient who had incurable cancer shows:

> For my part, I was like a bookmaker taking bets on the Grand National. Through my mind were running statistics about the likely outcome of her disease. In *her* case, there was a less than 1 per cent chance of a cure; a 70 per cent chance that she already had liver secondaries . . . [and] a less than 50 per cent chance of being alive for the marriage of her son [in three months' time] . . .
>
> She asked me if there was any hope of a cure, and I told her that this was unlikely – although not impossible, because there are no certainties in medicine. She then stated she wanted the complete truth, whatever that was.

The complete truth would have been everything that was going on in my head, including the feeling – only an educated guess – that she only had a few weeks left. In a court of law, anything less would be seen as withholding vital evidence.

(Whipp 1983: 177)

As it turned out, the doctor in this case appeared to have made the right decision in telling the patient as much as she wanted to know. They were then able to discuss a plan to manage the illness, and the patient survived just long enough for her son's wedding. In other cases, however, it is not always right to tell the patient, as other examples (below) show.

The nature of the patient

There are sometimes grounds for concluding that some patients are better off without full knowledge of their conditions. However, this may not be an argument for withholding *all* information. Children who have serious illnesses, for instance, could be given simplified accounts of what is happening to them (especially as children find uncertainty of any kind difficult). Similarly, adults with learning difficulties who fall ill could be given 'edited' or simplified explanations, though again this does not mean that such explanations should lack sensitivity or awareness of the individual's need to know.

An example of a case in which a patient did not benefit from being told everything is given by the same doctor who treated the patient mentioned above:

Some years ago, I had a patient who had cancer of the larynx. Six years later, he was definitely cured. He had never known his diagnosis, his family feeling that he could not bear it. He continued to smoke, increasing the risk of a second, new but similar cancer enormously. He could not understand why he should not smoke, and so I took it upon myself to tell him that he had had cancer.

He became acutely depressed and would not listen to any assurance that he was cured. He committed suicide a year later. His family blame me. I felt he should know the chances he was running, and should be in charge of his own destiny. Suicide had struck me as a negligible risk.

(Whipp 1983: 177)

The nature of the illness

As far as many illnesses are concerned, there is arguably a need for patients to be given only limited information and fairly simple explanations of what treatment options are available. This could be the case for many 'routine' and common illnesses, or where there are relatively few choices to be made about what is to be done for the patient.

However, some illnesses – chronic illnesses in particular – demand a high level of patient involvement in the treatment plan if treatment or management of the illness is to be successful. Diabetes, for example, is a good illustration of this. Diabetic patients need to be given quite extensive information about the nature of their illness and the way it is affecting them as individuals, and about diet and ways of managing the illness.

Another important category of illnesses is those which carry a social stigma, such as mental illness and sexually transmitted diseases, or which have major consequences for the individual's functioning in society, such as epilepsy. Again, all these kinds of illness require close involvement of the patient with the doctor and other professionals if treatment or management of the illness is to be successful.

Patients in these circumstances need to know a great deal about how they can be helped, though unfortunately it can be the case that professionals, just like general members of the public, hold negative views of certain illnesses (see, for instance, Scambler 1984, for a discussion of how **stigmatizing illness** is perceived).

Thus the patient's need to know may be most often disregarded in those cases in which the need is greatest, and where patients particularly need the help of professionals to cope with negative responses from people around them, such as family members or their employers. Arguably, it is for these reasons that an explicit policy or set of guidelines on 'the patient's need to know' is required most of all.

THE EXAMPLE OF VOLUNTARY EUTHANASIA

Any debate about this example divides opinion between those who maintain that medical and personal care must be given unstintingly to everyone up to the point at which 'natural' death occurs, and those who argue that, *if* voluntary euthanasia is acceptable morally, its benefits should not be disregarded. Apart from purely moral or religious arguments about voluntary euthanasia, what criteria have been seen as important in developing a policy on this difficult question?

Economics

First, economic criteria may help to explain why voluntary euthanasia has become such a 'headline issue' in recent years. This is despite the fact that the very idea of linking the (voluntary) termination of life with saving economic and medical resources is abhorrent to most members of the medical profession, as well as to the general public.

However, economic criteria are an important influence upon decisions about any health dilemma and, if euthanasia became more common, they would enter this debate as well. This is because medical costs and expenditure on patient care in the final six months of life often far outweigh costs at other times of life. There is an uncomfortable but dawning realization that, if episodes of terminal illness could be shortened, there would be enormous cost savings to the health service. Scarce medical resources and equipment could be freed more quickly than at present to help those whose illnesses are not terminal.

At the time of writing, medical professional opinion in most countries is firmly against any move towards a more open or explicit policy of allowing voluntary euthanasia. Exceptions are found in the Netherlands, where there have been cautious changes to allow 'mercy killings' in certain cases, and the Northern Territories of Australia – although, in the latter case, the state law permitting voluntary euthanasia has recently been suspended. However, where voluntary euthanasia has been openly discussed by medical practitioners, it is nearly always justified on medical or quality of life grounds, and the concept of an economic rationale is firmly denied.

Professional codes of conduct

These are another set of criteria affecting policy on euthanasia, and clearly they are linked to the previous point. By what legal criteria could doctors and nurses override their codes of preserving life? How could the practice of euthanasia be separated legally from murder, or at least from failing to do one's utmost to help the patient live? From the patient's point of view, how could it be legally separated from suicide? And, if it is incorporated into the law, would this be a 'slippery slope' leading doctors towards the encouragement of euthanasia?

Quality of life

This is also important in weighing up the merits of a voluntary euthanasia policy. How much pain, suffering or depression do those who want a 'mercy killing' experience? Can quality of life be measured and, if so, how? These are difficult questions to address, but to begin with there is basic choice between deciding whether primarily *medical* definitions of quality of life should be given the most weight, or whether primarily social or psychological definitions, including the patient's own wishes, should be given prominence.

This is not to say that doctors and nurses are unable to recognize patients' feelings or to take non-medical criteria into account. However, there is considerable evidence to suggest that, because medical practitioners get used to seeing the world from a medical viewpoint and to applying a 'medical model' or solution to problems, they are prone to disregarding patients' views of illness and its social consequences (see, for instance, Tuckett *et al.* 1985).

Accordingly, there is a case for suggesting that, even though voluntary euthanasia is not allowed, medical practitioners could benefit from greater opportunities to discuss the philosophical side of their work, how patients see serious and possibly terminal illnesses and how best to address the needs of patients who say 'I don't feel life's worth living, doctor, and I don't want any more treatment.'

Individual freedom of choice

This represents another area of potential conflict between patients, or users of health services, and professionals. If this criterion was supreme and if public opinion put individual choice before all other criteria, then doctors would simply have to comply with any seriously ill patient's wish to have his or her life ended.

However, as with other contexts in which individual choice is held up as an important value in life, we must ask how far individuals are ever able to choose in a free, unconstrained way, or to choose in their own interests. How 'voluntary' is voluntary euthanasia? How can it be ascertained that an end to life is really what the patient wants? Could counselling of patients by experts be provided in an impartial and sensitive way, or would any advice inevitably push the patient one way or the other? If we begin to have doubts about the answers to these questions, the more likely it is that we will begin to fall back on medical practitioners – the 'priests' of the modern age, as Kennedy (1983) put it – to act as arbiters and to provide 'medical' judgements upon what we want to do.

Who would implement the policy?

This is a key criterion because, whatever conclusions we reach about the other criteria, the question of who would actually take the steps to end a life concentrates the mind upon the desirability or otherwise of voluntary euthanasia. In the case of **active euthanasia**, would the family doctor, a hospital doctor, a nurse or even (with assistance from medical staff) patients themselves administer a lethal dose of pain killers or use other means to end their lives?

As far as **passive euthanasia** is concerned – that is, a decision not to strive actively to keep someone alive – should doctors or other health professionals continue to be mainly responsible? As mentioned above, this is the unstated or inexplicit policy we already have on euthanasia. Quite rightly, doctors often do not use aggressive and invasive therapies to prolong patients' lives once it becomes clear that such treatments would do so for only a few weeks, or would lead to a great deal of discomfort or pain.

The problem with an unstated policy such as this, however, is that it gives professionals a great deal of power when this may not always be in the best interests of patients or their relatives. Individual doctors' approaches to the treatment of terminally ill patients vary. In some cases, patients will be led through a series of operations and relatively aggressive, painful treatments even though they will gain little from these. On the other hand – and especially with older patients – doctors may give up too soon and fail to prolong patients' lives when this would have been in their interests, if only for a few months. Although the present policy of 'not having a policy' on passive euthanasia has certain advantages, therefore, it also brings the disadvantage of inhibiting debate on the appropriate role for medicine when people are terminally ill.

> **Box 7.2 Love and let die**
>
> Nancy Cruzan, now 32, has done nothing for the past seven years.
> She has not hugged her mother or gazed out of the window or
> played with her nieces. She has neither laughed nor wept, nor spoken
> a word. Since her car crashed on an icy night, she has lain still for so
> long, her hands have curled into claws; nurses wedge napkins under
> her fingers to prevent the nails piercing her wrists . . . The Cruzans
> could slip into Nancy's room some night, disconnect her feeding
> tube, and then face the consequences. Instead, they have asked the
> United States Supreme Court for permission to end their daughter's life.
> (*Telegraph* Weekend Magazine, 29 April 1990: 32)

The relative importance of the criteria for assessing the value of a policy
on voluntary euthanasia varies case by case. You may care to think about
how, or whether, 'right-to-die' legislation would be helpful in any of the
following cases.

- As a result of a climbing accident, a young person is paralysed from the
  neck down and cannot move. For over a year she has begged nursing
  staff to end her life.
- A man makes a third serious attempt on his life by taking a potentially
  fatal overdose of drugs. He has left a note saying that he does not wish
  to be revived, but is rushed to hospital before death has occurred.
- An older woman has terminal cancer. She is completely lucid, and she
  wants her life ended.
- A young woman is in a coma and has suffered irreversible brain damage
  as a result of a road accident. She is being kept alive by a life support
  machine, but it is unlikely that she will ever regain consciousness (see
  Box 7.2).

THE EXAMPLE OF SCREENING

Screening is an interesting example of the role of the medical profession
in our lives because, at first sight, it would appear to be a preventive
approach to health which, by helping to identify illnesses before they
become serious, would challenge reliance on curative medicine and the
idea of medical experts being our saviours once we have fallen ill.

Screening may be defined as the search for and identification of disease
in its pre-symptomatic form: that is, before there are obvious signs of
the disease. Examples are cervical cytology (smear tests to detect pre-
symptomatic signs of cancer of the cervix), breast cancer screening by
mammography and screening to detect hypertension. Screening is usually
carried out among particular 'target groups' thought to be particularly at
risk from a certain disease (for instance, men or women in certain age

> **Box 7.3   Criteria to evaluate the merits of screening**
>
> - Can we offer effective treatment for patients positive on testing?
> - How many positive tests will prove to be false alarms (and is this acceptable)?
> - How many patients will need follow-up over the next five years (and can we sustain this workload)?
> - How are we going to audit routinely the quality of the test, of the intervention and of follow-up?
>
> (Mant and Fowler 1990: 916)

groups), though it is also possible to carry out mass screening, where whole communities are tested for signs of disease.

Although screening appears to be a sensible measure helping to prevent the development of illnesses and saving lives, it needs to be viewed with great caution. As Mant and Fowler (1990: 916) explain, 'screening has the potential to do more harm than good.' They point out how, in the 1950s, there was considerable enthusiasm for mass screening tests for lung cancer. Despite earlier detection and treatment of this disease in the screened population, however, it was 'a great disappointment that 10 years after screening began cumulative mortality from lung cancer was identical in the screened and control populations.'

This does not mean that all screening is useless. There is evidence, for instance, that both breast cancer screening and cervical cytology can save lives 'if properly organised' (Mant and Fowler 1990: 916). But there is concern among health researchers that screening must be subjected to rigorous tests of its possible benefits and effects. In other words, as with other health policy dilemmas, certain *criteria* need to be laid down to determine what would be the best policy on screening for particular diseases or health problems.

What criteria are important in the case of screening? First, some important minimum standards can be applied to doctors (see Box 7.3).

Other important questions about a policy on screening can be asked, and these follow.

Are the subjects of screening to be fully informed?

To address this question, we must bear in mind what the purpose of a screening policy is. Is it for public health and preventive reasons? For example, testing blood samples of randomly selected patients for the HIV virus can help to show how widespread this virus is. However, if it is a procedure which is conducted without patients' knowledge, it raises the question of whether individual patients who are found to be HIV-positive should be told about their condition. Would it be ethically wrong *not* to inform them?

On the other hand, is screening an option for the *individual* to know more about his or her health and then to take appropriate steps? (For example, amniocentesis is a test routinely offered to women who are aged over 35 and who are pregnant. It can show whether the unborn child is likely to have spina bifida or Down's syndrome. Amniocentesis cannot be performed until after 16 weeks of a pregnancy, and results are not normally available for a further three to four weeks, raising the dilemma of termination at a late stage.)

What is the target group?

Does everyone have a right to some form of basic screening at regular intervals, or would this represent an unwarranted medicalization of social life? Should everyone in a certain category, such as drivers over a certain age, all pilots or food handlers, be *required* to undergo screening?

Costs, feasibility and health gain

Is a particular screening programme relatively cheap and easy to administer? What can the screened population and/or the health services do with the knowledge gained, and will discovery of formerly untreated illness lead to unmanageable demands for treatment, leading to costs and workloads in the health services which cannot be met? In the longer term, will screening result in relatively little improvement to health, or will it successfully enable secondary prevention to reduce the illness and death rate (as in breast cancer screening)?

Reliability

Will the screening procedure (including record-keeping), as well as the actual medical tests carried out, give clear and reliable information to the screened population? Could 'false positive' results create unnecessary worry among people who are well? Could 'false negative' results lead to dangerously optimistic and falsely reassuring messages being given to people who are in fact at risk?

Invasiveness

As with many health policy dilemmas, there are 'quality of care' criteria to be considered in judging whether a screening programme will be acceptable. This is a very subjective issue, because a test which is seen as invasive and distasteful by one person (for instance, screening for cervical cancer or prostate cancer) will not be seen in this way by another. As a result, the success or otherwise of a screening programme can be strongly influenced by the degree of sensitivity and awareness among medical practitioners or those administering the tests.

CONCLUSIONS: HEALTH POLICY AND PROFESSIONAL POWER

The three examples of health policy dilemmas show that medical professionals – doctors, nurses and other health service practitioners – are not merely caught up in these dilemmas but are often the key people that we call upon to interpret a policy and to take difficult decisions on our behalf, whether this is in respect of deciding how much to tell us about our illness, how actively to treat people who are terminally ill (or deciding whether to help them to die) or whether such activities as screening for illness are a good idea.

However, as pointed out at the outset, professionals – though given enormous responsibility in many situations – themselves operate in a world of constraints and uncertainties. The three examples of health dilemmas show that there is often confusion about what the best course of action should be. And in addition to ethical or moral dilemmas, there are the constraints of government health policy, the cost and feasibility of providing services and so on. Therefore, while health professionals can easily become too dominant or may be expected to have the final say in resolving a dilemma, it would be wrong to portray the medical profession as an all-powerful group which always acts in a single-minded, unified and self-interested way.

Thus there are at least two key lessons to learn from studies of the role of the professions in maintaining health. The first is that health professionals cannot be expected to resolve all our health policy dilemmas. As Kennedy (1983) argues, medical expertise does not make doctors and other professionals uniquely competent to take ethical decisions. A doctor can give advice about the physical and mental abilities a severely disabled baby is likely to have, for instance, but there is no technical or medical answer to the question of whether that baby's life is worth living. Following Kennedy's line of reasoning, there is a role for the layperson to establish *guidelines* or *criteria* for the professionals to act upon (and the three examples of health dilemmas above illustrate what sort of criteria might be involved). In short, there is a strong argument to suggest that all the responsibility for the shaping of health *policies* should not be handed over to the health professions.

The second lesson to emerge from recent research on the nature of health and illness is that doctors, nurses and other health workers can do relatively little to improve health or to reduce rates of disease. If all health practitioners were suddenly removed from our society, and if every hospital and doctor's surgery were to be closed, their absence would hardly be noticed in terms of the amount of illness or the death rate. What *would* be noticed, of course, is a great deal more pain, discomfort and uncertainty. The health professions and health services play a very important role in managing illness and in helping us to come to terms with it, both physically and mentally.

Health professions and the health service reforms

Despite the limitations of modern medicine, government policies to improve health still place a lot of emphasis on the role of the medical and nursing professions. As mentioned above, the government target of reducing suicide, for instance, is based on the questionable policy of relying upon the GP to play a central role. Many of the growing health inequalities in modern Britain are attributable to environmental influences and to poverty, yet official policies to prevent illness barely mention these basic causes, preferring to emphasize lifestyle or cultural choices and the need for experts such as health professionals to educate people into healthier lifestyles.

Whether for political convenience or for other reasons, therefore, faith in the health professions is still strong and they will continue to play a pivotal and powerful role in health policy. However, there is one important aspect of recent change in health services which prompts the question of whether the power of the health professions is quite as strong as it was: the government's health reforms following the NHS and Community Care Act of 1990 (see Chapter 9 for discussion).

Well before these reforms were introduced, Sir Roy Griffiths – an independent adviser to the government and chief executive of Sainsbury's supermarkets – had written an influential report (DHSS 1983) on the need for management reform in the NHS (not to be confused with Griffiths's later report on community care – see Griffiths 1988).

Sir Roy's 1983 report paved the way for a great deal of internal change in the structure of the NHS during the 1980s, and it introduced the concept of the *general manager* – a powerful role which Griffiths had envisaged as leading and controlling the competing interests of the various occupational groups in the health service (doctors, nurses and the various therapeutic professions).

However, as Cox (1991: 97) notes, 'the Griffiths Report [was] very respectful of medical power' and it sought to 'co-opt the doctors into management and budgetary responsibility.' According to various research studies of the impact of management reform in the 1980s, which Cox summarizes, there was little evidence that general managers had begun to control directly the consultants, who still continue to take the key decisions over such matters as clinical targets (the number of patients to be treated over a given period) and resource issues. This does not mean that general management had *no* impact, only that there is no sign that the medical profession has been marginalized in the policy and resource decision-making processes (Cox 1991: 104).

Thus there is little evidence in today's NHS of a fundamental shift in the balance of power towards the patient. There are signs that patients are becoming more questioning and are prepared to be more critical of doctors than they used to be, but despite such apparent readiness to challenge traditional professional attitudes, the policy making and administrative machinery is simply not in place to give patients an effective voice at the *policy* level of the NHS.

For the other health professions, such as nursing, changing priorities in health policy have brought mixed fortunes. NHS reforms brought increased uncertainty and job insecurity. For example, a 1994 pay review body found that managerial issues and job security worried nurses more than pay (Wainwright 1994: 2). Doctors have also faced considerable changes in the way in which hospitals and health authorities are run. In particular, there has been the challenge of coming to terms with a much more powerful breed of general manager – a role which has carried a good deal more executive authority than managers had in the 'traditional' NHS.

For a variety of reasons, however, the idea that professional power has been seriously dented or reduced in recent years can be questioned:

- An increasing number of doctors will become experienced in the newer forms of management (Hunter 1992). Instead of being 'frozen out' of vital decisions by non-medical managers, it is just as likely that they will adopt new strategies to retain their professional influence.
- Some doctors may come to have more, not less, power over their patients. For example, patients now have more freedom than they used to if they wish to change their GPs. But to counterbalance this, there is the danger of 'cream-skimming' by some GPs: that is, deterring the more costly patients and attracting the healthier, less costly patients. According to recent research, the NHS market gives financial incentives for GPs to do this, and it will be difficult to arrive at a formula for funding GPs which compensates their practices for costly patients (Robinson and Le Grand 1994).
- From the beginning of the first Conservative administration of the 1980s, it was made clear that doctors would have a freer hand than before to combine private fee-for-service work with NHS work.

These points refer to very general trends. They refer to doctors and to the medical profession as a homogeneous group, which it is not. The other health professions (e.g. nursing and the various therapies, such as physiotherapy) have always been divided in their attitudes towards health policy, as shown by the history of the NHS, and in the arguments and divisions between them and doctors about the recent health reforms.

This is not to say that no altruistic, caring or public-spirited professionals exist: there are many. Nor is it to say that professional interests are always narrow, or self-seeking, or against the public interest: often, the professional approach benefits the patient, and the interests of the profession and the patient coincide (for example, in raising standards of care or investment in medical research). However, in promoting a curative approach to medicine which downplays the economic, social and environmental causes of disease, the professional tradition in medicine inevitably draws doctors and other health professionals into defending a health system which does relatively little to improve health.

KEY TERMS AND CONCEPTS

acute illnesses
chronic illnesses
curative medicine/the curative
    model of medicine
euthanasia (voluntary and
    involuntary; active and passive)
iatrogenic disease

inexplicit policies
medicalization
outcomes
preventive health policies/services
screening
stigmatizing illness

SUGGESTIONS FOR FURTHER READING

Ian Kennedy's *The Unmasking of Medicine* (1983), though now rather dated, still offers one of the best critiques of the dominant role of the medical profession in health services and in thinking about medical and ethical issues.

Similarly, Thomas McKeown's *The Role of Medicine* (2nd edn, 1979) remains a classic historical study of the changing nature of disease and the limited role of medicine.

There are now a great many general texts on health policy, the health services and related areas such as the sociology of nursing and other health professions. One of the best is Steve Taylor's and David Field's *Sociology of Health and Health Care* (recently revised and published in a second edition, 1997). This book will provide you with a succinct and stimulating policy-related overview of key health issues. It is written for both the general reader and nursing students. Other useful texts are *Health and Health Care in Britain* (1994) by R. Baggott, *Women and the Health Care Industry* (1995) by P. Foster, and W. Ranade's *A Future for the NHS?* (1994).

Radical critiques of the medical profession can be found in a wide range of books, but the following offer fascinating historical evidence as well: Jane Lewis's *Politics of Motherhood: Child and Maternal Welfare in England, 1900–1939* (1980) and Jean Donnison's *Midwives and Medical Men* (2nd edn, 1988); on a different tack, Illich's *Limits to Medicine – Medical Nemesis* (1990) is also worth looking at, but needs to be taken with a pinch of salt.

Finally, although general texts such as Taylor and Field's (see above) provide some discussion of recent health policy and of reforms in the NHS, more detailed and comprehensive perspectives on recent health policy can be found in Rudolf Klein's *The New Politics of the NHS* (3rd edn, 1995) and in *Evaluating the NHS Reforms* by Robinson and Le Grand (1994).

8   UTOPIAS AND IDEALS: HOUSING

POLICY AND THE ENVIRONMENT

INTRODUCTION

Of all human needs, shelter is one of the most fundamental. But housing is also important because it can give the sense of security which stems from bonding with 'home'. Satisfactory homes help personal development and also help people to develop roots: a fusion of personal identity with place, neighbourhood and family. Establishing a home of one's own can also give a sense of responsibility and achievement. Not least, the economic investments people make in their homes represent important goals. These are not necessarily selfish: many people wish to pass on their property to their descendants.

Given the deep significance of housing in the human psyche as well as in society or the economy, it is not surprising that government policy in this area is subject to more than the usual amount of commentary and criticism. Government action which succeeds in meeting people's housing aspirations offers considerable political reward and electoral popularity.

On the other hand, anything which seems to threaten people's homes or their ability to obtain a home can immediately land a government in a great deal of trouble.

This chapter is therefore titled 'Utopias and ideals' because, before every disillusion or disappointment with housing policy, there are dreams and ideals. Before the property crash of the early 1990s, for example, there was the aspiration of home ownership for virtually everyone, and the dream of a housing market in which everyone would gain and no one would lose.

In this chapter we will examine other kinds of housing utopias and ideals, together with the inevitable disillusion and reassessment which follows them. In some cases, housing ideals are connected to much wider visions, involving dreams of ideal communities and environments. Although space will not permit detailed examination of these broader concerns, it is important to be aware of housing in its wider context, and the ways in which social planners in the past have linked policies for better housing with policies for better communities or environments.

Before returning to these broader questions near the end of the chapter, however, we need to examine definitions of housing policy in more detail.

HOUSING POLICY: DEFINITIONS AND SIGNIFICANCE

'Housing policy' refers to a wide range of government action. It covers any government action, legislation or economic policies which have a direct or indirect effect on housing, whether this relates to the supply of housing, house prices, tax policies affecting house purchase, housing standards or patterns of **tenure** ('tenure' being the legal definition of a person's right to reside in a dwelling, such as a rental agreement or ownership).

However, definitions in themselves do not indicate *why* housing is of special significance in social policy. Three main reasons may be identified. First, housing is an area of welfare in which the *market* is far and away the most important means of settling who gets what, or how needs are to be met. The other four of the five great social services (health, social security, education and personal social services) are increasingly being run on market lines. However, they are still basically public services and many people's needs for health services, social security etc. are still being met from public funds and not according to what they can personally afford, as is mostly the case in housing. Therefore, a focus on housing provides an important test of how well or badly the market serves people's needs.

Second, housing is an area of special interest because it highlights the complex nature of *needs* and how needs can be defined. 'Having a roof over your head' is an attractively simple but insufficient definition of housing needs. To define housing properly, we have to use concepts of *quality* and **autonomy**.

Thus, if someone has a roof over his or her head but lives in a severely overcrowded dwelling which is hazardous to health, we do not necessarily have to accept that he or she has a proper home. Depending on the standards of housing quality being used, someone in this position could be defined as homeless. Similarly, there is an argument that adults who have virtually no independence or autonomy in their dwelling are homeless: for instance, if such a person does not have any say in when he or she may enter or leave the dwelling, or in how he or she can use the space or rooms in the dwelling. People living in hostels, residential institutions or 'bed and breakfast' accommodation may fit into this category, and could therefore be regarded as homeless.

Thus, official statistics on **homelessness** should be treated with caution, because it is in any government's interests to argue that this is a problem that it is reducing and dealing with effectively. For this reason, official definitions of homelessness are likely to concentrate on categories of people who live on the streets or 'sleep rough' more than upon the larger group without proper homes (see the final section for further discussion).

A third reason for seeing housing as a key area of social policy is that it is intimately connected with a wide range of other welfare issues, such as health. According to historians of public health (see, for instance, McKeown 1979), housing policy, along with other environmental improvements such as the introduction of effective sanitation, did much more to improve health and life expectancy in the nineteenth and early twentieth centuries than anything achieved in medicine or health services. Poor housing conditions are still with us, however, and the effects of damp, poorly ventilated or poorly heated homes upon health can still be observed.

In terms of social division, housing policy may contribute to either a lessening or a heightening of racial tensions, for instance, or to either preventing or encouraging the formation of 'underclass' housing estates, where people on low incomes and experiencing high rates of unemployment may be concentrated.

This is not to say that housing policy alone could solve every problem of poor health, racial conflict or social deprivation, but it is true that, more than in any other area of social policy, decisions made in housing policy have a directly territorial impact. Visible, spatial inequalities can be either lessened or accentuated (as illustrated by the gulf between run-down council estates and spruce, security-conscious housing developments for the better-off).

Housing also stands out as an area in which change has been particularly marked and dramatic. Three interlocking factors help to explain why housing has been subject to so much change.

- There have been enormous changes in living patterns and family structures in the twentieth century. Population growth has accounted for some of the rapid increase in demand for housing, but even more important has been a trend towards smaller households and family groups. Many more people live alone or in couples than they used to do, and each new household creates extra demand for separate housing.
- British people's expectations and wants from housing have also gone through a revolution in the twentieth century, especially as far as home ownership is concerned (see Figure 8.1). Housing has also become an extremely important symbol in a status-conscious society – a way of marking, and possibly raising, one's status in the class system.

Figure 8.1   Housing tenure in Great Britain, 1950–1991

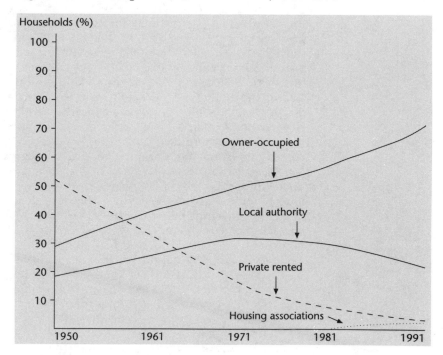

(Adapted from Balchin 1995: 6.)

■ Connected with the latter point, government policy in the second half of the twentieth century tended to reward the trend towards owner occupation by giving generous incentives in the form of tax relief to householders paying off mortgages. As a result, the housing market became a way of making money and houses became ever more valuable commodities.

HOUSING UTOPIAS AND IDEALS

To put recent changes in perspective, it helps to look first at how housing has been the subject of utopian plans and ideals for a long time. Therefore, in this section we will consider the main landmarks in the development of housing policy. Three broad phases of 'housing dreams' and ideals can be discerned in recent British history:

■ First, the nineteenth-century period, in which 'model housing' schemes were like beacons in a sea of squalid, overcrowded accommodation for the masses. Most of these schemes were the results of **industrial paternalism** – enlightened employers building good quality housing for their workers – but some were associated with charity and with efforts to provide 'decent' accommodation for people in poverty.

- Second, the period after the First World War and up to the 1960s, in which housing ideals developed around concepts of **social engineering**. The idea of planned new towns and 'garden cities', for instance, predates the 1914–18 war, but became influential in housing policy and the design of suburban housing in the 1920s and 1930s. In addition to planning ideal communities in the physical or environmental sense, this phase of idealism encouraged socialistic ideas about housing, including the ideal of mixing together people of different social classes. In practice, examples of such social engineering were few and far between. However, this 'middle period' in housing policy was one in which the idea of local government as a provider of housing (through rented **council housing**) was strongly endorsed by Conservative, as well as Labour, governments as part of an overall welfare programme.
- Third, the period after 1970, in which *the market and home ownership* have become even more central to housing policy than before. Mrs Thatcher's governments of the 1980s were chiefly responsible for widening the base of home ownership in Britain, but the percentage of households in council housing had already reached a plateau before 1979 (see Figure 8.1) and the percentage in private rented accommodation was also in steep decline. The policy of selling council houses to tenants had existed before Mrs Thatcher came to office. Although usually only a few thousand dwellings were sold by local authorities in England and Wales every year, nearly 46,000 were sold in 1972 (under a Conservative government) and over 30,000 in 1978 (under Labour), compared to 201,015 in 1982, when Mrs Thatcher's council house sales policy gained momentum (Forrest and Murie 1988: 110).

Housing ideals, philanthropy and the market: the nineteenth and early twentieth centuries

Although housing standards were generally very poor in the Victorian period, housing did gradually improve as the nineteenth century progressed and as larger numbers of working people became better-off than before. Further, although much housing was squalid, conditions and types of housing varied.

Rural housing gave most cause for concern. Chadwick's *Report on the Sanitary Condition of the Labouring Population of Great Britain* in 1842, for instance (see Chapter 3), documented in vivid detail the uniformly low housing conditions of agricultural workers. As will be recalled, Chadwick was particularly concerned with the connection between poor housing and ill health. The report showed how, in Tiverton in Devon, malaria had broken out where cottages had been built on marshland; in Dorset, a serious outbreak of typhus was reported; and in rural areas of Somerset, over 5000 people had died of fever in 1841. The hovels and tiny cottages in which farmworkers and their families lived were damp, smoky and overcrowded, and were often situated next to stagnant ponds and pigsties.

In the rapidly growing towns and cities, poverty, disease and squalid housing were also intimately linked together, but in the urban areas housing conditions were more varied than in the countryside. In London,

Glasgow and Edinburgh, tenements were common; in industrial areas north of Birmingham, 'back-to-back' terraced housing grew rapidly, while in mining and industrial towns of north-east England, workers often lived in single-storey cottages.

Lodging houses for the poor and for new arrivals in urban areas were particularly hazardous to health. As in the rapidly growing 'megacities' of poorer countries today, lodging houses in Victorian Britain had not only multi-occupied rooms but also multi-occupied *beds*, with shift workers each paying for a few hours' use of a bed. A Lodging Houses Act (1851) attempted to regulate this form of accommodation and to set some basic standards of sanitation and limits to overcrowding, but the huge number of lodging houses and the unwillingness of local authorities to implement the provisions of the Act made any progress difficult.

In both rural and urban areas, however, there were isolated but significant attempts to improve housing by employers, philanthropic organizations and the growing number of 'respectable' working-class families. Each of these groups had somewhat different housing ideals, though they shared a common determination to bring about greater security of tenure and a healthier environment with better sanitation.

Employer housing ranged from basic (by today's standards) terraced housing, often built by railway companies in towns like Crewe and Swindon, to 'model villages' in rural areas and housing in leafy urban estates, as built in the early twentieth century by the Cadburys, the chocolate maufacturers in Bournville, Birmingham. The latter was an example of a fashionable trend among 'enlightened' employers, who combined self-interest (a well housed workforce raised productivity and commitment to the employer) with genuine concern to improve not only houses but also the whole environment. Parks and recreation areas, wide and sunny avenues, gardens and allotments were often part of the overall plans of such housing schemes. They prefigured later concepts of the ideal urban environment (see next section).

Thus some industrial employers, especially those driven by religious convictions, such as the Quaker families who owned and ran Britain's chocolate firms (the Rowntree, Cadbury and Fry families), shared **philanthropic** ideals with other housing reformers working for charitable trusts and organizations.

Well known in the field of housing improvement was the Peabody Trust, a philanthropic organization named after its American founder. This trust built blocks of flats in London, each one strictly regulated: for example, children were not allowed to play in corridors and hallways, the entrance was locked and the gas supply was turned off at 11.00 p.m.

Concern with moral standards and strict control of residents' behaviour were the hallmarks of Victorian and Edwardian housing charities, and the Peabody Trust was not unusual in wanting only tenants who were 'deserving' cases: any signs of alcohol abuse, immoral sexual behaviour, failure to keep the property clean or reluctance to send children to school could result in eviction. Perhaps the best known of the housing reformers, Octavia Hill (see Box 8.1), developed a particularly strict code for tenants and shared a common feeling among Victorian reformers that it was fundamentally people, not economic conditions, that made slums. The key to

Box 8.1   Octavia Hill (1838–1912)

Octavia Hill could be seen as one of the key founders of modern social work, as well as a pioneer of housing policy and management. The daughter of a middle-class but not particularly well-off family, she concentrated on trying to find housing solutions for slum-dwellers and the very poor. This involved social casework and developing a relationship with families as well as finding them housing.

She hit upon the idea of developing an organization to *manage* rented properties which could be let to 'deserving' poor people in need of accommodation. Property owners handed over management responsibility to Octavia Hill's scheme, which guaranteed them a fair financial return and which was staffed by middle-class women volunteers who collected rents and supervised tenants and properties. Owners could be assured that their properties would be well looked after, thus encouraging them to let to people from the poorest backgrounds. Otherwise, landlords were reluctant to let rooms to the poor. Usually, high rents were charged for inferior accommodation, and as a result tenants at the bottom end of the rented accommodation market tended to 'flit' or default on rent.

After the opening of Paradise Place in Marylebone in 1865, Octavia Hill's housing scheme spread to include a large number of properties in London. Although it only ever reached a minority of people in need, it was an imaginative breakthrough in providing basic accommodation for poor families. However, her scheme was far from being 'pro-poor'. Its philosophy was governed by rather authoritarian ideas about how the behaviour of the poor could be improved: tenants were expected to follow the advice of their social superiors, the volunteer women who called to collect rents and to instruct them how to conduct their lives.

Hill's philosophy did not challenge the economic principles of the housing market. She opposed the idea of using charity to help poor people with their rents, or of subsidizing the cost of housing in other ways. Octavia Hill was against the early experiments with subsidized council housing in London in the 1890s, for example (Malpass 1984: 35).

If Hill's philosophy meant that a poor family had to struggle to pay rent for a single room (and, according to Hill's standards, one room per family was usually 'adequate'), then this was quite proper in a market system and the only way to develop independence among the poor. On the other hand, Hill wanted a fair housing market with legislation to guarantee basic standards. She successfully lobbied Parliament to improve housing: for example, through the 1875 Artisans' and Labourers' Dwellings Improvement Act. However, Octavia Hill's views of the causes of poverty remained fundamentally individualistic and moralistic, and these perspectives were clearly evident in the stance she took as a member of the Royal Commission on the Poor Laws (1905–9).

housing improvement, Hill and many other reformers thought, lay in improving the behaviour of the poor. Interestingly, there have been echoes of these ideas in recent times, with calls from Labour politicians for stricter policies to deal with 'problem tenants' in housing estates and for curfews to be imposed on children and young people (Bedell 1996).

Although the housing experiments of Victorian philanthropy and industrial paternalism were important in providing better conditions for a few, almost all (except Hill's) were restricted to helping working families in regular employment. Houses built to model standards raised building costs, and unless employers or charities were willing to subsidize rents, this meant that only a few could afford the resulting high rents.

Nor was the third Victorian ideal, the working-class solution of *self-help* through the formation of building societies, sufficiently widespread to bring better housing for the majority. Building societies, which began to increase in number from the middle of the nineteenth century, were cooperative groups set up by working people to pool their resources, through savings, and to build houses for their members. They were most often found in areas such as northern England and South Wales, where relatively high wages for skilled manual workers encouraged a higher rate of home ownership. In most of Britain, however, renting was the norm: 90 per cent of Britain's households were still in rented property by the beginning of the twentieth century.

Housing ideals and planning: the era of social engineering

The period from the end of the First World War in 1918 to the 1970s can be regarded as the heyday of state intervention in housing. Even though the market remained the key element in housing, and home ownership dramatically increased during this period, there was widespread acceptance that the market alone could not satisfactorily provide enough housing of acceptable quality.

More than this, there was a revolution in ideas about housing and the environment. Individualistic British notions of *laissez-faire* and letting people find their own housing solutions remained strong, but they were challenged by new ideas about architecture and planning. These ideas suggested that, in an ideal world, the state could plan everyone's housing needs and design an environment in which social divisions could be minimized.

Such ideas came from a variety of sources. Before the First World War, the concept of 'garden cities' had been developed by Ebenezer Howard, a radical liberal thinker who advocated a new kind of urban living. He had worked in Chicago in its pre-skyscraper days and had been impressed by the idea of a decentralized city in a spacious landscape. Howard believed that new towns could be built in the countryside of Britain; people could collectively own common facilities such as schools and workshops, for which they would pay a common rent, and they would be free to build their own houses in planned green spaces.

In 1899, the first garden city was commissioned at Letchworth in Hertfordshire. It was built with private capital and by 1914 housed 9000.

Another, Welwyn Garden City, had been built by 1920. Although these were small beginnings, the garden city idea had a profound effect upon politics and policy as the First World War drew to a close. As Fraser suggests, 'the "garden city" design with high-quality, low-density, "parlour" houses could genuinely be advertised as a reward to returning heroes' (Fraser 1984: 181).

Similarly, after the Second World War, the idea of building new towns and outer suburbs in green open spaces continued to have a strong effect on British planning and housing policy. In the 1950s and 1960s, a succession of new towns appeared in England and Scotland, and these, along with 'outer ring' housing estates, were usually part of a policy of clearing away inner city substandard housing and 'decanting' people to environments which were seen by planners as infinitely better than those they were uprooted from.

The early appeal of the garden city idea is understandable. For working people, living in separate houses with gardens offered the dream of escape from overcrowded conditions in which washing and toilet facilities had to be shared with neighbours or co-tenants. For middle-class reformers and politicians, this kind of housing seemed to fit with 'respectable' or conservative notions of family life.

For instance, it was in the housing of the 1920s and 1930s that the kitchen first appeared on a mass scale as a clearly defined space in the home; many pre-1920 houses used by ordinary people had no separate kitchen. Working-class women were able to shout 'Get out of my kitchen!' in a way that very few had been able to do before, and in so doing to colonize a space in the home for themselves. At the same time, the 'ideal homes' with separate kitchens, which so many women aspired to, had the effect of reinforcing a domesticated dependent role for many women.

Interestingly, some new homes in the 1920s combined a living room space with a kitchen area in which cooking was in full view of the family. For example, Unwin and Parker, two architects who were very active in the garden city movement, designed such 'open plan' kitchens in houses in Letchworth. However, this design met with working-class resistance in garden cities and suburbs, and later on in the new towns of the 1950s.

There were yet other alternatives in both house design and housing policy in the 1920s and 1930s, and among them was the important concept of mass housing in flats or apartment blocks. In the emergent Soviet Union and in Germany and Austria, where a strong socialist movement also developed, the architects of the 1920s wanted to do away with the bourgeois styles of the nineteenth century and to introduce blocks of flats that would be functional and efficient for the new 'socialist citizen'. In cities such as Berlin, Frankfurt and Vienna, there developed a connection between socialism and the building of such large apartment blocks.

Not surprisingly, given middle-class fears of socialist revolution and worker militancy, government policy in Britain in the 1920s and 1930s firmly rejected this kind of housing and the futuristic, social engineering philosophy of German and Soviet architects. The British response to a severe housing shortage after the First World War was to try to build millions of terraced and semi-detached houses with gardens and open spaces, not blocks of flats.

It is interesting to compare the attitudes of the 1920s in Britain with those of the 1950s and 1960s in this respect. In the later period, the solution to the housing crisis *was* to build 'tower blocks' of flats on a large scale, especially in redeveloped inner urban areas. The earlier fears of radical socialism breeding in blocks of flats had weakened, though the connection between Labour voting and the creation of large working-class council housing estates was not lost upon those who ran Labour-dominated councils in industrial areas.

Before the Second World War, however, the Labour Party was only beginning to flex its muscles as a force in local and central government. Yet although inter-war social policy was dominated by Liberal and Conservative ideas, a fundamental shift in attitudes towards favouring state intervention in housing took place after the First World War. By 1917, it had become obvious that the sacrifices of the population, and particularly of the armed forces, would have to be repaid. Lloyd George, Prime Minister of the wartime coalition government, formed a Ministry of Reconstruction with the object of coordinating the tasks of industrial redevelopment, demobilization of the armed forces and attending to Britain's urgent need for more housing.

The ambitious efforts of government to solve the housing crisis immediately after the First World War are often remembered as ending in failure. Rent control, introduced during the war, discouraged housebuilding because owners would not be able to recoup their outlay from the low rents chargeable. An impressive government programme to subsidize housebuilding by local councils and private builders ran into the buffers of spiralling costs and the decision to impose stringent cuts in government expenditure by 1922. By this date, there was still an estimated shortfall of over 800,000 houses in Britain.

However, looked at over a longer term, Britain's achievement in housebuilding between the wars was substantial, especially given the effects of economic depression and large-scale unemployment in those decades. Even the short-lived housebuilding programme between 1919 and 1922 resulted in nearly a quarter of a million new homes. 'Together with the private houses boom of the 1930s', Fraser points out, government action 'helped to solve the physical shortage of houses.' As Fraser adds, however, 'while the stock of houses increased, the problem of *bad* housing continued' (Fraser 1984: 203). The major task of slum clearance and rehousing fell to governments after the Second World War.

Between 1945 and the end of the 1960s, the twin ideals of state intervention in housing and government planning of the environment reached full bloom. The percentage of households in public rented (council house) homes rose from 12 to 31 between 1945 and 1971, while the percentage in private rented accommodation plummeted from 62 to 17 over the same period (Malpass and Murie 1994: 73). However, owner occupation rose from a quarter to a half of all households, and this represented a flowering of the private housing market as well, albeit greatly helped by government intervention through tax relief to mortgage payers.

As can be seen from the above figures, public sector housing played a major part in the huge effort to increase the supply of houses after the war. According to Malpass and Murie (1994), this was particularly the case

Figure 8.2   A mid-twentieth-century 'high rise' housing block in Bristol continues to dominate a local neighbourhood
(Photograph: Maggie Ainley ©.)

during the period of Labour government between 1945 and 1951, when four-fifths of all new houses were built by local authorities. The Conservative governments of the 1950s continued the council house building programme and were especially active in this respect between 1951 and 1954, but after 1955 they put a higher priority on encouraging private builders to meet general housing need.

Gradually, local authority council housing came to be seen as the sector in which poorer households would be *re*housed, and which was to carry the burden of slum clearance in the 1950s and 1960s. As Malpass and Murie point out, the official standards governing council houses were lowered after 1953, and council housing began to be seen as of significantly lower status and as having less appeal than privately built homes.

This was also the case during the period of Labour government in 1964–70, when owner occupation was endorsed as the favoured form of housing tenure for the majority. However, Labour combined this policy with a crash programme of public sector housebuilding, rehousing and slum clearance for the inner cities. Tower blocks and large housing estates were thrown together with great haste, while long-standing urban communities in inner cities were bulldozed to make way for new roads, open spaces and shopping centres.

The pace of public sector housebuilding at this time, combined with local government corruption and the patchy implementation of quality controls, meant that many problems were laid down for the future. Many of today's problems of leaking roofs, inadequate ventilation and corroding concrete date from the 1960s and 1970s rush to build cheap public sector housing. Poor building standards were matched by ill-conceived designs for housing estates. In many cases, either warren-like 'concrete jungles' were built, or bleak wastelands which are poorly serviced with shops and other community facilities.

The triumph of market ideals: housing policy in the 1980s

Despite these failures, the 'social engineering' phase of housing policy achieved a great deal. Not only did state intervention help to reduce severe housing shortages by subsidizing the market and providing public sector homes; it also introduced planning controls on land such as the Town and Country Planning Act (1947), which, though later replaced by other planning laws, established the concept of 'green belts' and protected the countryside from overdevelopment.

However, the 1980s saw the tide turning against the ideas of social engineering and planning which had come to dominate housing policy. In practice, both Conservative and Labour governments *before* 1979 had increasingly looked to the private market as the main supplier of housing, despite differences of emphasis between the parties. But it was the housing policies of Mrs Thatcher's government after 1979 that marked a decisive change in policy ideals and assumptions. Planning restrictions on the sale of land would be eased. No longer would council housing remain as a major player on the scene: this kind of housing would be increasingly **residualized** (see Box 8.2).

Mrs Thatcher's housing policies 'went with the grain' of public attitudes and aspirations (Cole and Furbey 1994), which in Britain – and particularly in England – favour owner-occupied housing for the reasons mentioned at the beginning of this chapter.

In some other European countries, social attitudes do not encourage owner occupation as much as in Britain, whereas in others owner occupation is even more common. In Germany, for instance, only two-fifths of

---

Box 8.2   Residualization

This is a useful general concept in social policy. It refers to a process whereby public services are increasingly used by a 'residual' or excluded minority of poorer people, rather than by the community as a whole. Two-tier services or facilities develop, with the better-off majority using private sector services (including housing) which they have paid for. Poorer families and individuals are left with public welfare services which, because the middle-class and better-off working-class families no longer use them, tend to become run-down, poorly funded and socially stigmatized. If council accommodation is becoming a residual category of housing, for example, this would mean that a certain stigma would be attached to living on a council estate – it would be a sign of social descent.

dwellings are owner-occupied, compared with the United Kingdom's two-thirds (CSO 1996: 177), while in France owner occupation is also lower than in the UK, at about 55 per cent of dwellings; in Italy, owner occupation is slightly more common than in the UK, while in Greece, Spain, Norway and the Irish Republic it is substantially higher – about four-fifths of dwellings are owner-occupied in these latter countries.

Rates of owner occupation, private renting and public rented or **social housing** therefore seem to vary considerably, according to cultural preferences and economic conditions in different countries. However, it is also likely that national variations in both taxation policies and housing policies have played a leading role in bringing about these differences. For instance, the long-standing desire of many British people to buy a home has been encouraged by government policy from the mid-1950s onwards, which has treated council housing as 'second best' accommodation. As mentioned above, this is something which began well before Mrs Thatcher's arrival in government. But there was more to housing policy in the 1980s than council house sales. Continuing tax relief on mortgages and the decontrol of rented accommodation were also key features. The radical changes to housing policy in the 1980s can be summarized as follows.

The *1980 Housing Act* gave both council tenants and some housing association tenants the statutory right to buy their homes. Housing association tenants' right to buy was affected by the status of their landlord: if the housing association was registered as a charity (as in the case of about half of housing associations), they did not have the right to buy.

As far as council tenants were concerned, this law gave substantial government discounts on the price of homes as an incentive to buy: these were discounts of between a third and a half of the property's value, depending on the tenant's length of tenure. Local authorities were required to provide mortgages of 100 per cent for buyers. For people who remained as tenants in local authority housing, the 1988 Act introduced a tenants' charter, which put 'tenancies in the public sector within a precise legal framework. This included security of tenure and procedures and grounds for obtaining possession', but not 'crucial areas of rents or mobility' (Malpass and Murie 1994: 120).

In the private rented sector, the 1980 Housing Act also introduced shorthold tenancies (giving landlords the right to evict tenants after a contracted period of between one and five years) and 'fair rents', a procedure through which former rent controls were abolished and landlords could more easily charge higher rents than before. The aim of these policies was to stimulate the private rented sector by offering greater incentives to landlords.

The *1985 Housing Act* reflected increasing concern about rising numbers of homeless people (see below). This Act endorsed the statutory duty for local authorities to help the homeless (which had been in force since 1977) as long as they are classified as not making themselves 'intentionally' homeless *and* if they fit a category of being in 'priority need' (such as pregnancy, being a homeless parent with young children or vulnerability as a result of mental or physical illness). Local authorities may advise and assist people claiming to be homeless and who are not judged to be in priority need, but are not required to do so.

The 1985 Act also consolidated and extended the powers of central government to force local authorities to sell council accommodation to tenants; similarly, the *1986 Housing and Planning Act* forced the pace of council house sales by increasing discounts to buyers and by making it easier for whole blocks of housing estates to be sold off (see Malpass and Murie 1994: 106).

The *1988 Housing Act* sought to break up further what was seen by Conservatives as a 'municipal monopoly' of council estates by: (a) giving individual tenants the right to choose another landlord, such as a housing association; and (b) introducing a policy of large-scale voluntary transfers (LSVTs) of council estates from local authorities to housing associations or even to private landlords. These policies were attempts to privatize 'problem' council estates – those which are particularly run-down and where very low market prices for accommodation made it difficult to purchase or sell under the former 'right to buy' legislation.

The 1988 Act also introduced housing action trusts (HATs), another device to try to renovate social housing in deprived areas and at the same time to prise council estates from local authority control. HATs were to be set up in selected areas. The housing estates affected were to be run by central government appointees in partnership with management boards, the latter including elected tenant representatives and local government representation. In return, each trust would receive substantial sums of central government money to improve the housing and the local environment.

The concept of HATs has been paralleled in education by that of state schools being able to 'opt out' of local authority control, thereby receiving extra central government cash for improvements. In the case of HATs, though, the initial areas selected did not cooperate with central government: there were local authority objections and, when balloted, tenants also rejected the proposals. However, as Balchin (1995) explains, by 1992 HATs had been established in four urban areas because local authorities themselves realized the advantages to them of receiving large injections of money to help to renovate very poor council housing. Tenants of HATs would not have to be paid housing benefit by the local authority but would instead receive it directly from central government – another saving to the local authority.

The above steps in housing policy in the 1980s were aimed to stimulate market solutions to Britain's housing needs, and have been contrasted with the former mentality of 'social engineering' and planning which had held sway over housing policy. However, in some ways Mrs Thatcher's policies were also examples of social engineering, if by this we mean a paternalistic use of the state to bring about changes which are seen as beneficial for people. It was not as though Mrs Thatcher's government simply relaxed local authority control over housing and let the market run free in the private rented or owner-occupied sectors. Rather, pro-market ideals and solutions had to be brought about – engineered – by all kinds of government incentives such as discounts to council house purchasers.

The most immediate achievement of this state-directed and state-subsidized market was an explosion of sales of council houses and housing association homes, which rose from under 50,000 in 1979 to 120,000 in 1981 and almost a quarter of a million in 1982 (Malpass and Murie

1994: 117). After the initial 'gold rush', sales declined sharply, but they revived markedly again after 1988 Housing Act, reaching the 200,000 mark in 1989–90.

Mrs Thatcher's years were also those in which mortgage interest tax relief, despite small reductions, remained relatively high throughout the decade: for instance, the percentage was 28.2 in 1979–80, 28.3 in 1982–3, 26.5 in 1986–7 and 21.2 in 1988–9 (Bell 1996). In Bell's words, this state subsidy of the housing market stimulated 'the get-rich-quick scheme of the 1980s, a giant national lottery in which everyone won – as long as the numbered balls kept bouncing around.'

In retrospect, housing policy in the 1980s stands out as the one area of social policy in which Thatcherite ideals of individual ownership, pro-market values and privatization had a substantial impact. In other areas, such as education and the NHS, 'the task of restructuring state welfare proved to be a longer-term project than initially envisaged' (Cole and Furbey 1994: 196), and the government approach to reform was much more cautious than with housing.

THE MORNING AFTER: HOUSING POLICY AS A NEW CENTURY DAWNS

In the early 1990s, the housing market suffered from a serious hangover, following the 'party' of property speculation and booming house prices in the 1980s. House prices fell most steeply in regions such as the South East and South West of England, where they had been highest, while they flattened out in areas such as the North of England and Wales (Balchin 1995: 217). Thus there was a convergence in house prices between regions.

At the time of writing, house price rises are being recorded again. However, there have always been rather distinct housing markets; in the forseeable future it looks as though house sales and purchases among the affluent will gradually pick up, while the housing market in cheaper houses will remain stagnant (Bell 1996).

The early 1990s collapse in the housing market was the result of a range of factors, some of which were 'market' causes: the dizzy rise in house prices in certain regions led to a house price 'bubble' which had to burst. At the same time, sharp reverses in economic policy played a large part. As a result of a huge deficit in the government's finances and a desperate need to limit public expenditure, mortgage interest tax relief was reduced to negligible levels by 1993, and this, along with other increases in indirect taxation and housing costs, had a very significant dampening effect on the housing market.

Limiting mortgage interest relief took away one of the major subsidies of the 'middle-class welfare state', and thereby achieved, incidentally, greater fairness in the welfare system (see Chapter 4). However, given the heavy loss of political popularity that the government had to bear for carrying out this policy, one suspects that cutting mortgage interest tax relief was brought about by sheer necessity (reducing public expenditure) rather than a commitment to either social justice or the free-market ideal of getting rid of a subsidy which had distorted the housing market.

The housing market collapse was widely perceived as a failure of government policy, despite the fact that some market pressures, such as high interest rates (which are set by the international markets and which directly affect mortgage rates), are only partly under any government's control. Between 1988 and 1990, for instance, interest rates set by building societies for first mortgages rose from about 9.5 to almost 15 per cent.

Whether or not governments are fully responsible for bringing about housing outcomes, however, a brief summary of the results of the late 1980s boom shows very mixed results from the pro-market and privatization dreams of that period.

Perhaps one of the sorriest outcomes was of *newly built houses unsold*: 230,000 in 1992, for instance (Balchin 1995: 214). A failure of the market led building firms to cut back the output of new homes, and there was a general depression in the construction industry.

Another obvious sign of problems in the housing market was the rate of *house repossession*, which had already risen to 19,300 in 1985, and then rose to over 75,000 in 1991 (Balchin 1995: 214). Houses are repossessed when householders with mortgages have repayment difficulties which cannot be resolved and, though they affect only a tiny minority, they are a significant indicator of a much wider and growing problem of *mortgage arrears*.

Market failure also became evident in a widespread problem almost unheard of before the 1990s – that of *negative equity*. This occurs when house values fall so steeply that householders face having to pay back a loan or mortgage which is greater than the property is now worth. Clearly, the amount of negative equity varies, depending on how much an owner paid for the house and how much house values have fallen in the intervening period. By 1992, over a fifth of all British households were affected by negative equity to some degree, so that for a while the market was, 'to an extent, ceasing to work' (Balchin 1995: 214).

Repossessions, mortgage arrears and other financial difficulties for homeowners are connected with what has been seen as another problem directly arising from the failure of the housing market: the growing problem of *homelessness*.

In the case of homelessness, however, it is easy to jump to conclusions. First, only a small part of the problem can be traced to the rising number of people who have lost their homes as a result of repossession or other financial difficulties associated with owner occupation. Most homeless people have never been owner occupiers.

Moreover, a number of social trends have combined to increase homelessness: high rates of divorce, separation, family conflict and break-up. These wider changes in values and ways of life can be influenced by government policy, but are beyond the ability of any government to control. Arguably, there would have been a rise in homelessness and of people living in temporary accommodation whatever kind of government had been in power or whatever social policies had been implemented.

However, while homelessness is not *all* the fault of government, there are clear signs that certain housing policies have either directly caused some homelessness or made the problem more difficult to solve than it would otherwise have been. Official rates of homelessness rose steeply in the 1980s, directly reflecting the effects of a range of new policies: for instance, the reduction of social security benefits to people aged under 25, the removal of benefits from 16- and 17-year-olds (unless participating in a Youth Training Scheme), the loss of 'low-rent' housing as a result of council house sales and the failure of the private rented sector to meet housing demand from low-income families.

As all housing commentators point out, the actual rise in homelessness was steeper than official estimates show. Homelessness is only officially counted if people have not made themselves 'intentionally' homeless (thus discounting many of the teenagers who run away from home) and have priority needs as defined under the 1985 Housing Act (see above). According to these limited definitions, homelessness almost tripled between 1979 and 1991, from 57,000 to 146,000 households, or almost half a million individuals. However, Shelter and other organizations with experience of the field maintain that the number of people either sleeping rough or tolerating highly inadequate temporary accommodation is far higher. As pointed out at the outset, much depends on the definition of an 'adequate' home, but official definitions do not take account of people who are forced to share accommodation with friends or relatives who barely tolerate them, or people who face abuse and violence in their homes.

The *disappointing performance of the private rented sector* must also be counted in any assessment of housing policy since the 1980s. It will be recalled (see above) that various items of legislation were brought in to add flexibility to rental agreements and to reduce restrictions on private landlords. Through the 1988 Housing Act, for instance, the government had hoped that decontrol and giving landlords the freedom to charge high rents would reverse the steady decline of private renting, but this did not prove to be the case. Private landlords still often prefer to make money through property speculation and sales of dwellings rather than through renting them out, and as yet there are few signs of a revival in the private rented sector. In 1994, for instance, there were under two and a half million privately rented dwellings in the United Kingdom (a slight decrease from 1981), whereas there were sixteen million owner-occupied dwellings, an increase of a third over 1981 (CSO 1996: 176). Rental from housing associations, though increasing by nearly a tenth every year, is even less common than private renting – under a million dwellings in 1994.

Finally, the impact of *council house sales* needs to be assessed, especially as far as the possibility of greater *residualization* of the public rented sector is concerned.

By 1994, the number of dwellings rented from local authorities had fallen to its lowest level since 1963 – about one in five of the 23.7 million dwellings in Great Britain (CSO 1996: 176). However, this decline can be seen in two ways. First, the sale of 1.3 million council homes between 1980 and 1990 could be portrayed as a considerable achievement of Thatcherite housing policy. Despite the financial problems experienced by some of those who bought council properties, for many there were substantial gains.

On the other hand, it is not as though rented public housing has disappeared. Despite the haemorrhage of sales, it is still a substantial sector, accounting for almost five million homes. Such a large sector is bound to include wage earners and younger households, not just a residualized minority of older households or those dependent on benefits.

Although people who live in local authority housing cannot be portrayed as a 'housing underclass' or as a completely residualized group, however, there has undeniably been a *trend* towards residualization as a result of the selling of council accommodation. Between 1983 and 1990, for instance, the proportion of 'economically inactive' people in Britain as a whole increased from 32 to 38 per cent, but among council house heads of household the proportions were already much higher (50 per cent in 1983), and increased more quickly, to 61 per cent in 1990 (GHS 1983, 1992). In other words, during the period of maximum council house sales, the proportions of people 'left behind' in council accommodation were increasingly those out of work or older people. Over the same period, the proportion of skilled manual workers (householders) in council accommodation fell from 24 to 15 per cent, another indicator of residualization and a sign that council housing is now only rarely the type of home occupied by higher-paid working-class people.

Thus opponents of council house sales point to what they see as several negative consequences: for instance, the cost to the public purse from sales which, far from saving public expenditure, have added to it (Balchin 1995: 166). This was mainly because the cost of giving tax relief to first-time buyers with mortgages cancelled out the gains from house sales and from cutting back council house building. Further, it should not be forgotten that large subsidies had to be given out to make purchases feasible for low-income families.

In terms of the social effects, critics of council housing sales point to the 'creaming off' of better council properties by purchasers. It is mainly the more popular two-storey houses with gardens that have sold well, and this makes it increasingly likely that poorer families with young children must be housed in unsuitable accommodation in high rise blocks. Communities also face break-up, according to the critics, because families who have purchased their homes 'trade up' for a better house elsewhere and leave the neighbourhood.

Whether or not the sale of local authority housing will inevitably have these effects, however, is a matter of debate. Much seems to depend upon the types of area and community in question. For instance, an interesting study of council housing and the African-Caribbean community by Peach and Byron (1994) shows that, although black tenants often had a raw deal in council accommodation, the right to buy was more likely to improve their position than further to 'residualize' them as a community (with the exception of single Caribbean women with dependent children, who *were* found to be disproportionately represented in inappropriate housing and often lacked the option to purchase). But rather than contributing to the break-up of community life, householders who purchase their flat or house are more likely to stay in the neighbourhood and to seek improvements in the local area.

This finding about one minority community could have implications for everyone living in council estates. 'Since it is the more economically able and entrepreneurial who buy,' Peach and Byron (1994: 381) conclude, 'it could be argued that the act of purchase ties them to the locality more strongly.' Conversely, they add that in public 'housing projects' in the United States, where all tenants must be on welfare benefits to qualify for housing, and no accommodation is sold, anyone who 'makes good' and improves his or her income is automatically ineligible for housing and is removed. Thus, 'improvers are eliminated and the social composition of the [housing] projects is always depressed. House purchase, it could be argued, could have the opposite effect.'

The African-Caribbean example is important, because it shows the dangers of generalizing about the longer-term effects of 1980s and early 1990s housing privatization. While there are clear trends towards a degree of residualization, or the concentration of the poor and workless in council housing estates, this is far from being a universal phenomenon.

CONCLUSIONS: HOUSING IN A 'POSTMODERN' SOCIETY

No other aspect of social policy in Britain reflects dramatic change in quite the way that housing does. Alcock describes housing as 'a kind of policy football – first kicked one way and then another' (Alcock 1996: 36), but in fact the housing policies of the two main political parties in Britain have converged over the past thirty years – and that convergence has been towards the idea of the private market being the dominant way of supplying housing, and the aim of owner occupation being the desired tenure for all but a few. Any real differences in approach have been more a matter of emphasis or of the speed with which governments have implemented policies such as the sale of council housing. Currently, the Labour government's plans for housing differ little from those of the Conservatives: there will be no reversal to a policy of providing local authority housing on a big scale, nor a reintroduction of mortgage subsidies (in fact, in the first budget after the general election of 1997, there was a further reduction in mortgage interest tax relief).

However, it is our very reliance on the market which has given housing its 'roller coaster' feel up to now. As Bell (1996) points out, Britain has experienced 'two house price booms in the past 25 years: in the mid-1970s and the late 1980s.' The latter was followed by one of the most serious slumps in the housing market in the twentieth century. But although house prices are again starting to recover, Bell concludes that 'the financial landscape has changed dramatically in the UK and the speculative excesses seen in the past two booms are unlikely to be repeated.'

Thus, while we do not know exactly what will follow the three main phases of housing policy of the past hundred years, housing will probably continue in the quieter and more depressed phase that has so far characterized the 1990s. Except in the South East of England, lack of confidence continues to affect the housing market, and this may lead to a revival in interest among younger people in renting rather than buying property (though, as we have seen, there is little sign of growth in private renting). A slow-down in the pace of change is also reflected in the relatively slow rate of housebuilding completions (CSO 1996: 178), which at 3.3 new houses per 1000 population in 1994 was lower than in 1981 (3.6) and certainly much lower than in the phase of rapid housebuilding in the 1960s and 1970s. As Balchin concludes, reliance on free-market signals to stimulate housebuilding has led, in a period of economic uncertainty, to undercapacity in the construction industry, a quarter of a million building workers remaining unemployed and 'housing needs which [are] very far from being satisfied' (Balchin 1995: 56).

The last point about housing needs is a key one, because although housing *policy* may be entering a more quiescent or less dramatic phase, housing *needs*, and the 'postmodern' society from which they emerge, are changing rapidly.

As mentioned at the outset, a number of social trends are combining to put additional strains on the housing market and to increase the need for extra dwellings: a high rate of divorce, separation and family break-up, increasing mobility and the need to move to realize job opportunities, and an ageing population in which more of the very old will continue to live in their own homes than they did in the past. At a time when the population needs an ever more flexible supply of housing to meet rapidly changing family and work demands, the inflexibilities of the market system are becoming particularly evident: for instance, difficulties in selling houses in many parts of the country.

However, not everyone is frustrated by the failures of housing policy and nor has everyone lost from the workings of the housing market. Owner occupiers aged over 40, who bought their properties at relatively low prices, have often gained the most from a lengthy period of mortgage interest relief (before it was reduced to negligible levels) and from rising house prices.

There is also continuity in the public sector of rented accommodation and, despite the problems of neglect, poor maintenance and the residualization of council housing noted above, not all council estates are synonymous with social deprivation and a breakdown of community life. We have noted, in this chapter, how the tenure of about one in five dwellings in Britain is public sector rented. Within what is still a substantial housing sector, there are clear distinctions between 'sink estates' with very high levels of unemployment and social deprivation, often situated on the outer edges of urban areas, and more favoured areas of council housing on smaller-scale estates.

There are even signs that, in areas such as inner London, where the demand for affordable housing is very high, some council estates are losing what has been unfairly termed their 'piss-and-pitbull' image (Bennett 1996). In the year in which English Heritage listed 67 council estates or tower blocks for architectural merit, Bennett adds, 'there are signs that certain council blocks are becoming coveted places to live. By way of purchasing or letting schemes, council flats are socially mobile as never before.'

While such trends may never amount to more than a passing fad, they do indicate a deeper swell of changes in attitudes to housing which will come to affect housing policy in the near future. On one hand, there is some dissatisfaction with owner occupation, especially among the young, and a search for more flexible housing alternatives. On the other, there appears to be a growing concern with *environmental* aspects of housing.

Some of this concern is emerging as a kind of consumerism. It is connected with the development of a more fragmented, postmodern society, in which people wish to identify with more narrowly defined groups than they did in the past. In age terms, for instance, the market is responding to a growing demand for housing developments which are tailor-made for older affluent people who wish to settle with their own age and income groups. In the United States, this kind of housing development is now quite widespread and, with American investment, it is likely to spread in the United Kingdom also.

However, not all the public concern with the environmental aspects of housing is consumerist in the ways described above. There is also growing concern with 'green' issues: for instance, with the ways in which house design could be improved to limit energy loss and emissions of 'greenhouse' gases; with environmental sustainability (for instance, improvement of public transport and cycle paths in new housing developments); and with possibilities for developing new kinds of partnership between businesses and voluntary or 'grassroots' organizations to regenerate cooperative community ties (Lewis 1992; see Atkinson 1995 for more radical discussions of community and environmental issues).

Finally, though, no conclusions about housing policy would be complete without a reminder that a postmodern society includes the **marginalization** of the poor in substandard housing as well as the opening up of a range of different kinds of housing for well-off consumers. Britain has become a more socially polarized society over the past two decades, and this trend is very evident in housing conditions in the poorest neighbourhoods. Even the Victorian problem of inadequate sanitation has re-emerged as 'water poverty'. There is firm evidence that this problem is increasingly affecting people in England and Wales (Huby 1995), and it occurs where water metering is introduced and families on low incomes are unable to pay steep rises in water service charges. According to one survey of low-income households on estates, almost three-quarters were taking serious measures to reduce water consumption, including washing clothes and flushing toilets less often. This had increased the risk to children of disease, 'including dysentery, hepatitis and body lice' (Donegan 1996).

This example is as much an economic or social security issue as it is one of housing, but the point of this chapter has been to draw attention to the connections between housing, the environment and inequalities in welfare. Whereas in the period of rapid housebuilding from the 1940s to the 1960s most of the attention was focused on 'bricks and mortar' issues – the design and cost of houses themselves – it is to be hoped that, in the future, the wider welfare and health implications of different kinds of housing policy will be increasingly appreciated.

KEY TERMS AND CONCEPTS

autonomy	philanthropy
council housing	residualization
homelessness	social engineering
industrial paternalism	social housing
marginalization	tenure

SUGGESTIONS FOR FURTHER READING

For authoritative guides to the history of housing in Britain and to recent housing developments, consult Peter Malpass and Alan Murie's *Housing Policy and Practice* (1994) and Paul Balchin's introductory but comprehensive book, *Housing Policy* (1995).

A more specialized study of the fate of council housing and the prospects for the future can be found in Ian Cole's and Robert Furbey's book *The Eclipse of Council Housing* (1994).

Built to Last?, a book of short readings edited by Carol Grant (1992), gives a readable and stimulating overview of housing history, including chapters on Octavia Hill, the development of building societies and the history of 'prefabs', as well as chapters on current issues, such as the housing experience of black people. Similarly, *Cities of Pride*, edited by Dick Atkinson (1995), provides a set of imaginative and interesting views on topics related to housing and urban regeneration: for instance, there are chapters on community development and the sustainable city.

9   COMMUNITY AND CARE

INTRODUCTION

Imagine whisking someone from the 1940s forward in time to today. Though many things in the welfare system would be vaguely familiar – NHS funding crises, for one – a puzzling change would be heated debates about something called **community care**. 'What or who is a **carer**?', the 1940s person might wonder (the rather specialized meaning of this term only appeared well after the 1940s – see Bytheway and Johnson 1997). She would be similarly puzzled over terms such as 'continuing care' and even 'community' itself, for what exactly is a 'community' social service: a service provided by local government, or perhaps by central government, through a Ministry of Community Care?

Our visitor from the past could also be forgiven for being puzzled by holes in the net of 'caring' services. She would be able to catch up with newspaper and television reports on 'community care scandals', including sad stories of mentally ill people who have harmed themselves when released into 'the community' with inadequate support. Walking through certain urban areas, it would be a shock to be accosted by people begging for money – a definite return to the 1930s – and to see, in the doorways of glittering shops, so many homeless and ill-clad people.

If our visitor had just read George Orwell's *Nineteen Eighty-Four* (it had just been published – the title deliberately reversed the digits '4' and '8'), she could be forgiven for thinking that something Orwellian had happened to the social services. She might think that a Ministry of Community Care was presiding over the opposite, Community Neglect, just as a Ministry of Love was overseeing perpetual war and political repression.

If our time-traveller from 1948 did form this impression, would you wish to reassure her that things were not quite as bad as they seemed; that the words 'community care' are not just empty government rhetoric but do, at least to some degree, represent a genuine policy of trying to improve care arrangements? Or would you argue that, in your view, community care policy represents one of the most glaring failures of the welfare system set up in the 1940s?

It is these opposing points of view, and what we would decide to tell our imaginary person from the past, that are the focus of this chapter. At the end, you should be better able to decide how far community care policies have succeeded in reaching the goals that have been set by governments and other interested parties. As with other areas of social policy, we will find that conclusions are 'messy' – inevitably so, as judgements partly rest upon political values and evidence is conflicting. However, an informed view is possible, and can be developed in two ways. First, we can examine the way in which community care has been *implemented* in Britain: that is, what type of care reforms were brought in and what the implications were, for both carers and the cared-for, of the market framework that was designed for service provision. Second, we are able to assess the *outcomes* of various community care policies. However, as implementation began relatively recently (from 1993), research studies are only just beginning to give a picture of the results of policies. To understand fully these two main aspects of community care, though, a little more historical background is necessary.

THE DEVELOPMENT OF COMMUNITY CARE

The Victorian legacy: care in institutions

We have just imagined a view of today's policies of community care from the perspective of the 1940s. A shrewd observer from the *1840s* might see, in today's community care debates, echoes of the nineteenth-century problems of how to provide care or protection on a long-term basis and how to meet the costs of care for older people, disabled people and the chronically sick. For 'community care', the nineteenth-century observer would probably read 'outdoor relief' (see Chapter 3), while today's residential care would be the equivalent of the workhouse or an institution for the destitute, such as an infirmary or a lunatic asylum.

Although the language and the social conditions have changed a great deal, therefore, the age-old tension continues: what are the benefits, to society at large and to the people who are the objects of care and control, of residential or institutional solutions on the one hand, and 'community' solutions on the other? Community care cannot be understood without reference to the alternative, **residential care**.

The main difference between now and 'then' (the nineteenth century), however, is that policy over the past forty years has been to **deinstitutionalize** care and to rely increasingly on the community. In the nineteenth century, the main aim was to build institutions and to separate paupers, the destitute and those judged to be either mad or morally wayward from the rest of 'respectable' society. As we saw in Chapter 3, however, a large majority of those who received help under the Poor Law system did so outside Poor Law institutions. The sheer expense and organization involved in putting everyone who needed help into institutions thwarted the Victorians' aim. By the same token, one of the main causes, if not *the* cause, of deinstitutionalization and the modern policy of community care is the cost savings that result from closing residential care institutions (Scull 1984).

At the beginning of the twentieth century, a much higher proportion of those in need of care were in institutions, compared to the proportion today. For instance, about three times more older people (about 8 per cent of over-65s) were institutionalized in workhouse accommodation, homes for the aged or hospitals or infirmaries, compared with under 3 per cent in residential or nursing home care today.

Gradually, geriatric medicine emerged as a specialty, there was a boom in hospital building and, with the coming of the NHS, older frail people were more likely to be hospitalized than in the past and less likely to be placed in workhouse-type accommodation.

The 1950s and 1960s: deinstitutionalization gains momentum

With the medicalization of problems of ageing came the pressure to reduce length of stay. Hospital and nursing care are expensive, and in the medical world older people began to be seen as 'bed blockers'.

There were parallel trends in other areas of care, such as psychiatric medicine and hospital care for the mentally ill. In fact, as the welfare system developed in the 1950s and 1960s, a number of factors worked together to put increasing pressure on residential and hospital care: first, there was mounting concern about spiralling increases in public spending; second, the costs of residential care were rising particularly rapidly; third, there were worries about the demographic and economic outlook (rapid increases in numbers of very old people combined with a slowing down of economic growth); and fourth, there emerged a strong critique of the negative and controlling aspects of residential and long-stay hospital care, as exemplified by liberal sociologists such as Goffman and critics of psychiatry (see Chapter 5).

Such critics of institutions had a point. A series of well publicized scandals about abuse of older people and children in residential homes, and revelations of the brutal degradation of people with learning difficulties and mentally ill patients in long-stay hospitals (see Chapter 5) seemed to bear out the oversimplified view that residential care is always a bad thing, and that allowing those in need of long-term care to live freely in the community is always preferable.

As Scull (1984) concludes, this consensus emerged during the 1960s. Both liberal or progressive opinion on the one hand and conservative opinion on the other could agree that, on grounds of either human liberty or saving money, residential institutions of all sorts should be closed down.

It is possible to trace the development of this thinking, and of community care as the alternative, in a number of official studies of policy and in significant pieces of legislation: for example, in the 1950s a Royal Commission studied the care of 'the mentally handicapped', and proposed living arrangements in community settings; the 1959 Mental Health Act sought to establish community care for the mentally ill, and this led to a significant reduction in long-stay hospital facilities, especially in the old Victorian asylums which were still a predominant feature of the health service; in 1963, the Conservative government produced a White Paper on the development of community care (Cmnd 1973), though an incoming Labour government in 1964 did not follow this up with legislation; and in 1968, local authorities were required (under the Health Services and Public Health Act) to provide a home help service to older people.

Some of these policies led to improvements in services and show that it would be wrong to conclude that governments cynically closed institutions solely in order to save public money. There *are* strong reasons for concluding that the needs of those who are frail, ill or disabled can usually be better met with help in their own homes or in some other community setting. However, nothing like a concerted policy on community care emerged in the thirty years after the welfare state was born. Although the benefits of well organized community care were acknowledged, the priority was more to close institutions than to divert substantial resources into personal social services for community care. As one indication of this, for instance, many local authorities never managed to provide home help services on the scale required by official targets before 1980 (Tinker 1981: 101).

Finding ways of getting health and social services departments to work together at the local level to plan, pay for and provide community services proved to be difficult – despite the introduction of joint financing arrangements in 1976 (Challis *et al.* 1995: 10). This underlined the point that health authorities in particular were more concerned with shifting the 'burden' of long-stay patients or residents than in developing a flexible policy of community care.

Thus, as a result of these attitudes, a basic idea that all institutional care is bad became firmly entrenched policy. However, in the closing down of many of Britain's Victorian asylums and other long-stay facilities, quite a lot has been lost as well as gained. Take Bill Bryson's memory (from 1973) of the effects of a large mental hospital – now closed – on an affluent commuter area near London, for instance. It offers a different perspective on both patients and local residents:

> what lent Virginia Water a particular charm back then, and I mean this quite seriously, is that it was full of wandering lunatics. Because most of the patients had been resident at the sanatorium for years, and often decades . . . most of them could be trusted to wander down to the village and find their way back again. Each day you could count on finding a refreshing sprinkling of lunatics buying fags or sweets, having a cup of tea or just quietly remonstrating with thin air. The result was one of the most extraordinary communities in England, one in which wealthy people and lunatics mingled on equal terms. The shopkeepers and locals were quite wonderful about it, and didn't act as if anything was odd because a man with wild hair wearing a pyjama jacket was standing in a corner of the baker's declaiming to a spot on the wall or sitting at a corner table of the Tudor Rose with swivelling eyes and the makings of a smile, dropping sugar cubes into his minestrone. It was, and I'm still serious, a thoroughly heartwarming sight.
>
> (Bryson 1996: 80–1)

The 1980s: 'community' and 'care' redefined

Bill Bryson's sketch of the relationship between a local community and a large mental hospital show us that the boundary between 'community' life and 'residential' or institutional life can be blurred. Unless inmates are incarcerated in prison-like conditions, there is bound to be a degree of interaction between the two. This point is important, because it is all too easy to assume what is meant by the respective terms 'community' and 'residential' care, when in fact their meanings are problematic.

In Knapp *et al.*'s study of 28 community care pilot projects, for instance, living in the 'community' is assumed to mean anything except long-term hospital care: for instance, 'community' projects included residential homes, **sheltered housing**, hostels, staffed group homes and home care (foster) placements (Knapp *et al.* 1992: 342). Similarly, Parker notes that in a government consultative document of 1977, *The Way Forward* (DHSS 1977),

> the term 'community' covered a range of provisions which included community hospitals, hostels, day hospitals, residential homes, day centres as well as domiciliary support. The major priority was to avoid admitting or keeping the old, the mentally ill or the mentally handicapped in the increasingly expensive district general hospitals or in long-stay hospitals: community care became defined as any other way of dealing with the problem.
>
> (Parker 1990: 11)

In the 1980s, however, official policy came to define community care in a different way. It was no longer to be regarded as the struggle to extend local authority social services or district health services into people's homes, decentralized community facilities or **day centres**. The new policy was to aim for care *by* the community (primarily through family and neighbour-hood support) in partnership with the state, rather than care *in* the com-munity (the provision of state-run services to people in their homes or nearby).

These significant changes in policy occurred partly because the trends noted above were still at work: that is, concern about rising numbers of very old people coupled with lack of resources, and so on. However, the 1980s in Britain ushered in additional pressures to find cheaper altern-atives, not only to institutional care but also to expensive care services delivered by public services to people in the community.

First, there was the impact of 'New Right' thinking about welfare. As discussed elsewhere in relation to the health service (see Chapter 7), Mrs Thatcher's government emphasized certain pro-market priorities and goals: for instance, taking service provision out of the hands of the state and local authorities wherever possible; relentlessly seeking value for money in government expenditure; using the strong powers of central govern-ment to set up market-style arrangements for purchasing and providing services at the local level; and seeking to treat users of social services as **consumers**. Though expressed in impartial and diplomatic language, these goals were woven into the two most influential government reports on community and residential care in the 1980s, the Audit Commission Report (1986) and the Griffiths Report (1988).

Second, however, the push for fundamental reforms in community care did not come solely from changing government priorities and the right-ward shift in thinking about welfare. The need to expand community care was made particularly urgent by the increasing costs of public spending on private *residential* care. In 1979, the cost to the public purse of subsidiz-ing older people's use of private residential homes was only £10 million. By the mid-1980s this figure had increased alarmingly to *£500 million* per year, and by the end of the 1980s it was approaching £1000 million per year.

It was an interesting case of conflict between the three main goals of Thatcherism as summarized above. Official policy did stimulate the pri-vate market in residential care by allowing residents of old people's homes to claim social security payments for residence fees. As the Audit Commis-sion and the Griffiths Report soberly reminded everyone, however, this open-handed subsidy had broken one of the principal tenets of Mrs That-cher's economic policy, that of good housekeeping and of reducing public expenditure. The flow of social security money into residential care had created 'perverse incentives' not to develop community care alternatives, which, as well as being cheaper, would as likely as not be a better form of care.

The party had to end, therefore, and both reports succeeded in convin-cing government and the social services community that there had been an unplanned drift into providing too much residential care – even though another government report (Firth 1987) showed that the overall provision of residential home places for older people (by private, local authority and voluntary sectors) had *not* risen very much in the 1980s in proportion to rising numbers of people aged over 75.

Therefore, the notion that large numbers of healthy, active older people were moving into private residential homes at public expense was wrong. Actually, Britain has long had a comparatively low proportion of people in residential care, and there is an argument for expanding residential accommodation. The main reason for a public perception of rapid growth in such accommodation is the boom in private homes (and the advertising of their facilities), whereas in fact, as Wistow *et al.* (1994) show, the ratio of beds in residential homes to older people (aged over 75) was rather static in the 1980s, mainly because local authority and voluntary sector provision stagnated.

As far as organizing community care more effectively was concerned, the Audit Commission's report and especially the Griffiths Report were very influential in shaping government thinking about how to reform the funding and provision of care services. Their influences are clearly apparent in the government White Paper *Caring for People: Community Care in the Next Decade and Beyond* (Cmd 849, 1989), which prepared for the legislation of the 1990 National Health Service and Community Care Act.

Key aspects of these reforms are discussed below but, before this, how may we assess the general thinking behind the Griffiths Report?

First, Griffiths did show awareness of the resource implications of developing fully effective community care. The Griffiths Report is sometimes held up as an example of ideologically biased thinking, predisposed to finding cheaper solutions to the 'care problem' and being more concerned with control of public expenditure than with human welfare. Such criticisms have some justification, but Wistow *et al.* (1994: 5) remind us that Griffiths was 'not entirely unsympathetic with the views of those critical about the adequacy of funding.' They quote from Griffiths's report, as follows:

> The Audit Commission on the one hand were satisfied that better value could be obtained from existing resources. On the other hand, many social services departments and voluntary groups grappling with the problems at local level certainly felt that the Israelites faced with the requirement to make bricks without straw had a comparatively routine and possible task.
>
> (Griffiths 1988: iii)

Second, while the Griffiths Report did show a concern that community care provision should be 'needs-led' rather than entirely dictated by financial considerations, there was a failure or an unwillingness to spell out the full *social costs* of community care. The Griffiths Report was remarkably unsociological. It made little or no attempt to examine social trends which have serious implications for the supply of people either able or willing to provide care in the family. These trends include geographical mobility and changing family residence patterns, high rates of divorce and separation, and a changing age structure which is leading to a shortfall in numbers of people aged 45–60, the main age group of carers.

While there is firm evidence to show that families are resilient and that support for dependent relatives is not ebbing away (Qureshi and Walker 1989), the rather bland assumptions about family support that underlie government policy need to be questioned, especially as an unequal burden of care often falls upon women in families, as Qureshi and Walker – and other researchers on caring responsibilities in families – have confirmed.

IMPLEMENTING THE COMMUNITY CARE REFORMS

Although the NHS and Community Care Act was passed in 1990, the government decided to delay implementation of the community care reforms until April 1993, except for two requirements: by 1991, local authorities had to (a) work out and publish their plans for the new care arrangements and (b) set up independent inspectorates to monitor standards in residential homes.

Even these relatively minor changes cost local authorities substantial sums (with no extra money from central government to help them out), and the full cost of the reforms was a major reason for delaying implementation to 1993. Council taxpayers would have faced significant increases in their annual charges to foot the bill for community care reforms. With a general election in 1992, the government could not risk the unpopularity that would result from such tax increases, already a highly contentious area as a result of the former, much-resented, community charge or 'poll tax'.

Not surprisingly, the formula for funding community care assumes that it will cost much less than its institutional alternatives. This is so even though there is an argument that, for people who are highly dependent on care services, providing good quality services to their own homes could cost *more* than grouping people together in a residential setting.

The government decided to fund local authorities through a support grant that would increase annually over a five-year period as community care costs mounted. The plan, at the end of this period in 1998, is that the equivalent of *half* the annual amount of social security payments for people in residential care will be diverted to community care. Although these are substantial sums, there have been complaints from local authorities that they are insufficient for the full development of community care and will result in tighter rationing of services (see the section on outcomes below).

In sum, the NHS and Community Care Act can be portrayed as a new version of an old tune: how to save money by replacing expensive institutional care with cheaper alternatives. However, it has begun to transform the landscape of care and social services. It was at least partly a genuine attempt to rationalize a system of providing services that previously had been far too poorly coordinated. The main changes brought about by the NHS and Community Care Act were as follows.

It was the first attempt to treat community care as a distinct entity and to bring comprehensive change to this area of social policy. *The core aim of the Act is to give people the choice, wherever possible, of being cared for in their own homes.* To support this aim, people in need of care have the right to have their needs assessed by professional practitioners such as social workers.

As noted above, local authorities are required to draw up care plans for their areas. These plans include the development of ways of assessing clients' needs irrespective of the facilities or levels of service actually available. *Assessment is supposed to be client-led or* **needs-led**. If a frail old person, say, needs a wide range of services to be provided in her home, then the assessment should record this, even if some of the services are unavailable or unaffordable at the time.

Although local authorities had been encouraged throughout the 1980s to contract out services they had previously provided themselves (for instance, refuse collection), it was the NHS and Community Care Act which brought a full change towards the introduction of an *internal market in social services*. The community care reforms require local authority social service departments to act mainly as the *purchasers* of care services (though local authorities may continue to provide services where it is not possible to find other providers, or where people who have the highest levels of dependency are involved).

Thus, as in the health services, a **purchaser–provider split** was introduced, with local authorities being responsible for ensuring that care needs are being addressed (and purchasing services accordingly), but with a diversity of other agencies, either private (profit-making) or voluntary (non-profit), increasingly fulfilling the role of providing services and engaging in face-to-face work with service users and their families.

Sometimes the phrases **welfare pluralism** and **mixed economy of care** are used to describe these arrangements. The latter term arises from economics: 'mixed economies' are found in countries where there is a mixture of publicly and privately run industries or utilities. However, it would probably be more accurate to view the changes brought about by the NHS and Community Care Act as the introduction of a **social care market** (Wistow *et al.* 1994: 2). This is because the whole picture has been changed, rather than parts of community care remaining as islands of publicly run services. *All* services provided in the community are now thought of in market terms because all are affected by the purchaser–provider split.

The full picture of this purchaser–provider split and how community care is funded can be seen in Figure 9.1.

One of the main flaws in the organization of care to be identified by government before 1990 was the poor level of coordination between providers of services to people's homes. Imagine someone newly identified as a person in need of services – a stroke victim, for instance. Without proper coordination of service providers, it would have been quite possible (though not very likely) for that person to have been visited on the same day by various members of health and social service agencies (for example, a home help organizer, a speech therapist, a district nurse, a volunteer helper from a stroke victims' association, a social worker), each one unaware of the visits and the objectives of the others. Or, without a key worker to orchestrate assessment and service provision, it would have been more likely that *no one* would call on a day when the client needed help.

Thus, a central aim of the community care reforms was to establish key workers, or *care managers*, whose responsibility it is to draw up tailor-made

Figure 9.1   Financing community care services

Sources of funds:

[Diagram showing flow of funds for financing community care services]

NATIONAL TAXATION + INSURANCE

Department of Social Security

Department of the Environment

Department of Health

LOCAL TAXATION

Local government

Housing Corporation

PRIVATE INVESTMENT

Benefits Agency

NHS Trusts + Fundholding GPs   Health Authorities

Social Services Department

PAYMENT OF CHARGES + RENTS

Housing Department

CHARITABLE DONATIONS + NATIONAL LOTTERY PAYMENTS

National voluntary organizations

Private providers

Local voluntary organizations

Housing Associations

COMMUNITY CARE SERVICES

The flow of funds from | SOURCE |
The flow of funds from *Agencies*

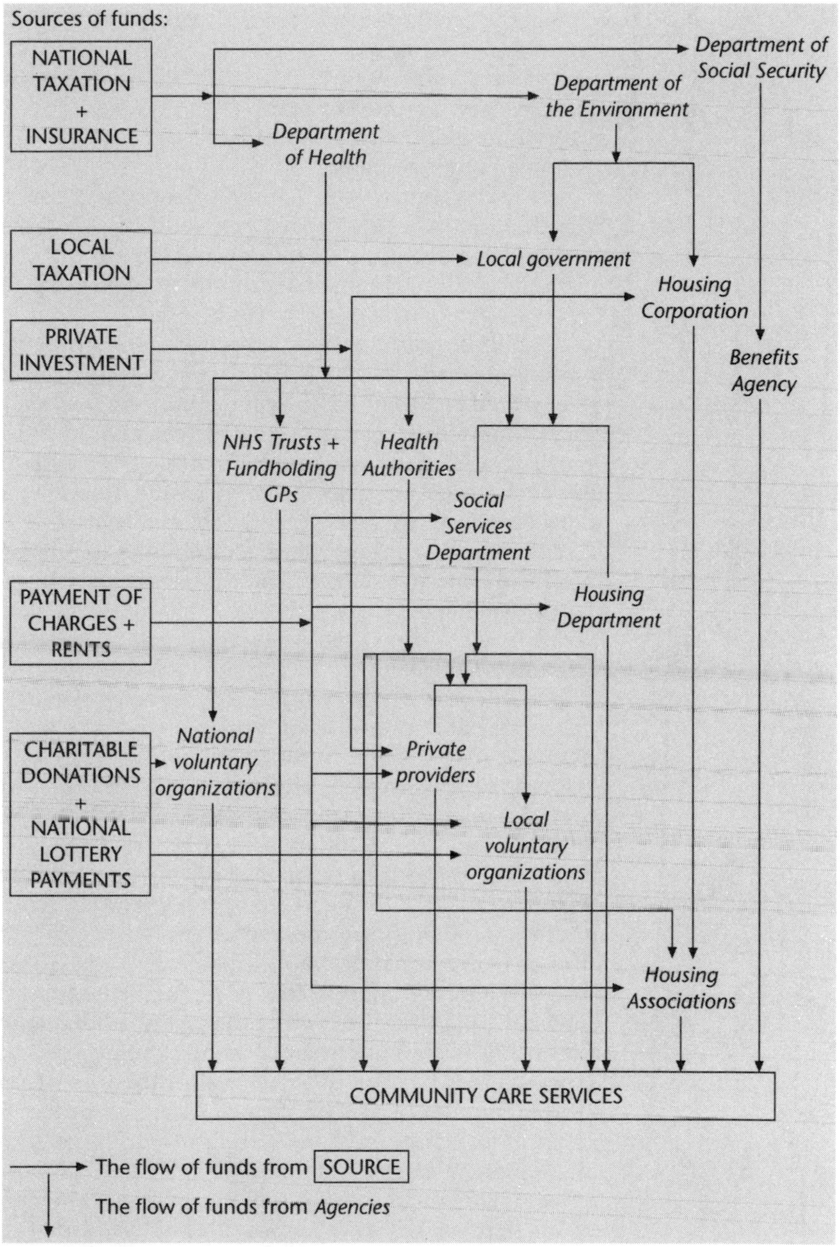

(Reproduced by kind permission of the Open University ©. The Open University is the original author and publisher of this diagram. *Source: Community Care* workbook K259 WB2, 1994: 89.)

'care packages' for individual service users. Building on the assessment made of a person in need of care and his or her carers' needs, the care manager is envisaged as someone who will:

- set targets and priorities, deciding who will get a service and what the aims of service provision are;
- give information to service users and carers to enable them to make choices about services;
- plan and manage the delivery of services to avoid either duplication and inefficient overlaps in services or gaps in provision of care;
- review and monitor the appropriateness of the services being provided in the light of changing circumstances and service users' changing needs.

In addition to these main functions, the government reform of community care encouraged the notion of care managers who would liaise with a range of care providers (private, voluntary and local authority organizations) to buy services, using the budget allocated to each case. However, central government guidelines to local authorities gave a choice of 13 different models or types of **care management**. In some local authority social service departments, both care managers and frontline care workers have been given considerable responsibilities for managing budgets, whereas in other authorities, where practitioners have been thought to have insufficient experience or expertise, control of budgets for community services has not been as devolved as this.

Another key change to be brought about by the 1990 Act was the return to local authorities of the power to decide who will receive long-term care in institutional or residential settings. No longer were people able to claim social security benefits directly from the Department of Social Security (DSS) to pay for private residential home fees. Local authorities now assess needs for institutional care. Only those who are judged to be in need may enter a private or voluntary sector home at public expense. If this happens, local authorities must first pay all the costs and then, following a means test of each resident, recoup some of the costs from users.

Where residents' incomes or assets fall below the means-tested level, local authorities may recoup some of the 'hotel' (board and lodging) costs of *private* and voluntary sector residential care from the DSS, though they must pay for all the 'care' costs in private residential homes. Thus, there is a disincentive to place people in residential care but, if local authorities do so, there is a financial incentive for them to place people in private or voluntary sector homes because, if local authorities' own homes are used, the local authority must meet the *whole* cost (i.e. 'hotel' and care costs) if the resident is unable to do so.

The rigging of the residential care market in favour of the private sector meant that the government was able to claim that it had not completely 'pulled the plug' on support for private home owners, who had previously been able to count on a steady flow of publicly funded residents into their homes. The abruptness of the government's change of policy was also lessened by the decision that people already receiving social security payments for residential fees in 1990 could continue to do so under the old arrangements (i.e. direct payment from the DSS).

OUTCOMES

Has community care improved as a result of the above changes in policy? As mentioned, it is rather difficult to reach cut-and-dried conclusions: implementation was delayed, it takes time for recent research on community care to be assessed and, besides all this, the reforms introduced changes in the social and health services which are all the harder to evaluate because of local variations in the way the reforms were implemented.

On the other hand, evidence is now beginning to emerge. It is possible to make out the broad outlines of what is happening, and the results of the first few years of the new policy may be summarized under three headings. First, there are the outcomes of the way in which community care has been implemented and managed – these could be described as the *outcomes for care managers* as well as the *practitioners and care workers* actually providing care services. Second, there are the *outcomes for people receiving care*, the most important group in terms of testing whether community care changes have made any significant improvements to people's lives. Third, there are the *outcomes for carers*.

Outcomes for care managers, practitioners and providers

In many ways the role of the care manager envisaged in the government's reform of community care differs little from that of traditional social work. Social workers have always been involved in setting priorities, acting as gatekeepers to resources and services, giving information and managing care in community or non-institutional settings. It was perhaps for these reasons that Sir Roy Griffiths saw local authority social service departments as the best choice for being the 'lead agencies' in organizing community care, rather than, for instance, health authorities.

On the other hand, care management, though it can be portrayed as 'a vehicle for effective resource management', has also been seen by some as 'a trojan horse introducing not just new management techniques but new values' (Jack 1992: 5). Whether or not one agrees with the changed role of social service departments, and of care managers in particular, it is undeniable that many of the people working in these roles have found it difficult to confront the new values that go with a market in social care.

In a recent survey of 600 care managers (Marchant 1995), however, it was found that although substantial numbers mourned the passing of traditional social work, a majority (69 per cent) felt that implementation of their departments' community care plans had been broadly successful, and just over half claimed that their work was more interesting and challenging than before. Therefore, the initial impressions are of mixed attitudes to the community care reforms rather than of widespread disillusion or collapse of morale.

On the negative side, the same survey found evidence of considerable levels of stress among care managers and associated staff. While stress levels have always been high in social service departments, there are several reasons to account for further increases in stress as a result of the community care reforms. First and foremost are the heightened stresses experienced as a result of budget cuts and financial restraints. As Marchant points out, 'it falls to the care managers to turn down a care package for a client if there is not enough money' (Marchant 1995: 16). In the past, social workers had to deal with the consequences of budgetary restrictions, but they often saw themselves as client advocates fighting 'management' or the local authority on behalf of their clients to obtain resources or better services. In their new roles as care managers and purchasers, however, they are now much more the rationers of care than before.

A second source of strain has emerged from the expansion of bureaucratic work involved in separating the three functions of assessment, purchasing and providing. In the survey reported by Marchant (1995), 96 per cent of care managers reported an increase in paperwork since the implementation of community care reforms began, and there were near-universal complaints about the large amount of form-filling that they now have to do. Stress results not so much from form-filling itself but from the restriction of opportunities for contact with service users and for providing assistance in the face-to-face way that many social service employees are motivated to do.

Third, additional stresses have been caused by the administrative confusion and upheavals which resulted from the changes in community care arrangements. As one respondent in Marchant's report said,

> People have moved into care management from other jobs – some have been occupational therapists and have moved from one professional environment to another and have found the transition quite difficult.
>
> (Marchant 1995: 16)

It seems likely that a substantial amount of the initial stresses and strains of the reorganization of care management will be significantly reduced as the changes 'bed down'; already there are several reports to indicate this, such as the government's own conclusions from Audit Commission reports (1993, 1994) and from monitoring of community care by the Department of Health which, while recognizing that 'there is considerable progress to be made', also reported 'a steadily improving picture' (Department of Health 1995).

Similarly, a report to evaluate changes in community care between 1994 and 1995 (involving discussions between care managers or purchasers and providers of care in the statutory, voluntary and private sectors) found that, in five representative boroughs, there had been certain improvements in management, as well as continued strains (Henwood 1995a). For instance, this study reported improved joint working between health and social services and better working relations between the local authority and the independent sector than in the previous year. It also confirmed that, while many social workers had experienced a sense of loss of direction and identity in 1994, by 1995 there was a growing recognition of the new skills of assessment and care management.

On the other hand, while Henwood's study found some improvement in joint working between social service departments and health authorities, other difficulties in managing care across the health and social care boundary remain. This is especially so where hospitals have increased pressure on care in the community by altering their discharge policies without liaising with social service and community health agencies. Furthermore, new problems have arisen in negotiations between community health service providers and home care providers on the matter of 'who does what' when caring for people in their homes. Thus, rather than ironing out old demarcation disputes between social service workers and district nurses or other health workers, the community care reforms have in some areas introduced new complications and inefficiencies.

In order to overcome this kind of problem, care management in some areas has been put in the hands of multidisciplinary teams of health and social service professionals. However, as Bland (1994) found in a study of multidisciplinary management, expected improvements did not always occur. Health and social service professionals did not work as closely together as expected. Where there have been attempts to develop a hybrid role which combines community nursing skills with home help, various administrative and financial problems seem to rear their heads to weaken the impact of such experiments. Clearly, differences between the health and social services in both skills and cultures are too deeply entrenched to be much affected by a few years of community care reform.

Finally, any consideration of outcomes for providers of care must include the independent sector. Private and voluntary organizations entered a period of uncertainty following the introduction of community care reform. As might be expected, there has been a fall in business for residential homes with the change in arrangements for funding (Henwood 1995a); further, a rise in the dependency levels of people being admitted to residential care has been reported (indicating that more people with moderate levels of dependency are staying in their own homes than before 1993).

Interestingly, many local authorities still seem to prefer to purchase care from their own residential homes despite the extra financial costs mentioned above. This is because local authorities are legally obliged to maintain at least some residential care establishments (they are required to find places in cases of severe need and may not always be able to rely on private establishments). Thus they have a contractual and financial commitment to their staff and, for the time being, seem to be maintaining these homes by channelling a substantial proportion of residents their way.

No headlong rush towards a private market in care is apparent in **domiciliary** and other community care services either. Private home care firms had developed in the 1980s, but not on a large scale and with a very uneven geographical spread. Leat (1993) suggests that there are discouraging barriers to private sector firms wanting to develop home care, including the managerial and administrative complexities involved in running a local home care service, the ever-changing patterns of demand in the areas covered and often a lack of economy of scale.

As with residential care, local authorities seem to prefer to purchase community care services either from their own providing units or from voluntary sector organizations. Local authority purchasers remain reluctant to embrace fully the ideas of market competition and of purchasing from a wide variety of providers, though in the long term this may change.

For the time being, it is the voluntary rather than the private sector which has experienced a significant rise in business, and in many cases local authorities seem to prefer to place contracts with a few of the larger organizations (for example, a contract to provide 'meals on wheels' with Age Concern) rather than a multiplicity of smaller competitors. This raises the prospect that, as has already happened in the Netherlands, the larger voluntary sector organizations will become quasi-state providers.

Outcomes for people receiving care services

Well before the White Paper *Caring for People* appeared, the government had commissioned research to find out how people receiving care would be affected by a greater emphasis on care in the community. The best known centre for research on the subject is the Personal Social Services Research Unit (PSSRU) at the University of Kent, which throughout the 1980s produced numerous reports on pilot community care schemes that were tried out in the surrounding area by Kent Social Services.

The Department of Health also funded a nationwide programme of pilot schemes to test the effects of replacing long-term hospital care with supported placements in the community for older people, physically disabled people and those with learning difficulties and mental health problems (Knapp *et al.* 1992). This programme was granted the equivalent of £25 million (1992 prices) to carry out 28 projects which resettled 900 people in the community – almost £30,000 per person, not counting additional contributions of resources and help from participating local authorities and volunteers. The authors of the report admit that this 'was itself impressive' (Knapp *et al.* 1992: 340), but in another way generous funding made the experiments somewhat unrealistic. In practice, few local authorities can devote as much money to community care schemes.

The applicability of experimental research on community care was also weakened by the fact that in two major projects (those studied by Knapp *et al.* and another set of projects reported upon by Challis *et al.* 1995), the client groups studied were being transferred from hospital accommodation or, in the case of the Challis *et al.* Darlington study, were frail older people on the brink of being transferred to institutional care. However, the majority of people being affected by community care reforms do not fall into these categories. They are not already in nursing homes or receiving long-term institutional care from the NHS. It may be relatively easy to demonstrate the benefits of care management and other experiments in community care for the people who have been in long-term institutional care, but one is left wondering whether the benefits apply to the majority receiving domiciliary care.

Discussing the research by Challis and his team, Sinclair concluded that:

> special schemes such as the Gateshead community care project do in certain respects 'better' than standard domiciliary services. They seem capable of preventing or delaying admissions to residential care and

they at least match the performance of residential care in terms of benefiting both carers and individual old people . . .

Yet, surprisingly, Challis and his colleagues' outstanding work is only dubiously encouraging to the supporters of community care. [It] was a state of the art project, yet in its effect on the morale of carers and old people it did not apparently out-perform 'ordinary' residential care . . . Given the difficulty of reproducing good effects of experimental projects in standard conditions, it is likely that replications of the Gateshead scheme will produce slightly worse results in comparison with residential care.

(Sinclair 1990: 223)

In sum, therefore, it would seem as though where resources are plentiful, well coordinated community care can deliver better outcomes than earlier forms of home care and support in the community. However, the value of residential care can be underestimated for older people, as Sinclair points out.

On the other hand, pilot community care projects seemed to show that other groups, such as people with learning difficulties or mental health problems, may be significantly better off outside residential or institutional settings. Knapp et al.'s study found, for instance, that community care projects for people with learning difficulties gave better outcomes in terms of gaining new self-care skills, social mixing and making more choices about daily activities (Knapp et al. 1992: 301). However, this was again at considerable cost – over half the projects cost more than hospital care – and the authors underline the point that community care can only improve over residential care if there are sufficient resources for staff training and adequate accommodation in the community.

The question remains, then, as to whether the implementation of community care reform since 1993 has improved upon previous patterns of caring for people at home, and particularly for the largest single group in need of home care, older people.

Again, much seems to depend upon the area one lives in and the amount of resources the local authority has been able to devote to community care, together with the service user's personal circumstances – the availability of support from family members, for instance. However, two main impressions of the early years of community care stand out: the first is the lack of any clear public endorsement or popular acclaim for the policy. If the new community care arrangements are working satisfactorily, they are doing so in a very quiet way.

The other main impression is of widespread dissatisfaction with the gap between the official rhetoric of community care as a 'needs-led' policy and the reality of stringent controls upon the resources available for home care and other community services. As deinstitutionalization gained pace in the early 1990s, local authority social service departments were faced with rapidly rising bills for services to people who would previously have stayed in hospitals or other long-stay institutions. As a result, they had little choice but to ration services to people, mainly older service users, who had previously been eligible for a range of domiciliary services such as 'meals on wheels', luncheon clubs and home help at relatively low cost.

Recently, Gloucestershire County Council sent out a standard letter withdrawing services from a block of service users (Thompson and Dobson 1995). In a high court case in 1995, five pensioners won a test case on this action and, as a result, local authorities may no longer cut community care services indiscriminately. However, the court judgement also ruled that local authorities 'can and ought to take resources into account both in the assessment of need and the provision of services' (Thompson and Dobson 1995: 20). As a result of this and other test cases affecting local authority responsibilities, it looks as though local authorities must honour existing decisions to provide community services once needs have been assessed. However, if it is faced with a shortfall in resources, it is quite within the rights of a local authority to reassess individuals' needs and withdraw services, even though it is forbidden to send out a standard letter to whole groups, as in Gloucestershire.

Financial constraints upon local authorities and the effects of a social care market mean that many individual service users are facing increased charges for home care and other services. Charges present a particular hardship to older people whose incomes fall just above the level at which they are eligible for social security assistance. An older person looking after a relative or spouse who is severely disabled, for instance, may try to struggle along with a minimum of home care because a few more hours of help each week would be too expensive.

Other aspects of community care reform are causing concern, and these also seem to reflect deep contradictions in the policy as a whole, rather than 'teething troubles'. For example, another major concern is that the ideal of consumer choice from a variety of service providers is not being addressed. As with the NHS reforms (as a result of which it is GPs and other medical practitioners who make 'consumer' choices on behalf of the patient, rather than patients themselves), the outcomes of community care policy seem to be putting more consumer power in the hands of care managers and their superiors than in clients' hands. Consumer complaints procedures, for instance, have been instituted by social service departments, but vary considerably in their effectivness and still have a long way to go before they are even known about by the majority of service users (Dean and Hartley 1995).

Involvement and participation of service users in planning community care services is also minimal, according to Henwood's (1995b) survey, in which discussion groups of both users and carers reflected on recent outcomes of the community care reforms. They called for more 'genuine involvement and empowerment', and a chance to make actual changes to the services provided, so that 'people get the help and support that they want, rather than the support which professionals believe they need' (Henwood 1995b: 19). But as North concludes, the previous Conservative government's definition of consumerism underpinning the NHS and Community Care Act was one in which empowerment had to take second place to its 'supreme aim of controlling public expenditure' (North 1993: 130).

Thus, North argues, the government's logic

depends on a conceptualization of service-users as greedy consumers rather than citizens and in the case of social care, access to services

as a privilege rather than a right. This . . . does not permit a responsible government to allow the public any definitive role in resource
allocation.

(North 1993: 131)

However, in saying this North is not suggesting that a policy of trying to
restrict public use of community care services is anything new, or that it
did not exist before the most recent policy reforms. As the incoming
Labour government of 1997 pledged to stay within the previous government's spending plans, we must assume that community care policy will
continue to be restricted by cost considerations before all else.

The point is that pressures upon community care resources have been
significantly increased since 1993. Moreover, government rhetoric about
choice and empowerment has set up certain tensions and public demands.
It is these contradictions and demands that must be managed by local
authorities.

Finally, while conflicts over lack of resources and charges for services
represent important issues, it is possible in some ways to overstate the
amount of change since 1993 in the way services are actually delivered
to service users. As Henwood suggests, community care reforms have
brought greater flexibility in service provision, but 'though perhaps an improvement on past practice, changes are still only marginal' (Henwood
1995b: 18).

In sum, therefore, we should beware of both over-optimistic and over-
pessimistic conclusions about the outcomes of community care as far as
service users are concerned. On the ground, the everyday experience of
people receiving care services from outside the home has not yet changed
a great deal, despite the original claims that community care would bring
great benefits because care would be channelled through 'one door'
(the care manager), rather than being poorly coordinated by a variety of
agencies.

The most important change, as far as clients or service users are concerned, is the rising cost of home care and other services. To many older
people, for instance, the levying of relatively high charges for community
care services represents a betrayal of welfare state values, and an apparent
withdrawal of care that many had believed would be provided free at the
point of use. Other than this, the most important changes seem to be
organizational or 'behind-the-scenes' changes in the ways that care managers, service providers and welfare professionals relate to each other.

Outcomes for carers

As mentioned at the outset, the identification of a specific group of people
called 'carers' is a relatively recent phenomenon. In the 1950s, a person
who provided a lot of care and attention to a close relative would not
necessarily have called herself 'a carer' or assumed that such a word summed
up her identity. Even today, people in minority ethnic groups, for instance, would not necessarily define themselves as 'carers' if they were

supporting and caring for dependent relatives. Their primary role would be that of son-in-law, daughter or whatever, rather than 'carer'.

To begin with, therefore, we should recognize that the term 'carer' is something of a label which can be imposed on people even if they do not primarily see themselves in this way. It is important to make this point, because, when one is examining 'outcomes for carers', it is all too easy to slip into an uncritical acceptance of one common image of carers when in fact there are many different kinds of people in a wide variety of caring relationships.

Perhaps the most common result of a stereotyped view of carers is to imagine that all are women. In fact, of Britain's approximate total of 6.8 million people who care for frail older people, disabled and ill people on a regular basis (Brindle 1995), only 58 per cent are women (Moore 1993: 162) – a clear majority of women, but not the overwhelming majority that is often assumed.

This is not to deny that women carers can be expected to shoulder a larger burden of caring responsibilities than men who provide care. Qureshi and Walker's (1989) study of patterns of care in a sample of families in Sheffield, for instance, shows that where there is a choice between male and female relatives, it is the latter who are more frequently expected to cut down or leave paid work and to perform a wider range of care tasks.

On the other hand, there are many households in which the only carer available is a man, especially as a high proportion of older people live as couples rather than in larger family groups. Arber and Gilbert's (1988) report, based on a nationwide sample of households and titled 'Men: the forgotten carers', showed that a marked pattern of gender inequality in favour of men does not exist, and that men take on almost as much care work as women do.

Interestingly, the same report showed that, with one or two exceptions such as 'meals on wheels', provision of domiciliary services is also more gender-equal than is often supposed. The proportion of men in need of care who receive domiciliary services is not significantly greater than the proportion of women who receive help from outside the home. Inequalities between households, however, are much more significant. Irrespective of whether the person in need of care is a man or a woman, those who live alone are much more likely to receive domiciliary services than people who live with others – even though there are substantial numbers in the latter category who are in greater need than some of those who live alone.

This finding underlines a very significant point about the relationship between the government's definition of community care and expectations of care in the family. Although officially each person in need has a right to be assessed in his or her own right, in practice community care assessments often put *family* circumstances before individual needs. Thus, the care plans for two disabled people with identical problems and needs will often be quite different if one happens to live with relatives in a household while the other does not.

It is only right, according to this definition of community care, that the family should be asked to step in to provide help wherever possible, while care funded by the state is targeted upon people living alone. However, the problem with this view is that it can lead to situations in which too many assumptions are made about the willingness or ability of carers to provide support. A care manager or social worker making an assessment of a disabled older person, for instance, must fill in a form which asks for details about the client's health, financial circumstances, housing, emotional and social needs etc., together with *basic* details about the client's relatives and carers. However, carers have needs too, and these may easily be missed in the initial assessment.

The Carers' National Association (Warner 1995) reports disappointment with carers' experiences of the reformed system of community care. Many carers do not feel that they are fully understood or appreciated by care managers, and a considerable number did not know that full-time carers (approximately 1.5 million in total) now have a right to have their own needs assessed. According to a Carers' National Association survey in 1994, only 13 per cent of carers had received a separate assessment of their needs (Brindle 1995). Similarly, many report that they have never seen or had an opportunity to discuss the written assessment of the person they are caring for. In general, carers do not appear to be treated as full partners in the process of making decisions about community care plans, despite the fact that so-called 'informal care' (support from family, neighbours and friends) is of enormous significance in ensuring the workability of government policy.

In recognition of their importance, though, it was government support of a Labour private member's bill (the Carers Recognition and Services Bill moved by Malcolm Wicks MP) that made full-time carers' rights to assessment a legal requirement. However, no extra money accompanies this legislation. Recording unmet needs among carers is an important step forward if recognition spurs local authorities into providing services such as respite care, but as with the community care programme as a whole, the severe financial problems that local authorities face will continue to hinder any substantial improvements for carers.

CONCLUSIONS

You will recall that at the beginning of the chapter you were confronted by the idea of someone visiting us from the 1940s – someone who would be rather confused about community care and who would need to know whether this policy had brought genuine improvements or not. How far is community care an ideological cloak masking a reduction in government commitment to public welfare services, and how far is it a realistic recognition of the fact that people are better able to look after themselves (or each other) at home?

First, the balance of evidence discussed in this chapter suggests that, despite government rhetoric about community care being a needs-led policy, it is in fact resource-led. This does not mean that we should point the finger only at recent policy as a way of explaining why community care has become a way of saving money. The history of community care from the 1950s onwards shows that there are long-standing pressures to deinstitutionalize care and to limit government commitments to providing services to people in their homes.

However, it would also be wrong to tell our 1940s visitor that no improvements have come about as a result of community care policy. Just because policy has been driven more by underlying economic pressures than need does not mean that the *idea* of care in one's own home is a bad one. Pilot schemes of community care in many different settings and with different client groups have demonstrated clear advantages of care at home over care in residential settings (though it will also be recalled that the advantages are not always clear-cut, and they depend on levels of funding which many local authorities are not able to meet). Community care can be 'cheaper and better' than residential care, as long as transition to the community is well managed and sufficiently well resourced.

The advantages of the new community care system over previous patterns of domiciliary care are much less clear, whether one is looking at the changes from the point of view of those who operate the system, service users or carers. Again, everything depends on finance and resources. Reports from around the United Kingdom show that many local authorities exceeded their community care budgets in the first three years of implementation. Services are being cut or rationed as social service departments run out of money (Hancock 1995). Therefore, it is not surprising that a strong tone of disillusion coloured early reactions to the implementation of community care.

On the other hand, some of the negative reactions to the reforms may die away as management changes 'bed down' and as care managers grow more accustomed to working in a social care market. From the point of view of users and carers, North suggests that, 'despite the rather bleak context',

> there exist opportunities as well as obstacles to user empowerment. The emphasis on individualized care packages hopefully will dissolve ossified approaches to the delivery of care ... The criteria on which decisions are based should be more visible and plans for future services will in theory become more accessible to the public.
> (North 1993: 131)

Examples of user empowerment referred to in this chapter are the recognition of carers' rights to their own assessment of need and the legal victory of six pensioners in the case against Gloucestershire County Council's withdrawal of care services. Neither example will transform the landscape of community care, but they do illustrate a combative and consumerist attitude among service users and carers. The emphasis on consumer rights and choice in a social care market is being continued by the Labour government elected in 1997. While it can be portrayed as empty rhetoric, it can nevertheless be exploited to criticize the limitations of official policy.

Changes have also occurred in one of the most contentious 'troublespots' in community care, the question of who should fund continuing care of people who are initially looked after in NHS facilities or by NHS staff. The confusion about who is responsible for paying and providing for long-term care was not resolved by the 1990 NHS and Community Care Act, and this opened up wider questions about the role of the NHS in the welfare system.

There is little doubt that our visitor from the 1940s would be extremely puzzled by present-day distinctions between health and social care, especially as some people with care needs can be treated as long-term NHS patients in one area, receiving nursing care paid for by the NHS, whereas in another area people with similar needs are treated as a local authority responsibility and, following a means test, could well have to pay all the costs of their care.

As nursing home fees reach £20,000 per annum, it is not long before those with assets of, say, £60,000 in the form of a house or other property will have to dispose of all their wealth to pay for their own care or that of a spouse. Under the rules at the time of writing, people who have more than £16,000 of assets must pay the full cost of residential or nursing home care. Consequently, not only confusion but also considerable anxiety has been caused by the lack of clarity in community care policy about who will qualify for free nursing care under the NHS. Central government guidelines to health authorities are only a restatement of the principle of using locally determined criteria – 'that is, health authorities, along with care providers and local authorities decide who is eligible for long-term health care' (Hancock 1995: 2).

Because of local anomalies and injustices, the question of who pays for long-term care will remain a sensitive political issue. Above all, worries about having to sell one's property to pay for long-term care threatens long-held assumptions about the importance of working to build up a 'nest egg' which can be passed on to one's heirs. Similarly, there is public concern over the rising number of older people who have been forced to transfer their homes early to sons and daughters, to avoid having to count them as assets and thus being charged accordingly for local authority care. As a result, the previous Conservative government proposed various ways to protect the assets of older people. It is likely that the present government will have to consider encouraging people in younger age groups to take out private insurance to cover future costs of residential or long-term care at home (Pole and Steele 1996).

In conclusion, our visitor from the 1940s would probably be left with the impression that something had been lost from the ideals of the welfare state that had been newly built in her decade. From a time in which the emphasis was upon collective responsibility, mutual support and access to 'free' health care, she would find our contemporary emphasis on the rights of the individual and the idea of community care as a 'package' of services in a market very strange.

On the other hand, the 1940s was a time in which no one had anticipated just how much chronic illness would replace acute illness as the main burden of the NHS, or how the needs for long-term care in the population would have grown tremendously with the ageing of the population. There would also be one element of continuity, despite changing needs and changing social policies: she would find, in the continued willingness of millions of relatives and others to provide care, a strand of altruism and responsibility which linked her decade with ours.

KEY TERMS AND CONCEPTS

care management

carer

community care

consumers (of care services)

day centre

deinstitutionalization

domiciliary care (home care)

empowerment

mixed economy of care

needs-led assessment

purchaser–provider split

residential care

sheltered housing

social care market

welfare pluralism

SUGGESTIONS FOR FURTHER READING

There is now a rich variety of books on community care policy and related areas, such as the social and economic contexts of community care. One of the best all-round books to consult is a reader edited by Joanna Bornat *et al.*, *Community Care: a Reader* (the 1997 second edition). Another useful text, which concentrates on the social context, is Anthea Symonds and Anne Kelly's *The Social Construction of Community Care* (1997).

For more detailed coverage of recent policy development in this area, see *Social Care in a Mixed Economy* by Gerald Wistow *et al.* (1994), and for a thought-provoking discussion of the nature of care and its relationship to social policy, it is well worth reading Julia Johnson's chapter, 'Care as policy' in *Care Matters*, a book edited by Brechin *et al.* (see Johnson 1997).

For historical background and discussion of the reasons for the development of community care, Scull's *Decarceration* (1984) is still an interesting read. Finally, the weekly publication *Community Care* provides a lively journalistic overview of topical issues in community care.

10 CONCLUSION: THE FUTURE OF SOCIAL POLICY

SOCIAL POLICY AND RAPID SOCIAL CHANGE

This book has aimed to introduce you both to the academic subject of social policy and to 'real' social policies evident in the world around us. It has included discussion of recent developments in social security, education, health services, housing and community care. It has also included discussion of key themes in the subject of social policy and some of the academic debates that have developed in the discipline.

In the years of welfare consensus (an overburdened term, but still of use in understanding mid-twentieth-century social policy – see Deakin 1994), studying social policy meant learning about the workings of the welfare state: the growing giant of welfare service provision in the 'post-war' years. In more recent years, though, fundamental changes have begun to undermine old assumptions about both the subject of social policy and the welfare state itself. As suggested at the beginning (see Chapter 1), it is probably better to think of welfare today as a *system* of more-or-less connected agencies in different sectors (the public, private, voluntary and informal) than as a 'welfare state' which is almost entirely a government-run operation.

As the old welfare state fragments and changes, it will be increasingly important to rethink the subject of social policy. If social policy continues to define itself as a subject which concerns itself only with traditional areas of study, focusing on need, inequality and social services in well demarcated areas such as education and health, important aspects of social change and social reform will be missed. The old association between the subject of social policy and the welfare state needs to be questioned seriously. 'Social policy' will become much more concerned than it is now with such themes as the role of non-government organizations in providing welfare, with the changing nature of work and equal opportunity (see Blakemore and Drake 1995) or with other aspects of human welfare, including leisure and patterns of consumption (see Cahill 1994).

Having said that, you will have noticed that this book has concentrated on the traditional fields of social policy, from education and health to housing and community care. This is because there are continuities in social policy and, though the pace of change has been very rapid in the context of welfare (the economic and political scene), it makes sense to look forward from a well understood base to developments on the horizon. It is also dangerous to make too many guesses, even about the near-future, when a week is as long in the politics of social policy as it is in the politics of anything else.

This concluding chapter therefore aims to encourage you to look over your shoulder at recent policy in such areas as education, the health service and community care, as discussed earlier in this book. However, it is important to try to reflect upon these recent changes in a way that helps us to think about the general direction of social policy today.

As a start, it may help to review the context in which British social policy finds itself following the landslide victory of Labour in the general election of 1997. What are the implications for social policy?

Second, and tied to the thesis that the old welfare state is crumbling away, is a set of debates about the emergence of a *postmodern* social order. Depending on one's viewpoint, the notion of **postmodernism** is either a very useful way of summarizing trends which have great significance for social policy, or a set of ideas which cloud the picture and obscure such realities as growing inequality and exclusion from welfare.

'New' Labour: a new dawn for social welfare?

The election of a Labour government in 1997 seemed to herald the dawn of a new political era. This was especially the case because Labour's victory over the Conservatives was so decisive and because it followed nearly twenty years of uninterrupted Conservative government.

As mentioned in Chapter 6, the British system allows governments with large majorities to do whatever they decide in a way that other constitutions (for example, the American) do not. Thus the new Labour government seemed to set out with a free hand to change policy. However, despite its large parliamentary majority, the Labour government's hand was relatively restricted, for a number of reasons. First, the Labour Party did not campaign on a platform of reversing the general direction of Conservative social policy; nor did voters seem to want this. The political mood in 1997 was anti-Conservative but not supportive of any kind of radical programme for social reform. The total of votes cast for Labour in

1997 was *lower* than the total for the Conservatives in Mr Major's election victory of 1992. The Labour landslide was a combined result of apathy (a relatively low turn-out at the polls) and of tactical voting to eject Conservative MPs from their seats, rather than a 1945-style Labour result based on a widespread mood of populist reform. Of particular note was Labour politicians' scrupulous concern to avoid any suggestion that a Labour government would significantly raise rates of income tax to fund an expanded welfare budget.

Were Labour and Conservative approaches to social policy therefore examples of 'synchronized swimming', rather than competing visions of the future? To argue against this, there were some clear differences between the two parties in 1997. A Conservative re-election would almost certainly have led, sooner rather than later, to privatization of the basic state pension scheme and the introduction of new personal pension funds; in education, to an expansion of grammar school places and of selection at the age of eleven; and, in social services, to large-scale privatization. This does not mean that any of the above 'Conservative' policies are ruled out of a Labour government programme, but at the general election of 1997 they did represent points of difference between Conservative and Labour policies.

On the other hand, there was plenty of evidence of 'synchronized swimming' in social policy by the two main parties. The Labour government planned to leave intact most of the Conservatives' social policy reforms achieved between 1979 and 1997. For example, despite changes to some of the terms upon which doctors and health authorities operate, the internal market system introduced by the Conservatives into the NHS will be retained; similarly, the education system will retain most of the changes introduced by the 1988 Education Reform Act (see Chapter 6), though one of the more distinctive aspects of Labour policy was the idea of diverting the proceeds of a one-off 'windfall tax' on privatized utilities to pay for 'welfare to work' and improved education and training schemes for young people aged between 16 and 18. In areas such as community care and the personal social services, the changes towards the greater involvement of the private and voluntary sectors in organizing and providing services will not be reversed.

In sum, therefore, and despite some innovative schemes for change in nursery education and 16–18 training and education, the broad outlines of Labour social policy at the beginning of the 1997 term looked very much like a continuation of former Conservative policies.

Social policy continuity in the early months of office contrasted with what has been termed a 'whirlwind of change' (Routledge 1997) in other areas, especially constitutional change (plans to set up a Scottish parliament and an elected assembly in Wales, and proposals for a radical reform of the House of Lords and for the introduction of proportional representation in European Union elections).

Some of the more radical changes in these other areas are likely to have marked effects on social policy. For instance:

- The setting up of a Scottish parliament with powers over spending priorities (and a limited power to alter taxes). This could increase

Scotland's divergence from England and Wales and accentuate differences in what is already a distinctive Scottish welfare system.

- The incorporation of the European Convention on Human Rights into British law, which will give British judges much greater authority than before to question government laws. In rulings over human rights, this may come to have important consequences in areas such as rights to social security for refugees.
- In economic policy, the bold decision of the Chancellor of the Exchequer (Gordon Brown) to pass to the Bank of England responsibility for setting interest rates might have important consequences for economic stability and thus for social policy in terms of government spending plans.

At the time of writing, however, the impact of these changes in economic policy and constitutional matters is yet to be seen. Of greater certainty are the economic problems the Labour government will face and the impact these will have on social policy.

As Aitken (1997) points out, the newly elected government inherited both 'cash-starved social services' and a 'grotesquely expensive budget deficit'. According to economics experts (see Coyle 1997), it was becoming clear before the 1997 election that either taxes would have to rise or the state-funded welfare system would have to shrink. But tight government spending plans were advanced by the Conservatives before the general election, and these were adopted by the Labour Party, which pledged to spend no more than the Conservatives would have done during the first two years of office. As a result of the current fixation with avoiding any substantial increase in direct taxes on individuals, the Labour government will either fail to keep spending below the limits set (resulting in continued costly budget deficits) or have to adopt a tough 'Conservative' stance on such questions as public sector pay awards in health and welfare services, or enforcing limits on access to health and social services.

One of the ways out of this continuing budgeting problem is illustrated by the government's 'welfare to work' policy which was launched nationally in April 1998 (the 'New Deal' programme). Although the plans for education and training of younger people will be relatively costly, there will also be an emphasis on 'workfare' measures which are explicitly designed to test claimants' willingness to work and their eligibility for benefits such as the Jobseeker's Allowance. Claimants face loss of benefit unless they accept a subsidized job or full-time education, or join an environmental task force. The appointment of Frank Field as a senior minister responsible for these measures was a significant development, because he is well known in the world of social security policy for his 'tough' (or 'realistic') stance on benefit fraud (see Chapter 5), such as bogus claims for NHS prescriptions, housing benefit and child benefit.

Interestingly, a pilot scheme to test workfare which was introduced in the final year of the Conservative government, Project Work, uncovered 'colossal fraud or deliberate idleness on a scale no one predicted' (Toynbee 1997). Almost half of the jobless included in the pilot scheme stopped claiming benefit or signed off within six months of its operation. As Toynbee adds, the surprising thing is that, despite large amounts of rhetoric about tackling the benefits culture, Conservative government between

1979 and 1997 did relatively little to reduce fraud; wary of adding to government expenditure on workfare and training schemes, the Conservatives preferred to freeze or lower the value of benefits in relative terms rather than engage in a full-scale (and politically popular) exposure of benefit fraud.

How far workfare 'really works' as a test of eligibility for benefit and whether it will actually succeed in reducing government expenditure on the scale envisaged by Toynbee remains to be seen. However, it seems very likely, at the time of writing, that one of the strongest themes in contemporary social policy will be the increasing tendency of government to *regulate* in the cause of human welfare rather than *spend*.

This trend was very noticeable in the early days of the Labour government elected in 1997. The new government's programme included bills to ban private possession of handguns, to introduce 'fast-track' punishment for young offenders, to begin new ways of assessing school standards and of providing student loans and to introduce a national minimum wage. Most of these examples have economic implications but do not involve the government directly in any large expenditure commitments. As McRae (1996) comments, Britain's trend towards greater regulation of social and economic behaviour is part of a worldwide trend: 'if they can't tax us, they'll boss us around.'

As noted above, a new consensus between the political parties has made it impossible to raise personal taxation, at least in direct or obvious ways. Thus, as the public sector is forced to contract, it is increasingly likely that 'social policy' will be about requiring people to safeguard their own welfare by being regulated: for instance, by being required to provide supplementary pensions for themselves, or (in the case of employers) to provide a minimum wage to safeguard a basic level of welfare for employees.

These observations are being made as if the government can act with a free hand by taking executive decisions on how to run the economy, regulate provisions for social welfare etc. But there is another important influence on Britain's social policy to bear in mind – the influence of the European Union (EU).

Britain and social policy in the European Union

Despite the importance of this subject, it was downplayed as an issue in the British general elections of both 1992 and 1997. Both main political parties were divided on the merits of Britain's membership of the EU and, in the case of the Conservative Party in particular, leading politicians were nervous about parading intra-party conflicts in public.

In the decade before 1997, the Conservative administration followed a policy of opting out of European social legislation and of determinedly opposing any signs of a 'federal' Europe or what was seen as the danger of a European 'super state' that would undermine British independence. In 1989, the United Kingdom dissented from the Social Charter (the Community Charter on the Fundamental Rights of Workers) approved in that year by the EU at Strasbourg. In 1991, the Treaty of Maastricht was agreed. This allowed a compromise: all the other EU states proceeded with a policy of adopting the 'Social Chapter' (that section of the Treaty dealing with employees' rights and employer–employee relations), but Britain was allowed to opt out of this part. At Maastricht, the EU also agreed that Britain could decide whether or not to join the single European currency.

With the election of a Labour government in 1997, British policy towards the EU and European social legislation changed. Within weeks of the general election, the British government was arranging for Britain to sign up to the Social Chapter. Along with other changes in domestic policy, such as the introduction of a minimum wage, Britain suddenly *appeared* to be moving much closer to a European corporatist model of social and economic policy (see the conclusion of Chapter 3), rather than the anti-regulation, free market approach favoured by the Conservatives.

However, appearances can be deceptive, and from the outset Tony Blair, the Labour Prime Minister, sought to disabuse his European counterparts of any idea that Britain would be following an old-style, pro-corporatist or socialistic approach to Europe. Just as his Conservative predecessor had done, Blair emphasized the importance of competition, relatively unregulated labour markets and the kind of social security policy which does not add unmanageable costs to employers (in the form of pension contributions, sick pay or other benefits), which could make European industry uncompetitive.

Whether Mr Blair's engaged but critical approach to the EU will succeed in modifying European Union policies remains to be seen. In any case, though, it would be wrong to overestimate the influence of the EU on any member state's social policies. There is no European 'juggernaut' about to flatten distinctive British social policies, for the following reasons.

First and foremost, the EU (which began its life as a 'common market') mainly legislates on social policies affecting employment. This is certainly an important area, because it includes rules about employment conditions, work-related social security and, most importantly from an expenditure point of view, pensions. However, there is no intention in the Maastricht Treaty to develop a Europe in which every country has the same kind of health service, education system or housing policy. Each country will continue to work out its own distinctive social policies, as recognized in the principle of **subsidiarity** (member states being expected to work towards the same goals, but in their own ways).

Second, the European Union is not a homogeneous group of countries which will be able to implement common policies on employees' rights, equal opportunities and other matters at a uniform rate. This is recognized in the Maastricht Treaty. Additionally, even EU countries which have well developed systems of labour market regulation and social security are beginning to question their value. It is increasingly realized in Europe that the social costs imposed upon European labour have resulted in Europe having the slowest rate of job creation in the world (OECD 1994). As a result, Mr Blair's drive for a more flexible and less interventionist approach to social and labour market policies in Europe may well be pushing at an open door.

Third, the requirements agreed to in the Maastricht Treaty, on equality and labour protection, are for relatively minimal standards. Many British employers already meet European requirements on such matters as working hours or the rights of part-time workers.

Where significant changes have had to be made to bring Britain in line with European law, to date this has mainly been because of *pre-Maastricht* agreements and legislation. At the time of writing, the only significant and immediate change resulting from Britain's signing up to the Social Chapter is the requirement that men and women are given equal rights to parental leave by employers. Therefore, it would be wrong to regard signing up to the Maastricht Treaty as a fateful step which has suddenly opened the floodgates to all kinds of European policy directives.

For example, the EU Social Security Directive was agreed in 1978 and, with Britain's consent, came into force in 1980. It requires equality of treatment for men and women in state-run social security schemes such as pensions and occupational insurance (and equal rights were extended in 1986 to cover private pension and occupational benefits). Another example is the 1976 Equal Treatment Directive, which relates to sex discrimination in employment.

Both of these directives have had a marked effect on the rulings of industrial tribunals in Britain (see Blakemore and Drake 1995) and, as a result of large compensation awards being given to individuals who have been discriminated against, they have begun to change the climate of opinion about the rights of women and other exploited groups in employment (though the success of European directives in combating discrimination against 'racial' minorities or disabled people is much less marked).

Thus, both Conservative and Labour administrations have subscribed to European legislation for a long time. It is easy to highlight individual cases which seem to show that Britain is being taken over by 'new' European rules, whereas in fact the rules are not new; nor is Britain's tendency to lag behind progressive European legislation on equal rights.

The changing context of social policy: a 'postmodern' era?

The 'modern' world has proved to be bewildering and confusing, if we take the twentieth century as representative. There have been two world wars, numerous acts of barbarism and mass murder, stupendous rises in agricultural and industrial production but also in human population, mighty clashes of political ideology accompanying the rise of mass democracy in many states – and, in the industrialized world – the rise of 'welfare states'.

On the brink of the twenty-first century, though, a possibly even more bewildering and rapidly changing world awaits us. It is therefore not surprising that, at the end of the twentieth century, commentators have increasingly referred to the 'end' of almost everything: the end of socialism, for instance, or the end of the industrial age (**postindustrialism**).

However, before we leap to the conclusion that social policy, along with everything else, really is being swept into a new world order, it is worth contemplating what theories of postmodernism are suggesting and whether they ring true in helping to explain both recent policy and emerging trends in policy. There are divided opinions among social policy experts about the value of the idea of postmodernism. For example, Mishra

(1993) finds the concept useful, while Taylor-Gooby (1994) is strongly critical.

First, it may be helpful to make a distinction between postmodernism, a general term implying the end of the 'modern' era as we have known it in the twentieth century, and *postindustrialism*, which refers more specifically to certain trends in the economy and the world of work (Penna and O'Brien 1996). The theory of postindustrialism can be summarized as:

- The collapse of manufacturing as a major source of jobs and the rise of service sector jobs.
- Associated with this, a fundamental set of changes in the ways both organizations and work itself are structured. The earlier industrial world provided work based on principles of mass manufacturing (Fordism). That is, people tended to work in organizations or factories run as hierarchies. Each worker had an allotted role and a predictable work pattern. But in the **post-Fordist** world, the old hierarchies based on traditional skills or on bureaucratic organizations are disappearing. Organizations have become 'flatter' (less like pyramidal power structures) and decentralized, while part-time work has expanded at the expense of full-time; people will increasingly move from one workplace to another and develop more flexible portfolios of skills.
- As a result of the first two trends identified above, old class and gender divisions based on industrial society are breaking down. However, new divisions are arising: there is likely to be a well rewarded section of the workforce who are the more skilled in postindustrial, knowledge-based employment, while a poorer section will be relegated to casual, temporary and part-time work.
- The postindustrial world, it is suggested, will also be reflected in an increasingly 'globalized' economy. This means that revolutions in production and information transfer permit production of goods and services on a worldwide basis. In the new world order, the nation state will become increasingly unable to manage or control the economy (or the social policies) within its own borders, and the pressures to compete in a global market will force the more 'expensive' countries to reduce their welfare and labour costs.

It is important to remember that the above points represent a *theory* about what is happening in the world today, not a set of firm conclusions. How much can be explained convincingly by this theory, and what use is the idea of postindustrialism in understanding social policy trends?

For those such as Penna and O'Brien (1996) and Fitzpatrick (1996), who believe that the concept does have some value, postindustrialism helps to explain a number of recent trends in the way the welfare system is developing: for instance, the **casualization** of employment in welfare services, as a result of the imposition of short-term and part-time work contracts, reflects wider changes in the workforce. The development of internal markets in most areas of welfare provision is resulting in the break-up of the old welfare bureaucracies; these changes also reflect the broader postindustrial trend towards working in fragmented, decentralized organizations. More generally, the emergence of a postindustrial type of economy is eroding the old norms of secure, permanent employment for men and leading to a situation in which the former 'Beveridgian' welfare state (see Chapter 3) is increasingly outmoded and unsuited to people's needs.

In addition to these arguments for using the concept of *postindustrialism*, there are suggestions that the more general concept of *postmodernism*, including study of how we think and perceive social problems and social policy, is useful (see, for instance, Hillyard and Watson 1996). For authors such as these, it is vitally important to include what are termed **post-structural** accounts and ideas in the study of social policy.

Poststructural views challenge the universalistic ways of thinking that underpinned the old 'Beveridgian' welfare state: for instance, the assumption that all people who fit a certain category (for example, older people, or women) have similar needs, and that a universalist welfare state should provide for everyone's needs in a similar way. As Hillyard and Watson suggest, poststructuralism may have applications in such areas as feminist critiques of the welfare system, leading to a **postfeminism** which disrupts former 'liberal' and 'radical' forms of feminism and rejects the idea that rational planning, more 'gender-neutral' approaches in welfare services and redistribution of resources in favour of women will necessarily reduce inequalities between the sexes.

Thus postmodernism contains a number of bold and interesting ideas. For some commentators on social policy, though, these ideas obscure more than they reveal. For instance, Carter and Rayner (1996) take as an example a particular area of social policy (education) to see whether concepts of post-Fordism and postindustrialism help to interpret recent changes in the education system. They conclude that these theories downplay important elements of continuity in British policy making: there is little evidence of radical change in either the way the education system is being run or the content of the system. Postmodernism may therefore exaggerate ideas of radical change from one era to another.

Taylor-Gooby (1994) also argues this point, suggesting that post-modernism is a set of ideas which is likely to deflect attention from such continuities as poverty and inequality. Far from ushering in a new postmodern era, Taylor-Gooby argues, the market economy and its accompanying values that now so dominate the world have led to a re-emergence of social conditions and relationships that are reminiscent of the period before the welfare state: a deregulated and exploitative labour market, and a retreat from the idea of using standard, society-wide policies to reduce poverty.

ENDNOTE: EMERGING TRENDS IN SOCIAL POLICY

As just mentioned, there are dangers in jumping to conclusions about the nature of the changes occurring around us. Postmodernism, postindustrialism and theories about all kinds of 'endings' exaggerate the idea that we are leaving behind one era and entering another. The beginning of a new millennium (in the Christian/Common Era calendar) has added to the fuss.

A more realistic view, at least as far as social policy is concerned, recognizes that rapid changes are indeed occurring (for instance, in the nature of work, or in the information revolution) but that continuity is also present, as demonstrated by the Labour government's decision to continue with and build upon most of the social policy changes introduced gradually by the Conservatives over their previous twenty-year period of office.

Recent changes are mixed up with more gradual, but perhaps equally profound, changes. The end of the 'old' welfare state did not begin recently, or even at the beginning of the 1980s, but in the mid-1970s under a Labour government. It is often forgotten that the highest point of public spending in Britain (48 per cent of GDP) was in 1975, just before a Labour Chancellor (Dennis Healey) made cuts in the welfare budget which have never been equalled since, even during Mrs Thatcher's period of office.

Since those days, *public* expenditure as a proportion of national wealth has fluctuated either just above or just below the 40 per cent mark, though *welfare* spending has crept up, proportionately and as a part of this, as areas of spending such as defence have been reduced (see Chapter 4, Table 4.2). However, in the present political climate it is hard to see how any government will be able to increase public spending on welfare.

This means that one of the more certain trends now emerging in social policy is the growth of the private sector. Pressure for more welfare and educational services will grow relentlessly in a society which is both ageing and tending to expect more out of life than in the past. If the public sector does not grow, demand will result in longer queues for services, rationing and oversubscribed services (for example, larger school class sizes) and, in turn, this will lead to increasing numbers of the better-off deciding to opt out of deteriorating public services. As one illustration of this, almost a quarter of households in Britain's most affluent region (the South East of England) are covered by a private health insurance scheme, while in Wales the proportion is below one-tenth.

As the 'middle-class welfare state' is slimmed down, the middle classes and the better-off are likely to experience social policies which regulate and encourage people to look after themselves much more than was the case in the past. As the better-off begin to shoulder more of the burden of their own welfare costs (for instance, higher education tuition fees), they are increasingly likely to talk about the responsibilities of the *less* well-off, as well as their own.

Thus, another emerging trend likely to be reinforced is that of a growing mood of **moralism** about welfare. 'Moralism' can be observed in a growing number of statements and speeches by religious leaders, politicians and other opinion-formers. For instance, a 1996 report from Britain's Catholic bishops, *The Common Good*, was representative of strong public support for policies that would encourage a more cohesive and 'responsible' society.

However, altruistic ideas and goals – as illustrated by this report – are likely to be coupled with tougher attitudes towards people in poverty and, as shown in recent American social policy, these attitudes will help to justify schemes that discipline and control those in receipt of public services. As Toynbee suggests (see above), a tougher approach to benefits may well be overdue. If moralism leads to enlightened social policies which help people to help themselves (rather than passively handing out public money to claimants), then one of the more encouraging outcomes of future social policies may be a reduction of welfare dependency and poverty.

On the other hand, one of the most disappointing signs of continuity in social policy is the failure to reduce poverty in any significant way. The government's Green Paper on welfare reform, *New Ambitions for Our Country: a New Contract for Welfare* (published by the Department of Social Security in March 1998), proposed 30 targets to measure the success of the welfare system in the coming decades, but these targets represent statements of intent rather than specific policies to tackle poverty. There is no commitment to a specific minimum pension, for instance.

Apart from radical proposals to reduce fraud by changing the way in which housing benefit is administered, the amount of continuity in the Labour government's current social policy is therefore quite striking. The long-awaited statement on welfare reform left intact the main architecture of the original Beveridge System: National Insurance remains, and in some ways the government's emphasis on 'welfare to work' reinforces the close link between employment and welfare benefits that Beveridge established. Also, the government's plans endorsed universalism (rather than means-testing and selective benefits) in all the main areas of greatest need – for instance in relation to child benefit, the state retirement pension (which, although shrinking in value is still seen as a foundation stone) and benefits for disabled people. Continuity of policy was also evident in the government's second budget (1998), which *increased* child benefit and retained mortgage interest tax relief (albeit at a low level, which is set to decrease further).

This does not mean that imminent radical changes are ruled out – for instance, it is likely that proposals for a compulsory second pension will be made – but that, just as the preceding Conservative government preferred incremental change, so will the present government (mainly for political or electoral reasons).

One of the most interesting aspects of social policy today and tomorrow is to see how far it will be able to moderate the sharp social divisions and growing inequalities inherent in the tough capitalist world. Persuading voters to pay even a little more in tax to achieve greater welfare and more social cohesion will be difficult, as will redesigning the welfare system in ways that will enable it to survive in the twenty-first century.

KEY TERMS AND CONCEPTS

casualization (of employment)
moralism
postfeminism
post-Fordism

postindustrialism
postmodernism
poststructuralism
subsidiarity

SUGGESTIONS FOR FURTHER READING

For interesting discussions of current trends in social policy which consider Britain in a European and international context, Catherine Jones's *New Perspectives on the Welfare State in Europe* (1993) and Cochrane and Clarke's *Comparing Welfare States: Britain in International Context* (1993) offer useful and interesting guides.

A more detailed coverage of social policy in Europe, focusing on gender issues, can be found in a chapter by Angela Glasner in Joe Bailey's *Social Europe* (see Glasner 1992), while my book (with Bob Drake) *Understanding Equal Opportunity Policies* (1995) includes discussion of the impact of European Union social policies on Britain, as well as a more general discussion of social trends and the changing context of social policy.

To follow the debate about postmodernism in social policy, try to obtain the issues of the *Journal of Social Policy* which include the articles by Taylor-Gooby, Penna and O'Brien, Fitzpatrick, and Hillyard and Watson, which were mentioned in this chapter (see Bibliography for details).

On a final and more general note, you will find that the *Journal of Social Policy* is well worth consulting for any research or coursework that you may have to do, or just to keep up to date with recent policy issues and debates. Each issue contains a section titled 'Digest', which helpfully summarizes key changes in various policy areas such as health services, education, personal social services, gender issues etc.

You may also like to note that the quarterly *Journal of Social Policy* is obtainable *free* if you become a member of the Social Policy Association. The annual membership fee is low (e.g. £12) if your annual income is below £15,000, and it brings other benefits (newsletter, access to grants, conferences etc.). Details are obtainable from SPA Membership, 16 Creighton Avenue, London N10 1NU.

GLOSSARY OF TERMS

The terms and concepts in this glossary are also listed at the end of the particular chapter(s) in which they have been most used. Therefore, by reading the text of the relevant chapter(s) you will be able to find examples of the ways in which they can be applied. Relevant chapter(s) are indicated after each definition with an abbreviation (for example, 'Ch. 1' for Chapter 1).

The definitions which follow are summaries of the way concepts are used in *social policy*. You may find different interpretations of terms in a dictionary or a reference book.

Where terms are closely related (for instance, 'maximalist' and 'minimalist' types of equal opportunity policy), they have been placed together for convenience. Otherwise, the following terms are arranged alphabetically.

acute illnesses   Serious life-threatening illnesses which are resolved in a relatively short period of time (usually a matter of days or weeks), either by death or by the patient regaining health. Medical intervention may help either to restore health or to manage acute illness, which may then become a chronic condition (see chronic illnesses). Acute infectious illnesses were common in Britain up to the early part of the twentieth century. (Ch. 7)

autonomy   When applied to individuals, this term refers to the ability of a person to decide his or her own fate; the autonomous individual has the freedom and the ability to make decisions independently or to exercise choices for himself or herself. 'Autonomy' can also be used to refer to government institutions or organizations (see *relative autonomy*). (Chs 2, 8)

basic needs   These are universal human needs which are considered to be fundamental, not simply to enable human beings to survive, but as basic requirements for the development of independent individuals. Autonomy (see above) has been seen as a basic need, as well as adequate nutrition and housing, for instance. (Ch. 2)

care management   A term associated mainly with the provision and organization of services in the community, or with managing services for people who are moving in or out of hospital or institutional settings. Care management is an approach which stresses the importance of coordinating health and social services in ways which (a) best serve the interests of service users and (b) maximize the efficiency of service delivery. Care managers are often social workers, but can be appointed from other fields, such as occupational therapy, and their job is to take the lead responsibility for coordinating the various services needed. (Ch. 9)

carer   This is a formal way of defining the role of someone who either willingly and voluntarily cares for someone, usually on a continual and permanent basis, or feels obliged to provide care or is paid to do so. The invention of the term 'carer' has had some unfortunate consequences, in that it tends to suggest that all the 'care' goes in one direction (from carer to 'cared for'), and it can overemphasize the helplessness and passivity of people who need help with managing their daily activities. (Ch. 9)

casualization (of employment)   A process of change in working conditions and work contracts. It refers to the way in which permanent work contracts and full-time jobs are replaced by short-term and part-time work. When work is casualized, employees tend to lose important rights and the protection of laws which safeguard their welfare: for instance, laws against instant or unfair dismissal, laws to ensure safety at work and contributions by employers to social security, insurance and pension schemes. (Ch. 10)

chronic illnesses   These are illnesses which are, in most cases, incurable. However, they may or may not be disabling and often they can be successfully managed by medical intervention. Chronic illnesses are thus long-term problems, in that they are not immediately life-threatening (for instance, Parkinson's disease), and they have replaced acute illnesses as the main causes of illness in modern society. (Ch. 7)

civil rights   The rights of individuals to liberty and security under the law: for instance, the right to move freely from one place to another, freedom from arbitrary arrest or detention without legal cause, and the right to own property. T.H. Marshall (1950) saw civil rights as a first step to the development of other rights (political rights and social rights). (Ch. 2)

coercion   This term can be used to define a wide variety of methods with which those with power constrain or force people without power to do something or to act in a particular way. Coercion may be subtle and may be exercised as a result of the way a particular organization or institution is run (for instance, a residential home for disabled people), or it may be direct and consciously applied by those with power. (Ch. 5)

community care   Refers to caring activities or services which exist outside large-scale institutions such as hospitals. The 'community' may be defined as a wide range of non-institutional settings (for instance, day centres, 'halfway houses' or sheltered housing schemes, foster homes), but in most cases 'community care' is another way of describing the care of people living alone or in families. (Ch. 9)

comparative need   A way of defining need in a group in relation to what other comparable groups have, or do not have. An observer may find that one group of disabled people, for instance, receive very little help in the form of social services even though it is clear that they need such services; finding a second comparable group which does receive services may help to establish a case for providing services to the first group as well. (Ch. 2)

consumers (of care services)   The idea of portraying users of public services as 'consumers' gained importance as a result of the introduction of market-style reforms of the welfare system in the 1980s. Its significance lay in the goal of giving individual service users greater choice of services or a greater say over how services should be delivered to them. Thus people who used public services such as the NHS were to be seen *as if* they were purchasing goods or services in the private market, even though (in the case of 'free' services) they were not paying for them at the point of use. (Ch. 9)

the contract state   A role for government which seeks to ensure that certain services are provided (such as education), but not by the government itself. Instead of public provision, the contract state draws up contracts with private and voluntary organizations to provide services. These organizations are then paid for services by government, which restricts its role to regulating providers and to making sure that value for money is obtained. (Ch. 3)

corporatist welfare states   A model or type of welfare state which is based upon the principle of legal or informal agreements between the major 'corporate groups' of society: for instance, organized labour (trade unions), employer organizations, voluntary organizations (such as a dominant Church) and government. Germany is an example of a corporatist welfare state. Some service and welfare provision is in the hands of Church organizations, while employers' and workers' organizations come to agreements with government over social security benefits and other aspects of welfare. (Ch. 3)

council housing   Rented accommodation provided and owned by elected local government councils. (Ch. 8)

critique   A critical discussion of a someone's idea, position, theory or set of findings. A critique appraises others' ideas and suggests new insights. (Ch. 1)

curative medicine   An approach in medicine which emphasizes the treatment of disease to effect cures and to restore health. The 'curative model' or approach implies a policy which puts more resources into treating sick people (with doctors, other medical practitioners, hospitals and drug therapy) than into preventing the onset of disease. (Ch. 7)

day centre   A social services term to describe a facility which provides services during the day (for instance, meals, recreation, therapy) for people who continue to reside in their own homes. (Ch. 9)

deinstitutionalization   A policy or process of change through which institutions such as mental hospitals and residential homes are closed down. It can also refer to a process of personal change in which former residents or patients lose their 'institutionalized' identities and behaviour patterns. (Ch. 5)

democratic pluralist model of power   This is one of several perspectives on the way power is distributed and exercised in society (see also *elite* *control* and *political economy* models of power). The democratic pluralist view suggests that power is distributed widely among a large number (plurality) of different groups in society (e.g. business interests, political parties, campaigning groups). No one group monopolizes power or decision making, and democratic elections make governments accountable to ordinary citizens. (Ch. 6)

the deserving (and undeserving) poor A term from the nineteenth century which implies a distinction between those who are destitute and have a moral right to state welfare or charitable support (for instance, orphaned children or disabled people unable to work), and those who could support themselves but do not do so, preferring to make undeserved claims upon the state or charitable organizations. (Ch. 3)

disciplines Used in this book to discuss the standing and identity of different academic subjects or fields of study, such as social policy. A 'discipline' is a recognized university subject which has generated its own body of research and has developed a distinctive set of theories. (Ch. 1)

dole One of the earliest terms related to welfare. 'The dole' was the daily or weekly payment (in bread or money) to the poor of the parish: that is, those who were regarded as the 'deserving' poor and who could receive 'outdoor relief' (assistance from the parish or Poor Law authorities while continuing to live at home rather than in an institution such as the workhouse). (Ch. 3)

domiciliary care Home care: that is, social services delivered by a local authority, voluntary or private sector agency to the home (domicile). (Ch. 9)

economic growth The size of an economy can be measured by statistical estimates of the total value of all the goods and services produced every year. Economic growth occurs when one year's total production exceeds a previous year's. However, economic growth measures can be criticized because they are usually based on what is known as the 'formal' economy or what has been statistically measured by economists. Official economic estimates often neglect the millions of hours and the resources devoted to family care and domestic work – an 'informal' economy of welfare. (Ch. 4)

egalitarianism A broad term which encompasses a variety of socialist points of view. However, all egalitarians believe in the importance of absolute equality and of creating a society which minimizes distinctions of rank or status and of income and wealth. (Ch. 2)

elite control model of power An analysis or view of power in society which suggests that power is concentrated in the hands of an elite, or several connected elites. Elites may be defined as extremely small groups of people who occupy the leading positions in business, government and political parties, cultural institutions and the military. (Ch. 6)

empirical research Research (of the natural or social world) which is based on observation, experience and testing of hypotheses against factual evidence. Empirical research is used to test theories, but is not itself highly theoretical. (Ch. 1)

empowerment A process of change in which oppressed groups discover their ability to challenge those who oppress them. Empowerment can be brought about by change in the power structures which govern communities and social service organizations. For instance, women living in a housing estate who were previously isolated and powerless might bring themselves together to form their own campaigning group to challenge street crime, domestic violence, a lack of community services and inadequate housing maintenance. (Ch. 9)

equality   When applied to human society, equality describes a state in which people are closely similar in social status, income, wealth, opportunities and living conditions. (Ch. 2)

equality of opportunity   Exists if everyone has the same or near-similar chances to achieve their ends or goals (for instance, through educational success or seeking employment). Therefore, equality of opportunity says nothing about final outcomes, which may be highly unequal in terms of success, educational qualifications or income. Equality of opportunity is a measure of how fair or equal conditions are at the 'starting gate' before the race. (Ch. 2)

equity   This term refers to justice and fairness in the distribution of something (for instance, social benefits, jobs, income and wealth). It may be just and fair for one individual or group to receive more than another because needs differ. (Ch. 2)

euthanasia (voluntary and involuntary; active and passive)   A method of bringing about death in a painless way. It is sometimes described as 'mercy killing', suggesting that it is someone other than the person or the animal that is suffering who takes the decision to end life. If this is the case, then we would be dealing with *involuntary* euthanasia. However, in cases where a person is conscious and wishes to end his or her life, euthanasia could be defined as *voluntary*. If death is brought about by the person himself or herself (either with complete independence or by activating a lethal injection, for instance), euthanasia can be defined as *active*, but if there is a termination of life by medical practitioners or someone else, it can be seen as *passive* euthanasia. In Britain, all forms of euthanasia are illegal. However, by administering pain-relieving drugs to patients with terminal conditions, medical practitioners commonly hasten death. (Ch. 7)

expressed needs   Needs which are publicly known and which have been identified as important by an individual or a group. Not all expressed needs are met, but the expression of need is an important first step in placing a demand on government or some other body.

external benefits   A term often used by economists to refer to additional benefits that could be gained from a particular policy or course of action. Rather than being a narrowly defined or individual benefit, an external benefit is likely to be something which brings a gain or payoff to the community as a whole. For instance, education brings individual benefits or payoffs (because it allows people with qualifications to obtain higher pay) but it also brings external benefits such as a general increase in productivity and efficiency.

felt need   This is need which (a) objectively exists (that is, there would be agreement among observers that a particular individual or group needs something) *and* (b) the people or groups in question realize that they have, and consciously express their feelings about. (Ch. 2)

flat-rate (contributions and benefits)   A rather old-fashioned term which refers to everyone paying in the same amount to a social security scheme and, if benefits are also flat-rate, all beneficiaries receiving the same amount. (Ch. 3)

freedom   May be defined 'negatively' as the absence of restraint or oppression (for instance, freedom from crime, freedom from arbitrary arrest), or 'positively' as freedom to do certain things, such as the freedom to follow educational courses to one's full potential. Positive freedoms have greater resource implications than negative freedoms because they often involve increases in welfare and educational spending (see *social rights*). (Ch. 2)

gross domestic product (GDP)   A measure of the total value, in money terms, of all the goods and services produced in a country, excluding exports and 'invisible' earnings (e.g. from insurance services provided to other countries). (Ch. 4)

homelessness   Lack of a home, which may exist even if people have a place to stay or a 'roof over their head'. People who inhabit overcrowded or hazardous dwellings, or who are unable to enjoy freedom of movement, may be described as homeless. (Ch. 8)

hypothesis   An assumption or guess which is used to explain something. Hypotheses are 'working assumptions' and need to be tested against evidence. They are developed as ways of finding out whether broader theories are correct. (Ch. 1)

iatrogenic disease   Disease which is caused or aggravated by medical treatment. (Ch. 7)

implementation (of policy)   The process of carrying out a policy and turning it from a written policy statement, law or guideline into action 'on the ground'. Note, however, that even when implemented, some policies do not bring about much change. (Chs 1, 6)

income (original, gross and final income)   The distinctions between original, gross and final income help to illustrate the effect of welfare provision upon people's incomes. Original income represents the sum that a household receives before taxes and other deductions are taken away; gross income is the sum that is left; final income is an estimate of gross income plus a financial estimate of the value of social/welfare services and social security benefits that the household receives. A year's primary schooling, for instance, might be valued at £5000 and added to the household's final income. (Ch. 4)

industrial paternalism   From the earliest days of the Industrial Revolution in the late eighteenth century and through the nineteenth and twentieth centuries there have been examples of employers who sought to improve the working and living conditions of their employees and their families. Such welfare concerns have been termed 'paternalist', because employers tended to assume that they knew what was best for their workers; further, in accepting improved conditions, workers were expected to show loyalty and deference to employers. Modern industrial paternalism can be seen in the management styles of Japanese companies operating in Britain. (Ch. 8)

inexplicit policies   This is a useful way to show that policy is not always official, stated or explicit. An inexplicit policy is one which is deliberately and consciously followed or one which 'emerges' from common practice. In either case, the aims of an inexplicit policy are never plainly stated or admitted. (Ch. 7)

justice In social policy, justice is discussed with reference to the fairness or rightness of policies. A socially just policy, for instance, will result in the fairest possible distribution of welfare, services or resources (see *equity*). (Ch. 2)

less eligibility A term used in the framing of the 'new' Poor Law legislation of 1834. 'Eligibility' in this old-fashioned usage can be taken to mean 'satisfactory'. The argument put forward by those who wanted to reform the old (pre-1834) Poor Laws was that the income and living conditions of those in receipt of public assistance (poor relief) should always be 'less eligible' (satisfactory) than the lowest-paid labourer's in work. (Ch. 3)

liberal welfare systems One of several major categories or types of welfare system. A country which has a 'liberal' welfare system is typically one in which state welfare provision is minimal. Where public services and welfare benefits are provided, they tend to be strictly means-tested and restricted to the poorest sections of society. The dominant philosophy is one of *laissez-faire*, and the majority make their own arrangements (through the private sector or reliance on family support) to safeguard their welfare. Gosta Esping-Andersen's *The Three Worlds of Welfare Capitalism* (1990) refers to this type of welfare system. (Ch. 3)

marginalization A social and political process in which weaker or poorer groups and individuals are excluded from, or pushed to the margins of, mainstream society. Marginalization means that the views and the needs of excluded groups tend not to be taken into account in policy making. (Chs 5, 8)

means tests Rules which are used to target benefits or services upon people whose incomes (means) fall below a certain level, so that only poorer groups are eligible. Means-tested benefits may be contrasted with universal benefits, which are available to all. (Ch. 3)

medicalization A process of social change in which perceptions of human and social problems shift towards the view that problems can best be explained as 'illnesses' which must be dealt with by medical treatment. For instance, much deviant behaviour which might once have been described as 'evil' or 'mad' is now portrayed as illness that must be treated. Natural phenomena such as childbirth have also been extensively medicalized. (Ch. 7)

minimalist and maximalist policies (of equal opportunity) The terms 'minimalist' and 'maximalist' could be applied to any kind of policy, in that the former suggests the idea of doing the minimum, while the latter suggests maximum government intervention and effort. In relation to equal opportunities, a minimalist policy is one which is typified by an employer or government seeking to ensure that competition for jobs or education is fair and is not openly discriminatory in any way. Maximalist policies are those which seek more ambitiously to change outcomes by equalizing numbers of men and women, ethnic and racial groups and other under- or overrepresented groups in the workforce. (Ch. 2)

mixed economy of care A phrase which summarizes the complex modern system of social and health services, which are provided and funded by a variety of different types of organization: local authority or government organizations, voluntary sector organizations and private sector organizations. The idea of a 'mixed economy' was developed originally to describe countries which combined capitalism with nationalized (state) industries. (Ch. 9)

models (of welfare or social policy) In academic discussion, the term 'model' is used to describe a set of ideas which summarize the essence or essential characteristics of something. A model is not expected to be an accurate or detailed description: it is a way of picturing or generalizing basic types. In welfare, we may therefore develop ideas or models of different types of welfare system, such as 'the Scandinavian model' of social policy. (Ch. 1)

moralism A set of values which are used to judge the desirability (or otherwise) of social policies on moral and religious grounds. (Ch. 10)

need In social policy, the term 'need' is usually reserved for objective definitions of resources, skills or other things which are required and which are lacking in an individual or group: for instance, psychological needs for security or personal development, or physical needs for adequate nutrition. (Ch. 2)

needs-led assessment A principle of basing assessment of people's eligibility for services or welfare upon an objective definition of their needs – as opposed to 'resource-led assessment', which works on the principle of assessing need on the basis of what services or resources are available. (Ch. 9)

normative needs Needs defined by professionals' standards and their judgement of what is lacking and what ought to be provided. (Ch. 2)

normative policies Policies which express social norms and strong public views of what ought to happen in society. (Ch. 2)

objectivity This is a key term in any discussion of social science. It is particularly important in social policy because the assessment of policies is often influenced by values and political opinion rather than by objective assessment. Although complete objectivity may be impossible, this does not mean that all statements have equal validity or that one person's observations are always as valid or reliable as another's. An objective appraisal or piece of research is one which is as free of prejudice as possible. Objectivity is attained when evidence and reasoned argument show that a particular phenomenon – a government policy, for instance – has certain characteristics which exist independently of the perceiver's mind or personal opinions. (Ch. 1)

oppression (see also *empowerment* and *social control*) 'Oppression' is a term now widely used in sociology and politics, as well as in social work training, where 'anti-oppressive practice' is a key training goal. Oppression refers to a wide variety of behaviours and practices which unfairly deprive others (the oppressed) of their rights to autonomy and self-expression. In traditional and wider usage, the term 'oppression' suggests tyranny and extremes of cruelty. However, in social science and social work, 'oppression' is used to imply a broad range of discriminatory behaviour which excludes and demeans powerless groups or individuals. (Ch. 5)

outcomes The results or achievements of policies: for instance, health policy outcomes can be measured in terms of rates of various illnesses, or education policy outcomes can be measured by rates of literacy or by percentages of the population attaining various skills. (Ch. 7)

parliamentary democracy A form of democratic government in which almost all elected representatives are members of political parties which compete for power (although independent representatives or MPs are sometimes elected). The party which has the largest group of elected members after an election then forms the government, though it may have to rely on the support of another party if it does not have an overall majority in parliament. In a parliamentary democracy, elected members are bound more by the policies and discipline of their parties than by the wishes of their constituents. If there were a democracy in which those elected to power *directly* represented the wishes of the voters (for instance, to restore capital punishment), representatives would become 'delegates'. (Ch. 6)

pauperism A state or condition of absolute poverty *and* of dependence on public welfare. The Victorians drew a distinction between general poverty, which many experience, and pauperism. (Ch. 3)

payment by results (in education) A phrase associated with education policy in the latter part of the nineteenth century. Public funding of schools was based on a system of assessing school attainment (the numbers of pupils passing tests in the 'three Rs' – mainly tests of numeracy, literacy and rote-learning of basic facts) and school attendance. The more pupils a school could 'process' successfully through the tests of rote learning, the more money was received from government. (Ch. 3)

philanthropy Charity and the practice of 'good works' in the community, either by donations or by benevolent action. (Ch. 8)

policy agenda The main public issues or topics which are seen as a priority by government and/or by the general public and the mass media. There is no completely objective way of defining which issues are on the policy agenda at any particular time, because there is a constantly changing list of concerns which drift into and out of the limelight. The absence of public issues from the policy agenda may have nothing to do with their importance: many important issues or examples of need are ignored and never reach the policy agenda. (Ch. 6)

political economy model of power (see also the *democratic pluralist* and *elite control* models of power) This view of power suggests that vested political and economic interests tend to be the dominant influences on decision making and policy. For instance, the deep-seated interests of capitalist business exert a strong influence on government decisions about public spending and social welfare. However, these influences may be subtle and hard to detect. For various reasons, including a political ideology which supports the prevailing economic system, those who are relatively powerless may support dominant interests (for instance, by voting for parties which are pro-business and which reduce welfare). The political economy model is primarily a Marxist view of power. (Ch. 6)

political rights These are rights to political expression and freedom: for instance, the right to organize and to hold political meetings, to demonstrate publicly in groups, to organize political parties, to publish political views, to hold elections and to vote without being intimidated. (Ch. 2)

positive action   A term used to define a particular approach to equal opportunities policy. Positive action includes measures which go further than minimalist policy (see *minimalist*). Positive action encourages people from underrepresented groups to apply for jobs or for educational places (whereas a minimalist policy would simply try to ensure fairness and similarity of treatment of applicants). However, positive action does not go as far as positive discrimination or 'reverse discrimination', which is a policy to ensure that formerly underrepresented groups are equally represented in the workforce or in educational institutions. (Ch. 2)

postfeminism   Feminist perspectives show how inequalities between men and women are constructed and maintained. While not denying that major inequalities remain as a result of traditional patterns of male dominance, postfeminist perspectives point to the growing instability of men's and women's identities in the 'postmodern' world (the identity and economic status of many men has been profoundly affected by changes in the nature of manual work, for instance). Rather than taking for granted the idea that existing gender divisions will continue, post-feminism suggests that a variety of male and female roles will develop. (Ch. 10)

post-Fordism   'Fordism' refers to the dominant pattern of work organization in modern society. Whether one works in a factory or not, 'Fordist' organizations tend to be large-scale, hierarchical and bureaucratic, and to divide work into specialized units. However, as a result of profound changes in the economy and in technology, the nature of work is changing. To manage these changes, organizations – whether private firms or public organizations such as NHS hospitals or social services departments – are also changing. A 'post-Fordist' economy or society is one in which the majority of organizations are becoming less centralized than before, and in which employees are expected to work flexibly with a range of skills rather than as specialized workers with narrowly defined skills. (Ch. 10)

postindustrialism   A term which sums up key changes in the world of work and work organization. It is held that, as the industrial society of the twentieth century gives way to a 'postindustrial' society, work and production will no longer take place in centralized plants or offices. Increasingly, work will be performed in decentralized units and in less hierarchical or bureaucratic working environments. Knowledge-based work and ability to use and control information will become increasingly important, while 'traditional' patterns of work in manufacturing industry will decline in significance.

postmodernism   A term which refers to a wide variety of ideas about the ways in which society is changing from a 'modern' period to an emergent, 'postmodern' period. Postmodern society is characterized by the breakup or fragmentation of all the major social institutions and social groups: for instance, working patterns, social class groups and even categories such as 'older people', a 'group' which will become increasingly diverse in terms of lifestyles and expectations. If a postmodern society is emerging, this will have profound consequences for social policy. The 'modern' notion of centralized government and universal policies may have to give way to more diverse patterns of government intervention (for instance, partnerships between business and government agencies) in an increasingly complex and diverse 'postmodern' society. (Ch. 10)

poststructuralism   A way of thinking which challenges the idea of universal truths. Poststructural ideas question the assumption that there is an underlying rationality in the social structures that we live with (such as government or the state). A poststructural approach would suggest that different ideas and views of a subject (such as poverty) all have a certain validity (even if they are not all equally valid). There may be no single, 'correct' view of a problem such as poverty and of what to do about it. Therefore, poststructural thinking, like postmodernism in general, poses questions about the basic idea of having a commonly defined policy which is based on a single, 'rational' set of goals. (Ch. 10)

preventive health policies/services   An approach to designing, planning and delivering policies which aims above all to prevent people from becoming ill. 'Secondary' prevention refers to the concept of preventing further illness among people who have already contracted a disease. (Ch. 7)

principles   As used in this book, the term 'principles' refers to the rules or guiding ideas which govern social policies. (Ch. 2)

public administration   The subject or field of study which is concerned with the ways in which government policies are administered: that is, how government is organized and run, how decisions are made and how services are delivered. (Ch. 1)

public health   This term refers to government and medical concern with maintaining a healthy environment and with preventing outbreaks of disease in the community. (Ch. 3)

purchaser–provider split   The formal separation of the two separate functions of purchasing (or paying for) services and of providing and delivering them. This term gained currency as the 'internal market' was developed in health and social services during the 1980s. Formerly integrated departments (for instance, social services departments in local authorities) were divided into separate units, some of which played the 'purchaser' role, while others provided services (such as home care teams). (Ch. 9)

quangos (quasi-autonomous non-governmental organizations)   These are public bodies or organizations which have been created and set up by government, but which are not actually part of central government. Therefore, the appointees who run quangos are not civil servants. Some are experts and professionals, but many are drawn from the business world. Quango managers usually work part-time for a quango while continuing to work for other employers or as managing directors for business firms. The phrase 'quasi-autonomous' means that these organizations are partially free of government control. (Chs 1, 6)

real increases/decreases (e.g. in spending, wages or benefits)   A technical term to indicate that, when amounts of money are compared from year to year, inflation and other distortions have been removed from the calculations. For instance, when government expenditure in 1950 and the year 2000 is compared 'in real terms', it means that like is being compared with like, in terms of the currency values which are referred to. (Ch. 4)

redistribution Simply, a distribution or sharing out which is different from before. It is important to remember that 'redistribution' of resources does not necessarily mean a shift from the rich to the poor; wealth and resources can be redistributed in favour of the better-off. (Ch. 4)

relative autonomy A term used in political science and in sociology to describe the relationship between the state, or government, and economic and business interests. It suggests that governments can act somewhat independently of these interests and may sometimes appear to act against vested economic or capitalist interests. However, this autonomy or free-dom of the state is not complete; in the final analysis, theorists suggest, the state's policies tend to support underlying vested interests. (Ch. 6)

residential care A broad term to describe a variety of living arrangements and social care for people who cannot, or do not wish to, live in their own family homes. 'Residential care' tends to be reserved for descriptions of social service establishments (including the private sector and voluntary sector), whereas 'institutional care' is an even broader term which can include not only social services but also health care estab-lishments such as hospitals and nursing homes. (Ch. 9)

residual (approach to provision of state services) A residual approach or policy is one which assumes that most people will purchase welfare services, care or social security from the private sector (the market), or look after themselves, or obtain help and care from their families. However, those who cannot fend for themselves or who cannot afford to do so form a 'residual' (remaining) group, and a 'residual' state or public service is provided for them. (Ch. 3)

residualization A process of change in which service is increasingly restricted to the poor, who cannot afford better quality private services or other forms of care. (Ch. 8)

screening This refers to the policy and practice of investigating the occurrence of disease in a population or a community. (Ch. 7)

sheltered housing A form of accommodation for people who are relatively independent and can manage most of the tasks of daily living by themselves, but who may be frail or vulnerable in some way. Sheltered housing is usually adapted in various ways to meet the needs of those who have physical and/or mental impairments, or who may benefit from having immediate access to a supervising warden. (Ch. 9)

social administration (see also *public administration*) The subject or field of study which focuses on the structure and organization of social welfare services (in particular, education, health, the personal social services, housing and community care services). While social administration has a theoretical element (administrative theory), it has traditionally been seen as less theoretical than the discipline of social policy, and more concerned with the study of the 'nuts and bolts' of service provision – the content of social services and how they are administered. (Ch. 1)

social care market (see also *mixed economy of care*) The concept of a 'social care market' suggests competition among a number of care providers; the 'consumer' of care, or service user, may therefore choose between providers (assuming that he or she has the means and resources to do so). (Ch. 9)

social consensus General agreement. When applied to welfare policy, the idea of social consensus suggests that there is no support for any reversal of or significant change to the direction of policy. (Ch. 5)

social contract An agreement between major social groups which may be binding (and expressed in legal terms) or may exist more loosely as a set of 'understandings' and political compromises. For instance, a social contract may develop in which trade unions expect government to follow certain economic and welfare policies in order to protect their members' livelihoods; in return, government may expect trade unions to moderate their wage rise demands. However, this is only one example; a 'social contract' may develop between government and any major sectional interests, or between government and the community as a whole. (Ch. 5)

social control Any kind of relationship, social process or social pressure in which an individual's or a group's behaviour is brought into line with social norms and general expectations. Social control may be highly visible, direct and coercive (as in police tactics which are brutal and confrontational), or it may be more subtle and generally accepted (as in preventive policing, such as community work with young people). (Ch. 5)

social democratic welfare states 'Social democracy' is difficult to define in precise terms, but all social democratic states stress the importance of equality, openness and participation. Social welfare in social democratic states therefore tends to be inclusive and available to all on an equal basis, and the best known examples of the social democratic model (such as Sweden) are renowned for the comprehensiveness and generosity of their social services and social security benefits. (Ch. 3)

social engineering A philosophy or approach to government which suggests that it is possible to plan solutions to social problems and to create a new social order. (Ch. 8)

social housing Housing provided for those who, for one reason or another, cannot purchase accommodation on the open market. Social housing may be built by and/or rented from private sector, voluntary sector (housing association) or public sector (local authority) organizations; in this sense it is a wider category than *council housing* (see above). (Ch. 8)

social rights These are rights which are associated with the development of a welfare state. In welfare states, full citizenship is represented by rights to certain services (such as a 'free' education) and social security. (Ch. 2)

social security benefits (contributory, non-contributory, income-related and non-income-related) Entitlement to and size of *contributory* benefits is worked out on the basis of need *and* how much an individual has previously contributed to the scheme through taxes and national insurance contributions. *Non-contributory* benefits are provided on the basis of need only; neither the amount of benefit nor a person's right to it are affected by a contribution record. *Income-related* benefits are adjusted in amount according to the recipient's means (a means test is applied so that poorer benefit claimants receive more and the better-off receive less).

Non-income-related benefits are standard and are calculated irrespective of income. (Ch. 4)

Speenhamland system   An informal system, widespread in Britain before the introduction of the 'new' Poor Law in 1834, to supplement the income of poorer agricultural and rural workers. Public money, gathered in the form of local rates or taxation, was used to subsidize poorer workers' pay on a 'sliding scale' (the lower the wage, the higher the subsidy). (Ch. 3)

stigmatization   Social stigmata are public and obvious signs of 'spoiled identity' or shame. Stigmatization refers to a process of applying such signs of deviant status and shame either to groups and individuals or to particular kinds of public services. In 'residual' welfare systems, for instance, both those who rely on public welfare and the services themselves are likely to be stigmatized. (Chs 5, 7)

subsidiarity   The concept of allowing policies to be applied or implemented in ways which are decided at a lower (subsidiary) level of decision making. The European Union, for instance, has developed a range of social policies and (depending on their status) some of these must be adopted by member states; however, the principle of subsidiarity allows each country to develop the policy in its own way, as long as the main aims and objectives of the policy are achieved. 'Subsidiarity' also refers to the idea (underlying many social policies in European countries) of expecting the family and local community to meet welfare needs wherever possible. (Ch. 10)

taxation (direct, indirect, progressive and regressive)   Income taxes are examples of *direct* taxation, while *indirect* taxes are levied on goods and services. *Progressive* taxes are those which become progressively higher as income and wealth rise, so that the better-off pay high taxes and the low-paid relatively little; *regressive* taxes, on the other hand, take similar amounts from everyone, so that the less well-off end up losing a higher proportion of their income in tax than the better-off. (Ch. 4)

tenure   A legal expression of the claim or right that someone has to live in a property: for instance, by ownership, or by leasing or renting. (Ch. 8)

theory   An idea to explain phenomena or facts that have been observed. (Ch. 1)

underclass   A sociological term to describe a category or group that is excluded from the labour force. This term is highly contentious because there is disagreement about: (a) whether such a group exists (the excluded comprise many different groups in poverty, such as older people, the long-term unemployed, some sections of minority ethnic communities, single parents); and (b) what the causes of exclusion are. For instance, some commentators suggest that members of the underclass exclude themselves from the rest of society by adopting a deviant and/or criminal lifestyle, while others suggest that if an underclass exists, it is composed mainly of people who wish to work and to join the mainstream but are prevented from doing so for various reasons. (Ch. 5)

utilitarianism   A school of thought which developed in the early nineteenth century, largely through the efforts of Jeremy Bentham. Utilitarianism aims to assess the value of all human action (including government policy) in terms of its 'utility' or use. Briefly, utility is itself assessed by the ability of an action or a policy to bring 'the greatest happiness to the greatest number'. (Ch. 2)

values   Ideas and standards which are highly important in a social group or a culture. Certain values may be evident in social policies: for instance, American policies on poverty may express core American values concerning self-reliance and individualism. (Ch. 1)

wants   Not to be confused with *felt need* (see above), wants are (in social policy terms) expressions of a subjective desire for something (resources, care, a service) irrespective of need. For instance, a person may want to have a particular surgical operation but not need it. Felt need occurs when the person subjectively feels an actual need for something. (Ch. 2)

welfare   An extremely difficult term to define briefly. This is because almost every commentator has a different definition of the main ingredients or components of human welfare. However, a comprehensive definition would include not only measures of well-being in the present, such as health and material well-being, but also opportunity and autonomy. (Ch. 1)

welfare capitalism   A 'late' stage in the development of capitalist society in which the provision of welfare becomes an integral and essential part of that society and its market economy. (Ch. 5)

welfare dependency   A term which suggests not only financial dependence upon welfare benefits and services but also a state of mind – a psychological state in which those dependent on welfare lose motivation, skills, independence and self-reliance. (Chs 3, 5)

welfare pluralism   This is a useful term, which sums up the way in which many observers see the future of welfare. 'Welfare pluralism' suggests that welfare provision will increasingly become the responsibility of a number – a plurality – of providers (state, voluntary, private and informal) rather than mainly being the responsibility of the state.

welfare system   A phrase which can be used to suggest that a structure of welfare services and social security exists, but that this is not provided by, or organized solely by, government. Where welfare *is* still mainly a government-run concern, we may continue to use the term 'welfare state'; otherwise, 'welfare system' may be more appropriate. (Ch. 1)

welfarism   A set of political and social values which strongly support the existence and continuation of a comprehensive welfare state. (Ch. 1)

'whole system' comparisons   As an alternative to comparing individual social policies in one country with those of another (for instance, policies on secondary education in Britain and France), it is possible to compare the 'whole systems' of each country (or groups of countries): that is, their economic systems, political systems, belief or value systems etc. This will help to put their respective social policies in context (see Jones 1985). (Ch. 3)

workfare   Policies which seek to make eligibility for benefits and welfare conditional upon willingness to work – in other words, claimants only receive benefits if they have completed a specified total of hours of work per week. (Chs 3, 5)

workhouse   A centuries-old social institution which provided shelter and subsistence to the poor if they were willing to work in the institution upon menial and/or back-breaking tasks. (Ch. 3)

BIBLIOGRAPHY

Abrams, F. (1995a) 'Parents get bigger role at school inspections', *Independent on Sunday*, 15 January, 11.

Abrams, F. (1995b) 'How Gillian Shephard gets her sums wrong', *Independent on Sunday*, 12 March, 19.

Acheson, R.M. and Hagard, S. (1984) *Health, Society and Medicine*. Oxford: Blackwell.

Addison, P. (1994) *The Road to 1945: British Politics and the Second World War*. London: Pimlico.

Aitken, I. (1997) 'A cunning plan to save the welfare state', *The Guardian*, 6 May, 13.

Alcock, P. (1993) *Understanding Poverty*. London: Macmillan.

Alcock, P. (1996) *Social Policy in Britain: Themes and Issues*. Basingstoke: Macmillan.

Andrews, R. (1992) *Collins Thematic Dictionary of Quotations*. Glasgow: HarperCollins.

Arber, S. and Gilbert, N. (1988) 'Men: the forgotten carers', *Sociology*, 23(1), 111–18.

Atkinson, D. (ed.) (1995) *Cities of Pride – Rebuilding Community, Refocusing Government*. London: Cassell.

Audit Commission (1986) *Making a Reality of Community Care*. London: HMSO.

Audit Commission (1993) *Taking Care: Progress with Care in the Community*. London: HMSO.

Audit Commission (1994) *Taking Care: Progress with Care in the Community*. London: HMSO.

Baggott, R. (1994) *Health and Health Care in Britain*. London: Macmillan.

Balchin, P. (1995) *Housing Policy – an Introduction*, 3rd edn. London: Routledge.

Barnett, C. (1986) *The Audit of War*. London: Macmillan.

Barr, N. (1993) *The Economics of the Welfare State*, 2nd edn. London: Weidenfeld and Nicolson.

Bedell, G. (1996) 'Their bedtime, our business', *Independent on Sunday*, 9 June, 21.

Bell, S. (1996) 'Hot property, but not too hot to handle', *Independent on Sunday* (Business section), 11 August, 4.

Bennett, O. (1996) 'It's really all right once you get inside', *Independent on Sunday* (Real Lives section), 8 September, 3.

Bentham, J. (1982) *An Introduction to the Principles of Morals and Legislation*, edited by J.H. Burns and H.L.A. Hart. London: Methuen.

Best, G. (1979) *Mid-Victorian Britain 1851–75*. London: Fontana.

Blakemore, K. and Boneham, M. (1994) *Age, Race and Ethnicity*. Buckingham: Open University Press.

Blakemore, K. and Drake, R.F. (1995) *Understanding Equal Opportunity Policies*. Hemel Hempstead: Prentice Hall.

Bland, R. (1994) 'EPIC – a Scottish care management experiment', in M. Titterton (ed.) *Caring for People in the Community: the New Welfare*. London: Jessica Kingsley, 113–29.

Bornat, J., Johnson, J., Pereira, C., Pilgrim, S. and Williams, F. (1997) *Community Care: a Reader*, 2nd edn. London: Macmillan.

Bradshaw, J. (1972) 'The concept of social need', *New Society*, 30, 640–3.

Brindle, D. (1995) 'Government backs bill to recognise carers', *The Guardian*, 3 March, 7.

Bryson, B. (1996) *Notes from a Small Island*. London: Black Swan.

Bytheway, B. (1994) *Ageism*. Buckingham: Open University Press.

Bytheway, B. and Johnson, J. (1997) 'The social construction of carers', in A. Symonds and A. Kelly (eds) *The Social Construction of Community Care*. London: Macmillan.

Cahill, M. (1994) *The New Social Policy*. Oxford: Blackwell.

Callender, C. (1992) 'Redundancy, unemployment and poverty', in C. Glendinning and J. Millar (eds) *Women and Poverty in Britain in the 1990s*. Hemel Hempstead: Harvester Wheatsheaf, 129–48.

Carter, J. and Rayner, M. (1996) 'The curious case of post-Fordism and welfare', *Journal of Social Policy*, 25(3), 347–67.

Carvel, J. and MacLeod, D. (1995) 'Learning swerve', *The Guardian*, 14 June, 15.

Challis, D., Darton, R., Johnson, L., Stone, M. and Traske, K. (1995) *Care Management and Health Care of Older People – the Darlington Community Care Project*. Aldershot: Arena.

Chew, R. (1992) *Compendium of Health Statistics*, 8th edn. London: Office of Health Economics.

Cmnd 1973 (1963) *Health and Welfare: the Development of Community Care*. London: HMSO.

Cochrane, A. and Clarke, J. (eds) (1993) *Comparing Welfare States: Britain in International Context*. London: Sage.

Cole, C. and Furbey, R. (1994) *The Eclipse of Council Housing*. London: Routledge.

Colwill, J. (1994) 'Beveridge, women and the welfare state', *Critical Social Policy*, 14(2), 53–78.

Coyle, D. (1997) 'Welfare state caught in tax tug-of-war', *Independent*, 10 April, 11.

Cox, D. (1991) 'Health service management – a sociological view: Griffiths and the non-negotiated order of the hospital', in J. Gabe, M. Calnan and M. Bury (eds) *The Sociology of the Health Service*. London: Routledge, 89–114.

Crowther, A. (1988) *Social Policy in Britain 1914–1939*. Basingstoke: Macmillan.

CSO (Central Statistical Office) (1994a) *Social Trends 24*. London: HMSO.

CSO (Central Statistical Office) (1994b) *Economic Trends*, No. 494. London: HMSO.

CSO (Central Statistical Office) (1994c) *Regional Trends 29*. London: HMSO.

CSO (Central Statistical Office) (1996) *Social Trends 26*. London: HMSO.

Dahl, R.A. (1961) *Who Governs? Democracy and Power in an American City*. New Haven, CT: Yale University Press.

Dale, J. and Foster, P. (1986) *Feminists and State Welfare*. London: Routledge.

Deakin, N. (1994) *The Politics of Welfare*, 2nd edn. Hemel Hempstead: Harvester Wheatsheaf.

Dean, H. (1991) *Social Security and Social Control*. London: Routledge.

Dean, H. and Hartley, G. (1995) 'Listen to learn', *Community Care*, 30 March to 5 April, 22–3.

Dearing, Sir Ron (1994) *The National Curriculum and Assessment: Final Report*. London: School Curriculum and Assessment Authority.

Department of Health and Social Security (1977) *The Way Forward*. London: HMSO.

Department of Health and Social Security (1983) *NHS Management Inquiry (the Griffiths Report)*. London: DHSS.

Department of Health (1995) *Community Care Monitoring: Report of 1994 National Exercises*. London: HMSO.

de Swaan, A. (1989) 'The reluctant imperialism of the medical profession', *Social Science and Medicine*, 28(11), 1165–70.

Dickens, C. (1982) *Oliver Twist*. Oxford: Oxford University Press.

Dickens, C. (1902) *Nicholas Nickleby*. London: Dent.

Donegan, L. (1996) 'Water meters "burden poor"', *The Guardian*, 23 January, 5.

Donnison, J. (1988) *Midwives and Medical Men*, 2nd edn. London: Heinemann.

Doyal, L. and Gough, I. (1991) *A Theory of Human Needs*. Basingstoke: Macmillan Education.

Drabble, M. (1988) *Case for Equality*, Fabian Tract 527. London: The Fabian Society.

Esping-Andersen, G. (1990) *The Three Worlds of Welfare Capitalism*. Cambridge: Polity Press.

Eurostat (1992) *A Social Portrait of Europe*. Luxembourg: Office for Official Publications of the European Community.

Field, F. (1995) 'The poison in the welfare state', *Independent on Sunday*, 14 May, 27.

Firth, J. (1987) *Public Support for Residential Care: Report of a Joint Central and Local Government Working Party*. London: Department of Health and Social Security.

Fitzpatrick, T. (1996) 'Postmodernism, welfare and radical politics', *Journal of Social Policy*, 25(3), 303–20.

Forrest, R. and Murie, A. (1988) *Selling the Welfare State*. London: Routledge.

Foster, P. (1995) *Women and the Health Care Industry*. Buckingham: Open University Press.

Fraser, D. (1984) *The Evolution of the British Welfare State*. Basingstoke: Macmillan.

GHS (1983) *General Household Survey 1983*. London: OPCS, Table 6.9.

GHS (1992) *General Household Survey 1990*. London: OPCS, Table 3.31.

Gilmour, Sir Ian (1992) *Dancing with Dogma*. London: Simon and Schuster.

Ginsburg, N. (1992) *Divisions of Welfare*. London: Sage.

Glasner, A. (1992) 'Gender and Europe', in J. Bailey (ed.) *Social Europe*. London: Longman, 70–105.

Glendinning, C. and Millar, J. (eds) (1992) *Women and Poverty in Britain – the 1990s*. Hemel Hempstead: Harvester Wheatsheaf.

Glennerster, H. (1992) *Paying for Welfare – the 1990s*. Hemel Hempstead: Harvester Wheatsheaf.

Glennerster, H. (1995) *British Social Policy since 1945*. Oxford: Blackwell.

Goffman, E. (1991) *Asylums: Essays on the Social Situation of Mental Patients and other Inmates*. Harmondsworth: Penguin.

Gordon, P. (1989) *Citizenship for Some? Race and Government Policy 1979–89*. London: Runnymede Trust.

Gough, I. (1979) *The Political Economy of the Welfare State*. London: Macmillan.

Grant, C. (ed.) (1992) *Built to Last? Reflections on British Housing Policy*. London: ROOF Magazine/Shelter.

Gray, J. (1995) 'Beggaring our own neighbours', *The Guardian*, 17 February, 12.

Griffiths, R. (Chair) (1988) *Community Care: Agenda for Action*. London: HMSO.

Guardian (1994) 'Blair conversion delights opt-out Tories', *The Guardian*, 2 December, 2.

Hague, D. (1995) 'The wrong debate on university standards', *Independent*, 30 August, 13.

Hallett, C. (ed.) (1995) *Women and Social Policy: an Introduction*. Hemel Hempstead: Prentice Hall.

Halsey, A.H. (1978) *Change in British Society*. Oxford: Oxford University Press.

Ham, C. and Hill, M. (1993) *The Policy Process in the Modern Capitalist State*. London: Harvester Wheatsheaf.

Hancock, C. (1995) 'Who'll take care of the caring?', *The Guardian* (Society section), 8 March, 2–3.

Harris, J. (1977) *William Beveridge: a Biography*. Oxford: Oxford University Press.

Hattersley, R. (1995) 'Labour's big, bad idea', *Independent*, 22 June, 19.

Hayek, F.A. (1944) *The Road to Serfdom*. London: George Routledge & Sons.

Hennessy, P. (1992) *Never Again. Britain 1945–51*. London: Jonathon Cape.

Henwood, M. (1995a) *Making a Difference? Implementation of the Community Care Reforms Two Years On*. London: Nuffield Institute for Health/King's Fund.

Henwood, M. (1995b) 'Measure for measure', *Community Care*, 6–12 July, 18–19.

Hill, M. (1990) *Social Security Policy in Britain*. Aldershot: Edward Elgar.

Hills, J. (1993) *The Future of Welfare – a Guide to the Debate*. York: The Joseph Rowntree Foundation.

Hillyard, P. and Percy-Smith, J. (1988) *The Coercive State: the Decline of Democracy in Britain*. London: Fontana.

Hillyard, P. and Watson, S. (1996) 'Postmodern social policy: a contradiction in terms?', *Journal of Social Policy*, 25(3), 321–46.

HM Treasury (1995) *Public Expenditure: Statistical Supplement to the Financial Statement and Budget Report 1995–96*, Cm 2821. London: HMSO.

Holtham, G. (1994) 'Britain languishes at the bottom of the class', *Independent on Sunday* (Business section), 23 October, 8.

Horowitz, R. (1995) *Teen Mothers: Citizens or Dependents?* Chicago: University of Chicago Press.

Huby, M. (1995) 'Water poverty and social policy: a review of issues for research', *Journal of Social Policy*, 24(2), 219–36.

Hunter, D. (1992) 'The lost tribes of the NHS', *Health Service Journal*, 20 August, 19.

Hutton, W. (1995) *The State We're In: Why Britain Is in Crisis and How to Overcome It*. London: Jonathon Cape.

Illich, I. (1990) *Limits to Medicine – Medical Nemesis: the Expropriation of Health*. London: Marion Boyars.

Independent on Sunday (1995) 'Poor results of an elite system', *Independent on Sunday*, 27 August, 18.

Jack, R. (1992) 'Case management and social services: welfare or trade fare?', *Generations Review*, 2(1), 4–6.

Johnson, J. (1997) 'Care as policy', in A. Brechin, J. Katz, S. Peace and J. Walmsley (eds) *Care Matters*. London: Sage.

Johnston, P. (1995) 'Portillo attack on welfare state', *The Daily Telegraph*, 28 June, 2.

Jones, C. (1985) *Patterns of Social Policy: an Introduction to Comparative Analysis*. London: Tavistock.

Jones, C. (ed.) (1993) *New Perspectives on the Welfare State in Europe*. London: Routledge.

Jones, K. (1994) *The Making of Social Policy in Britain 1830–1990*, 2nd edn. London: The Athlone Press.

Joseph, K. and Sumption, J. (1979) *Equality*. London: John Murray.

Judd, J. and Abrams, F. (1995) 'Labour emasculates opted-out schools', *Independent*, 22 June, 2.

Kempson, E., Bryson, A. and Rowlingson, K. (1994) *Hard Times: How Poor Families Make Ends Meet*. London: Policy Studies Institute.

Kennedy, I. (1980) 'The Reith Lectures – Unmasking medicine', *The Listener*, 13 November, 641–4.

Kennedy, I. (1983) *The Unmasking of Medicine*, 2nd edn. St Albans: Granada Publishing.

Kesey, K. (1962) *One Flew Over the Cuckoo's Nest*. London: Methuen.

Kincaid, J. (1984) 'Richard Titmuss 1907–73', in P. Barker (ed.) *Founders of the Welfare State*. London: Heinemann Educational, 115–20.

Kitwood, T. (1997) *Dementia Reconsidered*. Buckingham: Open University Press.

Klein, R. (1984) 'Edwin Chadwick', in P. Barker (ed.) *Founders of the Welfare State*. London: Heinemann.

Klein, R. (1995) *The New Politics of the NHS*, 3rd edn. London: Longman.

Knapp, M., Cambridge, P., Thomason, C., Beecham, J., Allen, C. and Darton, R. (1992) *Care in the Community: Challenge and Demonstration*. Aldershot: Arena.

Leat, D. (1993) *The Development of Community Care by the Independent Sector*. London: Policy Studies Institute.

Le Grand, J. (1982) *The Strategy of Equality*. London: George Allen & Unwin.

Le Grand, J. (1995) 'The Strategy of Equality revisited: a reply', *Journal of Social Policy*, 24(2), 187–91.

Lewis, J. (1980) *The Politics of Motherhood: Child and Maternal Welfare in England, 1900–1939*. London: Croom Helm.

Lewis, J. (1983) *Women's Welfare, Women's Rights*. London: Croom Helm.

Lewis, N. (1992) *Inner City Regeneration: the Demise of Regional and Local Government*. Buckingham: Open University Press.

Lloyd, T.O. (1993) *Empire, Welfare State, Europe: English History 1906–1992*, 4th edn. Oxford: Oxford University Press.

Lowe, R. (1993) *The Welfare State in Britain since 1945*. Basingstoke: Macmillan.

Lukes, S. (1974) *Power: a Radical View*. London: Macmillan.

McKeown, T. (1979) *The Role of Medicine: Dream, Mirage or Nemesis?*, 2nd edn. Oxford: Blackwell.

Macleod, D. (1995) 'Hands across the sea', *The Guardian* (Education section), 30 May, 2.

McRae, H. (1996) 'If they can't tax us, they'll boss us around', *Independent on Sunday* (Business section), 8 September, 4.

Malpass, P. (1984) 'Octavia Hill, 1838–1912', in P. Barker (ed.) *Founders of the Welfare State*. London: Heinemann, 31–6.

Malpass, P. and Murie, A. (1994) *Housing Policy and Practice,* 4th edn. Basingstoke: Macmillan.

Mant, D. and Fowler, G. (1990) 'Mass screening: theory and ethics', *British Medical Journal*, 300, 916–18.

Marchant, C. (1995) 'Care managers speak out', *Community Care*, 30 March to 5 April, 16–17.

Marshall, T.H. (1950) *Citizenship and Social Class, and Other Essays*. Cambridge: Cambridge University Press.

Marshall, T.H. (1963) *Sociology at the Crossroads*. London: Heinemann.

Marshall, T.H. (1970) *Social Policy*. London: Hutchinson.

Mason, D. (1995) *Race and Ethnicity in Modern Britain*. Oxford: Oxford University Press.

Meikle, J. (1994) 'Puppets on a string?', *The Guardian* (Education section), 8 November, 2.

Midwinter, E. (1994) *The Development of Social Welfare in Britain*. Buckingham: Open University Press.

Mishra, R. (1990) *The Welfare State in Capitalist Society*. Hemel Hempstead: Harvester Wheatsheaf.

Mishra, R. (1993) 'Social policy in a postmodern world', in C. Jones (ed.) *New Perspectives on the Welfare State in Europe*. London: Routledge, 18–40.

Moore, S. (1993) *Social Welfare Alive!* Cheltenham: Stanley Thornes.

Murray, C. (1994) *Underclass: the Crisis Deepens*. London: Institute of Economic Affairs.

Nicholas, E.J. (1983) *Issues in Education: a Comparative Analysis*. London: Harper & Row.

North, N. (1993) 'Empowerment in welfare markets', *Health and Social Care in the Community*, 1(3), 129–37.

Novak, T. (1988) *Poverty and the State: an Historical Sociology*. Milton Keynes: Open University Press.

Nozick, R. (1974) *Anarchy, State and Utopia*. Oxford: Blackwell.

O'Donnell, O. and Propper, C. (1991) 'Equity and the distribution of NHS resources', *Journal of Health Economics*, 10, 1–19.

Office of Population Censuses and Surveys (1994) *General Household Survey 1992*. London: HMSO.

Oliver, M. (1990) *Politics of Disablement*. London: Macmillan.

Organisation for Economic Co-operation and Development (1994) *The OECD Jobs Study*. Paris: OECD Publications Service.

Orwell, G. (1954) *Nineteen Eighty-four*. Harmondsworth: Penguin.

Parker, R. (1990) 'Elderly people and community care: the policy background', in I. Sinclair *et al.* (eds) *The Kaleidoscope of Care: a Review of Research on Welfare Provision for Elderly People*. London: HMSO, 5–22.

Pascall, G. (1986) *Social Policy: a Feminist Analysis*. London: Tavistock.

Peach, C. and Byron, M. (1994) 'Council house sales, residualisation and Afro Caribbean tenants', *Journal of Social Policy*, 23(3), 363–83.

Penna, S. and O'Brien, M. (1996) 'Postmodernism and social policy: a small step forwards?' *Journal of Social Policy*, 25(1), 39–61.

Pepinster, C. and Castle, S. (1995) 'Half of British households now on means-tested benefits', *Independent on Sunday*, 14 May, 1.

Phillimore, P., Beattie, A. and Townsend, P. (1994) 'Widening inequality of health in northern England, 1981–91', *British Medical Journal*, 308, 1125–8.

Piven, F. and Cloward, R. (1971) *Regulating the Poor: the Functions of Public Welfare*. New York: Pantheon Books.

Pole, J. and Steele, J. (1996) 'Who will look after granny?', *The Guardian* (Society section), 6 March, 6–7.

Powell, M. (1995) 'The Strategy of Equality revisited', *Journal of Social Policy*, 24(2), 163–85.

Qureshi, H. and Walker, A. (1989) *The Caring Relationship – Elderly People and Their Families*. Basingstoke: Macmillan.

Ranade, W. (1994) *A Future for the NHS? Health Care in the 1990s*. London: Longman.

Ranson, S. and Travers, T. (1994) 'Education', in P. Jackson and M. Lavender (eds) *Public Services Yearbook*. London: Chapman & Hall, 223–35.

Rawls, J. (1972) *A Theory of Justice*. Oxford: Oxford University Press.

Robertson Elliot, F. (1996) *Gender, Family and Society*. Basingstoke: Macmillan.

Robinson, R. and Le Grand, J. (1994) *Evaluating the NHS Reforms*. London: King's Fund Institute.

Routledge, P. (1997) 'Take your marks, get set, govern!', *Independent on Sunday*, 18 May, 19.

Royle, E. (1987) *Modern Britain – a Social History*. London: Edward Arnold.

Rust, V. and Blakemore, K. (1990) 'Education reform in Norway and in England and Wales: a corporatist interpretation', *Comparative Education Review*, 34(4), 500–22.

Sampson, A. (1992) *The Essential Anatomy of Britain: Democracy in Crisis,* revised edn. London: Hodder & Stoughton.

Scambler, G. (1984) 'Perceiving and coping with stigmatizing illness', in R. Fitzpatrick, J. Hinton, S. Newman, G. Scambler and J. Thompson (eds) *The Experience of Illness*. London: Tavistock Publications, 203–26.

Scruton, R. (1984) *The Meaning of Conservatism*, 2nd edn. London: Macmillan.

Scull, A.T. (1984) *Decarceration: Community Treatment of the Deviant – a Radical View*, 2nd edn. Cambridge: Polity Press.

Simon, B. (1988) *Bending the Rules: the Baker 'Reform' of Education*. London: Lawrence and Wishart.

Sinclair, I. (1990) 'Promise and performance', in I. Sinclair *et al.*, *The Kaleidoscope of Care: a Review of Welfare Provision for Elderly People*. London: HMSO, 217–24.

Sinclair, I., Parker, R., Leat, D. and Williams, J. (1990) *The Kaleidoscope of Care: a Review of Welfare Provision for Elderly People*. London: HMSO.

Spicker, P. (1993) *Poverty and Social Security*. London: Routledge.

Stainton, T. (1994) *Autonomy and Social Policy*. Aldershot: Avebury.

Statistics Sweden (1992) *On Women and Men in Sweden and the European Community*. Orebro: SCB Publishing Unit.

Steintrager, J. (1977) *Bentham*. London: George Allen & Unwin.

Stevenson, J. (1984) *British Society 1914–45*. Harmondsworth: Penguin.

Stitt, S. (1994) *Poverty and Poor Relief: Concepts and Reality*. Aldershot: Avebury.

Symonds, A. and Kelly, A. (eds) (1997) *The Social Construction of Community Care*. London: Macmillan.

Tawney, R.H. (1964) *Equality*, 4th edn, with an introduction by R. Titmuss. London: George Allen & Unwin.

Taylor, S. and Field, D. (1997) *Sociology of Health and Health Care: an Introduction for Nurses*, 2nd edn. Oxford: Blackwell Scientific Publications.

Taylor-Gooby, P. (1994) 'Postmodernism and social policy: a great leap backwards?', *Journal of Social Policy*, 23(3), 385–404.

Thane, P. (1996) *The Foundations of the Welfare State*, 2nd edn. London: Longman.

Thompson, A. and Dobson, R. (1995) 'Death of an ideal', *Community Care*, 6–12 July, 20–1.

Timmins, N. (1995a) 'Think the unthinkable, Mr Smith', *Independent*, 9 November, 19.

Timmins, N. (1995b) *The Five Giants – a Biography of the Welfare State*. London: HarperCollins.

Tinker, A. (1981) *The Elderly in Modern Society*. London: Longman.

Titmuss, R.M. (1987) 'The irresponsible society', in B. Abel-Smith and K. Titmuss (eds) *The Philosophy of Welfare – Selected Writings of R.M. Titmuss*. London: Allen & Unwin, 60–86.

Toynbee, P. (1997) 'The Tories were right: workfare really works', *Independent*, 27 February, 19.

Tuckett, D., Boulton, M., Olson, C. and Williams, A. (1985) *Meetings between Experts – an Approach to Sharing Ideas in Medical Consultations*. London: Tavistock Publications.

Ungerson, C. (1987) *Policy Is Personal: Sex, Gender and Informal Care*. London: Tavistock Publications.

Vidal, J. (1994) 'Health over wealth', *The Guardian*, 'Society' section, 4–5.

Wainwright, M. (1994) 'Price to pay for public sector awards', *The Guardian*, 4 February, 2.

Walker, A. (1990) 'The benefits of old age? Age discrimination and social security', in E. McEwen (ed.) *Age – the Unrecognised Discrimination*. London: Age Concern England.

Walker, P. (1994) 'What happens when you scrap the welfare state?', *Independent on Sunday*, 13 March, 17.

Warner, N. (1995) *Community Care: Just a Fairy Tale?* London: Carers' National Association (unpublished report).

Warnock, M. (ed.) (1966) *Utilitarianism*. London: Collins/Fontana.

Whipp, E. (1983) 'Doctors, patients and the truth', *New Society*, 3 February, 177–9.

Wilkin, D., Hallam, L., Leavey, R. and Metcalfe, D. (1987) *Anatomy of Urban General Practice*. London: Tavistock.

Wistow, G., Knapp, M., Hardy, B. and Allen, C. (1994) *Social Care in a Mixed Economy*. Buckingham: Open University Press.

Worsthorne, P. (1971) *The Socialist Myth*. London: Cassell.

Wyn, H. (1991) 'Women, the state, and the concept of financial dependence', in J. Hutton, S. Hutton, T. Pinch and A. Shiell (eds) *Dependency to Enterprise*. London: Routledge.

INDEX

MAKING SOCIAL POLICY
THE MECHANISMS OF GOVERNMENT AND POLITICS, AND HOW TO INVEST-
IGATE THEM

Peter Levin

Making Social Policy is a new and original textbook on policy making in British
central government. Starting from first principles, it examines policy making through
concepts drawn not from academic theories and interpretations but directly from
the experiences and perceptions of the politicians, officials and others involved in
the decision-making process. Peter Levin sets out a range of techniques for doing
this, and applies them to five case studies of policy making by the Thatcher and
Major governments. He elegantly brings out the various *mechanisms* at work,
including the strategies deployed by the various participants. These case studies,
which bring together material from a variety of sources, cover:

- housing and education policy
- social security reform
- the poll tax
- the annual public expenditure cycle
- Europe: the Social Charter and the protection of women workers.

Making Social Policy is also about *how to study* policy making. It shows you how to
recognize a policy when you see one, and how to make your own analysis of the
mechanisms by which government produces and adopts policy proposals, and by
which legislative and other measures subsequently come about. Peter Levin also
demonstrates how many theoretical perspectives employed by academic writers
comprehensively fail to capture the reality of what actually takes place.

Making Social Policy is essential reading for students of social policy, politics,
government, and public administration.

Contents
*Introduction – The policy-making machinery – 'Policy' and 'social policy' – Approaches
and methods – Formulating intentions: housing and education in the Conservative 1987
election manifesto – The dependence of the Prime Minister: the 'poll tax' saga – Consultation
and pressure: reforming social security in the mid-1980s – The Treasury versus the spending
departments: the annual spending round – European social policy and the UK: the Social
Charter and the protection of women workers – Conclusion: the mechanisms of policy
making – Notes and references – Index.*

288pp   0 335 19084 7 (Paperback)   0 335 19085 5 (Hardback)